Food Blogging FOR DUMMIES®

Kelly Senyei

John Wiley & Sons, Inc.

Food Blogging For Dummies®
Published by
John Wiley & Sons, Inc.
111 River Street
Hoboken, NJ 07030-5774

www.wiley.com

Published by John Wiley & Sons, Inc., Hoboken, New Jersey

Published simultaneously in Canada

Library of Congress Control Number: 2012933619

ISBN 978-1-118-15769-5 (pbk); ISBN 978-1-118-22602-5 (ebk); ISBN 978-1-118-23938-4 (ebk); ISBN 978-1-118-26399-0 (ebk)

Manufactured in the United States of America

10 9 8 7 6 5 4 3 2 1

About the Author

Kelly Senyei is a multimedia food journalist, stylist, photographer, and chef. She joined the food blogosphere in 2008 with the launch of her blog, Just a Taste (`www.justataste.com`), which chronicles her culinary musings tied to everything from easy appetizers and creative cocktails, to quick-fix meals and endless desserts. Kelly is a big proponent of keeping things light in life (and she's not talking about calories) and was motivated to launch her blog to share her family's rich recipe history.

After receiving her master's degree in broadcast television from Columbia University's Graduate School of Journalism, she joined the editorial team at FoodNetwork.com as an intern, where she wrote features and blogged on Food2.com. Unable to quiet her longstanding desire to attend culinary school, she enrolled in the Culinary Arts diploma program at The Institute of Culinary Education (ICE), where she conceptualized and launched the school's first official blog, DICED. For seven months, she photographed and blogged about every intricate detail of life as a culinary student, and in 2010, she received the People's Choice Award for Food Photography by the International Association of Culinary Professionals.

Kelly graduated with highest honors from ICE and honed her culinary skills by externing in the Food Network Kitchens, where she cross-tested recipes, prepared food for photo shoots and TV productions, and had the lucky chance to cook in a practice battle of *Iron Chef America* (the secret ingredient was popcorn!). She was then invited to join Condé Nast in reimagining the iconic *Gourmet* magazine in digital form. Kelly presently works as the Associate Editor of *Gourmet Live* writing articles for the app and Gourmet.com, managing the brand's blog and social media presence, and art directing and prop styling for photo shoots.

Through her work at *Gourmet Live,* Kelly has interviewed everyone from Eric Ripert and Tom Colicchio to Wolfgang Puck and Frank Bruni. She's also written in depth about the topics of cooking in the 1800s, nocturnal sleep-related eating disorder, the frozen yogurt fallacy, extreme couponing, low-carb diets, kitchen traumas, and more.

Kelly makes regular, expert appearances in all types of food media and has spoken at BlogHer Food and Food Blog Forum. Her work is featured on *Gourmet Live,* NBC, FoodNetwork.com, Glamour.com, and Food2.com. When not busy keeping up with the latest food media news and trends, she can be found in her New York City apartment, experimenting with ingredients and creating recipes.

Dedication

This book is dedicated to my family, who are the most loving, supportive, and hilarious people I know.

Author's Acknowledgments

First and foremost, I want to acknowledge my family — Mom, Dad, Alison, Grant, Grandmom, and Julio. Thank you all for breathing life and inspiration into Just a Taste and into me. I cannot thank you enough for your patience over these past six months and for your constant encouragement to pursue my greatest passion. You are all my eternal support system on speed dial, and for that — and for keeping me well-caffeinated — I am forever grateful.

I also want to thank the entire team at John Wiley and Sons, Inc. who worked on the book, especially my acquisitions editor, Amy Fandrei, who sent me an e-mail on April 5, 2011 that turned a lifelong dream into an opportunity that has now become a reality. And not a single page of this book would exist in legible form without the tireless efforts of my editor, Nicole Sholly, whose inspiring ability to answer my 973 questions while embracing my incessant food puns continues to amaze me. I am honored and blessed to have worked with Amy, Nicole, and so many others at Wiley.

I owe much gratitude to my Condé Nast family, especially Tanya Steel, Juliana Stock, Jennifer Mason, Kemp Minifie, Kendra Vizcaino, Ma'ayan Rosenzweig, Patricia Reilly, Megan Steintrager, and Kerry Acker. It is an absolute pleasure to work and to laugh with each of you every day.

Finally, I want to thank all those who lent their wisdom, guidance, and inspiration, especially Elise Bauer, Jaden Hair, Diane Cu, Todd Porter, Elaine Wu, and the entire BlogHer team, Paul Grimes, William Carr-Hartley, Brian Aronowitz, and my agent, David Larabell. And last, but definitely not least, the countless food bloggers who took part in the nationwide The State of the Food Blogosphere survey and who serve as the centerfold and true heart of the book.

Without each and every one of you, *Food Blogging For Dummies* would not be a reality. I raise a glass to toast to you, that you all may enjoy reading this book as much as I enjoyed writing it.

Publisher's Acknowledgments

We're proud of this book; please send us your comments at http://dummies.custhelp.com. For other comments, please contact our Customer Care Department within the U.S. at 877-762-2974, outside the U.S. at 317-572-3993, or fax 317-572-4002.

Some of the people who helped bring this book to market include the following:

Acquisitions, Editorial

Senior Project Editor: Nicole Sholly

Acquisitions Editor: Amy Fandrei

Copy Editor: Jennifer Riggs

Technical Editor: A.J. Rathbun (www.ajrathbun.com)

Editorial Manager: Kevin Kirschner

Editorial Assistant: Amanda Graham

Sr. Editorial Assistant: Cherie Case

Cover Photos: ©iStockphoto.com / mattjeacock (computer and hand, utensils); ©iStockphoto.com / Megan Tamaccio (background)

Cartoons: Rich Tennant (www.the5thwave.com)

Composition Services

Project Coordinator: Sheree Montgomery

Layout and Graphics: Carl Byers, Timothy C. Detrick, Corrie Niehaus, Mark Pinto

Proofreaders: Rebecca Denoncour, Tricia Liebig

Indexer: Slivoskey Indexing Services

Publishing and Editorial for Technology Dummies

Richard Swadley, Vice President and Executive Group Publisher

Andy Cummings, Vice President and Publisher

Mary Bednarek, Executive Acquisitions Director

Mary C. Corder, Editorial Director

Publishing for Consumer Dummies

Kathleen Nebenhaus, Vice President and Executive Publisher

Composition Services

Debbie Stailey, Director of Composition Services

Table of Contents

Introduction *1*

About Food Blogging For Dummies....... 1
Foolish Assumptions....... 2
Conventions Used in This Book....... 2
What You Don't Have to Read....... 3
How This Book Is Organized....... 3
Part I: Whetting Your Appetite....... 3
Part II: Finding Your Voice....... 3
Part III: The Soup to Nuts of Design....... 4
Part IV: Eating with Your Eyes....... 4
Part V: Marketing & Monetization....... 4
Part VI: The Part of Tens....... 4
Icons Used in This Book....... 5
Where to Go from Here....... 5

Part I: Whetting Your Appetite *7*

Chapter 1: The Many, The Proud **9**

Assessing the Food Blogosphere....... 9
Food blogging on the rise....... 10
Surveying the scene....... 12
Making your move....... 12
Understanding the Varied Roles of Food Bloggers....... 14
Meeting Your Fellow Food Bloggers....... 16
Setting Yourself Up for Success....... 19
Finding your niche....... 19
Owning your voice....... 21
Six tips for sweet success....... 23

Chapter 2: Finding Your Niche **25**

Starting with a Spark....... 25
Streamlining your foodie interests....... 27
Identifying what makes you different from other food bloggers....... 29
Building your food blog skills....... 30
Joining the Food Blogging Community....... 31
Knowing Your Audience....... 32
Writing Your Own Recipe for Success....... 35
The Secret Sauce for Naming Your Blog....... 36
Brainstorming your way to a name....... 38
Gauging instant reactions....... 39

Chapter 3: Setting Up Shop 41

Registering and Hosting Your Blog 41
Registering your domain 45
Selecting a web host 48
Choosing a Blogging Platform 50
Knowing your blogging software options 51
Installing your blogging software 56
Claiming Your Social Media Space 58
Benefiting from social media 58
Strategizing your social media approach 59

Part II: Finding Your Voice.. 61

Chapter 4: Is This Thing On? 63

Finding Your Voice 63
Making a good first impression 64
Setting the tone 65
Mastering Good Food Writing 67
Descriptions 67
The basics 69
The Power of Going Public 70
Ranting and raving 70
Publishing your first blog post 71
Food Blog Legalese 101 75
Protecting your content 76
Being credible, not a copycat 78

Chapter 5: Setting Your Content Menu 81

Defining the Content on Your Blog 81
Brainstorming blog post ideas 83
Engaging your audience 87
Writing and Creating Recipes 89
Organizing Your Content 91
Creating categories and subcategories 92
Understanding pages versus posts 94
Gauging content and time commitments 96

Chapter 6: Branding Your Blog through Consistency and Frequency. . . .99

Envisioning You and Your Blog as a Brand 100
Creating consistency 100
Branding your blog 101
Establishing Your Style Guide 102
Post length 103
Attribution 104
Images 104

Links 105
Recipes 107
General grammar and spelling 108
Inserting Visuals into Posts 109
Focusing on Frequency 112
Implementing a posting schedule 113
Deciding what days to post 115

Part III: The Soup to Nuts of Design 117

Chapter 7: The Lay of the Land 119

Extreme Makeover: Food Blog Edition 119
Making the best first impression 121
Blogging templates for beginners 123
Utilizing a custom template 124
Beautifying Your Blog 128
Selecting a color palette 129
Determining font size, style, and contrast 131
Designing your header 133
Embracing negative space 134
Steering clear of common errors in design 135

Chapter 8: Your Blog's Roadmap 137

Understanding Navigation Essentials 138
Establishing your home page 140
Crafting your About page 141
Creating a Contact page 144
Claiming Your Blog's Prime Real Estate 145
Mapping out your blog above the fold 145
Mapping out your blog below the fold 148
Getting social or getting lost (literally) 151
Inviting Readers to Have a Voice 154
Adjusting your comment settings 154
Establishing comment guidelines 156

Chapter 9: Getting Your Garnish On 159

Exploring the Wide World of Widgets 159
Implementing widgets 161
Going beyond basic widgets 164
Displaying badges and buttons 167
Creating Your Own Blog Garnish 168
Hyperlinking a graphic 169
Memorizing common HTML tags 172
Building your blogroll 173

Part IV: Eating with Your Eyes 175

Chapter 10: Food Photography Basics **177**

Developing Your Photo Style 177
Starting with the Fundamentals 179
Seeing the bigger, clearer picture 179
Shooting in Manual mode 182
Putting on the "manual" training wheels 184
Wanted: Depth of field 184
Sticking to the Basic Photography Rules 185
Obeying the Rule of Thirds 186
Composing the perfect shot 188
Gaining perspective 189
Paying attention to backgrounds 191
Seeing the (Natural and Artificial) Light 191

Chapter 11: Gathering Your Equipment and Tools **195**

Knowing Your Camera Options 195
Camera phones 197
Point-and-shoot cameras 198
dSLR cameras 198
Building Your Studio 199
Enhancing your light 200
Repurposing household items 201
Freeing up your hands 204
Assembling Your Food-Styling Toolkit 205

Chapter 12: Styling and Photographing Food **209**

Finding Your Style 210
Going au naturale 210
Faking your food 212
Food Styling Like the Pros 214
Timing your process 216
Speeding up your process 218
The Power of Propping 220
Choosing props with a purpose 220
Orchestrating the extras 221
Constructing Your Setup 227
Photographing Food in Restaurants 230
Using Free Programs to Edit Your Photos 233
Typical editing tasks 233
Assessing free editor options 234

Part V: Marketing & Monetization 237

Chapter 13: (Super) Marketing 239

Envisioning Your Blog as a Brand 240
Becoming Your Own Publicist 241
Sharing Your Content..243
Feeding your readers' cravings..243
Promoting your visual content 246
The Ins and Outs of SEO 248
Clueing in to keywords..249
Giving and getting link love 252
Interacting Online and Offline..254
Building community 254
Meeting and greeting bloggers offline..255
Tracking Your Progress..256
Implementing a statistics tracker 256
Decoding basic blog statistics..258

Chapter 14: Bringing Home the Bacon 259

(Reality) Check, Please! 260
Making the Most of Your Content 261
Tapping into the Ad World..262
Evaluating the impact of ads 263
Putting profits in perspective..264
Keeping the Control with Direct Advertising..266
Joining an Ad Network..267
Google AdSense..269
PlateFull..269
BlogHer advertising network..269
Federated Media Publishing..270
Foodbuzz Featured Publisher program 271
Interacting with Sponsors 271
Establishing effective relationships with sponsors..271
Giving and taking with giveaways..273
Diversifying Your Online Portfolio 274
Squeezing income from your skill set 274
Opening up shop..279
Accepting Swag without Selling Out 281

Part VI: The Part of Tens 283

Chapter 15: Ten Things to Know before Starting Your Food Blog . . .285

Match Your Blog Name to Your URL 285
Look into Self-Hosting Your Blog 286
Embrace Editing 286
Log Your Ideas and Inspirations 286
Get Social Early in the Game 287
Know Your Free Resources 287
Blog with a Conscience 288
Let You Be You 288
Avoid an Obsession with the Numbers 289
Back Up Your Blog 289

Chapter 16: The Ten Hardest Foods to Photograph 291

Beef Stew 291
Hummus 292
Raw Meat 292
Melted Cheese 293
Oatmeal 294
Ice Cream 294
Chocolate Pudding 295
Meatloaf 295
Poached or Fried Eggs 296
Enchiladas 296

Index 297

Introduction

Food blogging. Five years ago those words carried little weight in both the culinary and digital worlds. There were plenty of food writers, and even more bloggers, but there were very few who actually combined the two crafts. What began as a handful of tastemakers who took their ideas to the web has since evolved into an epicurean explosion whereby food enthusiasts of every age and every skill set can lend their voice in text and visuals (or should I say victuals?) to a community growing at an unforeseen pace.

Where would anyone be without the invention of food blogs? A few things are certain: You'd never have witnessed the proliferation of cake pops. You'd never have read the first blog-to-book cookbook. You'd never have experienced food porn in all its hi-res digital glory.

This book is for anyone who has a love of food, and an even bigger love of sharing their food experiences with others. I designed this book as a resource that's hopefully entertaining. After all, you're blogging about food, not nuclear fission. I'll warn you that I'm not afraid of a good food pun to help convey a point (and luckily — or unluckily — for you, I'm not short on them either).

About Food Blogging For Dummies

I'm the type of person who eats breakfast while daydreaming about lunch, and who digs in at dinner while strategizing about dessert. If you love food as much as I do, chances are you also love sharing that passion with others.

Food Blogging For Dummies is the ultimate recipe for taking your passion from your kitchen to the World Wide Web. From strategizing your blog's name and designing an effective home page to editing your photos and making the most of social media, this book addresses all of the essential ingredients for creating and maintaining a successful food blog.

I begin by whetting your appetite with a look at the current state of the food blogosphere, which provides an insider's perspective of the robust online food blogging community bubbling with complementary and contrasting voices, visuals, opinions, and passions. Discover your place in the greater food blogosphere as you get your creative juices flowing.

Here's a sample of the tools and information included in the book, which will help you

- Set up the technical elements of your blog.
- Find your food niche while making the most of your layout and design.
- Determine your mix of content by evaluating a variety of post topics.
- Join the food community through online and offline interactions.
- Master the ins and outs of social media, marketing, and earning an income.
- Style, prop, and photograph food using resources you own already.

Foolish Assumptions

Everyone knows making assumptions is a bad idea. But because I'm writing a book on a topic as expansive as food blogging, I inevitably have to assume a few things about you, dear reader:

- You are interested in not only creating food-centric content, but also sharing that content with an online audience.
- You know what a blog is, but not how it is set up or maintained.
- You have access to the Internet and know how to surf the web.
- You like to eat (a lot).

Conventions Used in This Book

Conventions are a fancy way of saying that information presented to you in this book is done so consistently. When you see a term *italicized,* for example, look for its definition, which is provided so you can understand the meaning of the term in the context of food blogging. If step-by-step instructions are required to complete a process, they appear numbered with the actionable items designated in **bold.** And finally, all references to website addresses (or URLs) and e-mail addresses are in `monofont` so they're easily distinguished from plain text.

What You Don't Have to Read

I have written this book so that each chapter stands independent of the others, meaning you can scan and flip through to whichever topics interest you the most. You can also skip over any sidebars and stick to the main material, which provides insight for completing the task at hand or points you toward the next steps in a process.

How This Book Is Organized

Food Blogging For Dummies is divided into six parts. Although you don't have to read the chapters, or even the individual sections, in order, I advise you to stick to the chronological layout if you're really looking to build the ultimate food blog from the ground up.

Use the Table of Contents and the index for quick references to locate information about specific topics, and make sure you spend some time studying (or drooling over) all the colorful visuals in the book. In this section, I provide you with an appetizer-size version of each of the main parts.

Part I: Whetting Your Appetite

From preserving your family's food legacy on the web to kick-starting your culinary empire online, the motivations and goals for launching a food blog are vast and varied. Although some may be in search of fame, fortune, or even a cookbook deal, others strive to simply establish their voice and create an online community of food-loving enthusiasts. Regardless of your aspirations, knowing who already dominates the digital space, finding your niche, and strategically setting up the backend of your blog are all critical aspects that should be thought about well before your first post ever goes from private to public.

Part II: Finding Your Voice

Just because photography plays such a critical role in the digital culinary scene doesn't mean good old, plain text should be pushed to the back-burner. Establishing your voice and fine-tuning the tone of your blog is an evolving process that includes setting your content menu while paying particular attention to consistency and frequency. Discover the power of going public with your content, plus get a primer in food blog legalese as you discover the sticky world of recipe copyright law.

Part III: The Soup to Nuts of Design

Where is the search bar? Who is this person? Why can't I leave a comment? If you want to lose readers, just leave them asking any of those questions. Although the content you publish is undoubtedly an important aspect of your food blog, the bottom line is this: The superficial stuff matters. Enter the fabulous world of layout and design, from polishing your blog's first impression to crafting a confusion-free roadmap for your readers. Get ready to get your garnish on.

Part IV: Eating with Your Eyes

One of the biggest draws to any popular food blog is the photographs. Although a recipe for a sour cream chocolate chip bundt cake can make a reader reach for the Preheat button, what's really going to lead them from his couch to his kitchen is the drool-worthy photo of a cake that looks so moist he can almost taste the half-melted chunks of bittersweet chocolate and tender morsels of cake while scrolling down the page. But not everyone has the resources, space, or time to splurge on a professional photography setup. Find out about the power of the point-and-shoot, the insider's guide to Food Styling 101, and how you can create your very own in-home studio without blowing your budget.

Part V: Marketing & Monetization

After the creative stuff is under control, focus on promoting and distributing your content while entertaining the options for making bank from your blog. Discover the strategic steps for maximizing your blog's rank in search engines, extending your brand, tracking your progress, and diversifying your sources of online income.

Part VI: The Part of Tens

It wouldn't be an iconic *For Dummies* book without the inclusion of the Part of Tens. In this part, I serve up two essential ten-tip guides. Chapter 15 discusses the ten things I wish I had known before starting my food blog (with the eleventh tip obviously being that someone had written a guide to prevent me from making those mistakes). Don't miss that chapter! Chapter 16 introduces you to ten of the hardest foods to photograph. Go face-to-face with the divas of the food world and figure out how to prevent them from having meltdowns while maximizing their charm on set.

Icons Used in This Book

What's a *For Dummies* book without icons pointing out useful tips, interesting facts, and potentially dangerous pitfalls? Familiarize yourself with the three icons here and their identifying qualities to make sure you don't miss out on the meatiest parts of the book.

The Tip icon points out helpful information designed to make your job easier.

The Remember icon marks an interesting and useful fact — something you might want to keep in mind for later use.

The Warning icon highlights lurking danger. When you see this icon, I'm waving at you from the sidelines telling you to pay attention and proceed with caution.

Where to Go from Here

Hungry yet? Grab a fork and start digging in to any chapter you choose. Start by scanning the Table of Contents to discover which sections pique your interest and head straight to the source for the information — for example, head to Part III for the lowdown on setting up your blog's technical framework — or start with page one and devour the whole book from the beginning, savoring each section as if it were the next decadent dish in an irresistible six-course meal.

I want to be the first to welcome you to the expansive food blogging community! I hope *Food Blogging For Dummies* provides answers to all your questions and needs, but if you're ever stumped or are just looking to chat with an equally as passionate food lover (who once wrote a 750-word article entirely about parsley), please feel free to e-mail me at `kelly@justataste.com`.

Part I
Whetting Your Appetite

"It all started when I was researching recipes for Baked Alaska and frozen custard for my baking blog."

In this part . . .

Get your first taste of the food blogosphere by taking a careful look at how past moments in culinary media have shaped the present-day community. As you meet your fellow food bloggers, you'll discover that the motivations for launching a food blog are vast and varied, from perfecting your slicing and dicing to kick-starting your culinary empire online.

Although some bloggers may be in search of fame, fortune, or even a cookbook deal, others strive to simply establish their voice and create a network of food-loving enthusiasts.

In Part I, you begin to zone in on your own aspirations as you discover the key factors to think about before your first post ever goes from private to public.

1

The Many, The Proud

In This Chapter

- Assessing the current state of the food blogosphere
- Understanding the many roles of food bloggers
- Finding your voice in text and visuals
- Meeting other food bloggers
- Setting yourself up for the sweet taste of success

Creating, launching, and maintaining a food blog can be a casual hobby or a serious business. Regardless whether you're a home cook and amateur writer, or a professional chef and James Beard award-winning author, managing your food blog will lend you a spatula to help shape the growing culinary scene.

Whether your goal is preserving your family's legacy through food or becoming the next Pioneer Woman of the digital Wild West, the reach, popularity, and influence of food blogs is a rapidly expanding sector of the online realm that's impossible to ignore.

In this chapter, I introduce you to the wide world of food blogging by providing context in terms of its size, scope, and robust growth over the past five years. As you look to the past, you can find your food blogging place in the present while planning for a beautifully designed, easily navigated, one-of-a-kind online journal. Understanding the many roles of a food blogger helps you in crafting a strategic and realistic approach to success, no matter how you measure it.

Assessing the Food Blogosphere

The field of food blogging represents an explosion of popular culture, and in this case, popular cuisine. From Bakerella's cake pops to Hungry Girl's Fiber

One chicken strips, food blogs have cultivated some of the culinary industry's biggest trends.

Where else can you discover the current craze — in the form of Oreo-stuffed chocolate chip cookies or the latest incarnation of bacon — than the thriving world of food blogging? Every day a new tastemaker launches a blog and joins the growing throngs of impassioned, dedicated, and driven food enthusiasts who are ditching the ketchup-stained 3x5 cards and taking to the web to publish and share content.

Food blogging on the rise

Five years ago, Smitten Kitchen, Orangette, Homesick Texan, and Simply Recipes could very well have been the names of my favorite local hangouts — the corner café I go to for my morning coffee, the downtown diner with the key lime pie, the steakhouse with the famous filet, or the bakery with the unbeatable sticky buns. And the names Deb Perelman, Molly Wizenberg, Lisa Fain, and Elise Bauer might as well have been the names of my favorite singers, or painters, or even childhood friends.

But if you ask any food blogger in 2012 whether they've ever heard of Smitten Kitchen, you might as well be asking them whether they've ever heard of a guy named Elvis.

A few of my personal heroes — Deb, Molly, Lisa, and Elise — are among those who have helped usher the field of food blogging from a quiet corner of the web to one of the most rapidly growing sectors of the modern digital era. Elise, for example, launched her wildly popular food blog, Simply Recipes, in 2003 as a way to document her family's rich recipe history. Since, she has inspired countless readers whose eyes graze her page to do the same. Elise's clear and concise policy regarding comments on her blog has set the tone for transparency and accountability in food blogging, and her generosity in advising less-experienced bloggers has advocated for a supportive community surrounding the creation and sharing of content online.

Food blogging has become a phenomenon whereby impassioned foodies have come to know these bloggers' names, and countless others, through every typed word, every calculated recipe, every comment, every photo, *every single thought* — blogged publicly for the rest of the world to read, enjoy, react to, and most importantly, draw inspiration from.

So just how far-reaching is this epicurean explosion?

Technorati, an online search engine that tracks blogs, estimated in a *Times Online* article from February 2009 that there were roughly 33,000 food blogs on the web. That number has gone nowhere but up in the past three years.

BlogHer, one of the most expansive and robust communities of bloggers across every niche, reported a 70 percent increase in unique visitors — specifically to its Food Channel — from October 2010 to October 2011. As a result, the Food Channel has become BlogHer's largest category of blogs in the entire network.

Aside from dominance in the digital realm, food bloggers have extended their reach by making the reverse trek to the world of print via cookbook deals. Clotilde Dusoulier of Chocolate & Zucchini was the first food blogger to go from blog-to-book, and many others followed suit, including Adam Roberts of Amateur Gourmet, Amy Sherman of Cooking with Amy, Angie Dudley of Bakerella, and the list just keeps on growing.

If the cookbook craze isn't enough to demonstrate the power and proliferation of food blogging, just tune in to the Television Food Network for a look at the Pioneer Woman in action as food blogger extraordinaire Ree Drummond hosts her own cooking show.

The number of food blogs is growing, and so too are appetites — not only for food, but also for content that is entertaining, engaging, useful, and inspiring. Bloggers are following their passions to fill every niche, from budget-conscious meals on $5 Dinners, to gluten-free recipes on Celiac Teen, as shown in Figure 1-1.

Figure 1-1: Food bloggers follow their passions.

Over the past 15 years, food blogs have helped usher food from dinner tables to mainstream media channels by championing every topic from specialized diets and restaurant reviews to video tutorials and original recipes. The following timeline shows some of the most influential moments, and although not all-inclusive, it highlights turning points that represent moments of progress in the digital sphere. I've also noted the launch dates of a handful of the most popular blogs still in existence to this day so that you get a sense of the timing and evolution of the food blogging industry.

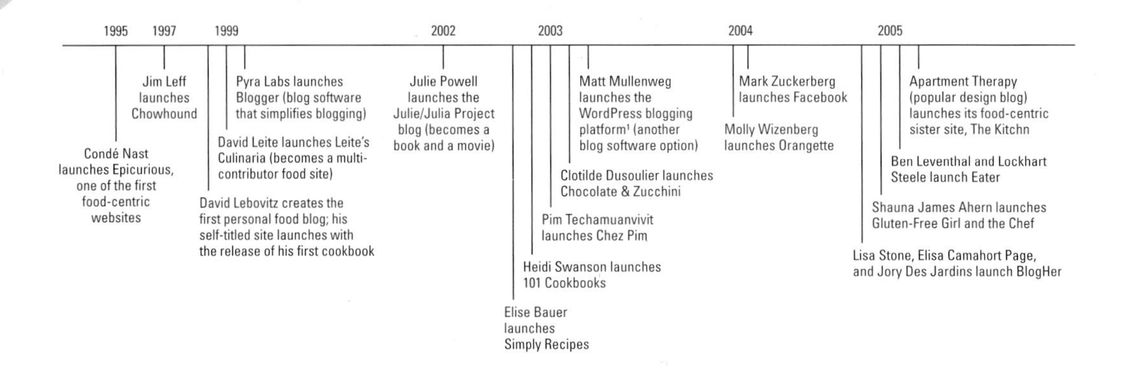

Surveying the scene

I could think of no better way to discover the who, what, why, when, and where of the current food blogging scenes than by going straight to the source with an exhaustive The State of the Food Blogosphere survey. I wrote this survey and then posted a link to it on Facebook and Twitter, asking food bloggers across the country and across the world to weigh in with their thoughts. Fellow food bloggers and food media industry professionals re-tweeted and re-posted the survey link, encouraging their followers to do the same.

Over a three-month period, more than 135 veteran and beginner food bloggers alike participated in the survey, which featured 20 questions tied to every aspect of food blogging, including the motivations for joining the community, the frequency and consistency of posting, the average monthly ad revenue earned, the preferred type of camera, and more. I've sprinkled the results throughout the relevant chapters to provide perspective on the thriving and inviting community you're joining.

Although respondents were required to provide their name and blog information to participate, all published results from the multiple-choice survey remain anonymous.

Making your move

Start preheating your oven because there's no time like the present to kick your food passion into action by launching your blog. Don't let the tens of thousands of food bloggers already in the online space prevent you from wanting to dive right in. The sheer number of impassioned foodies may be overwhelming, but it's also even more reason to not waste another minute getting started.

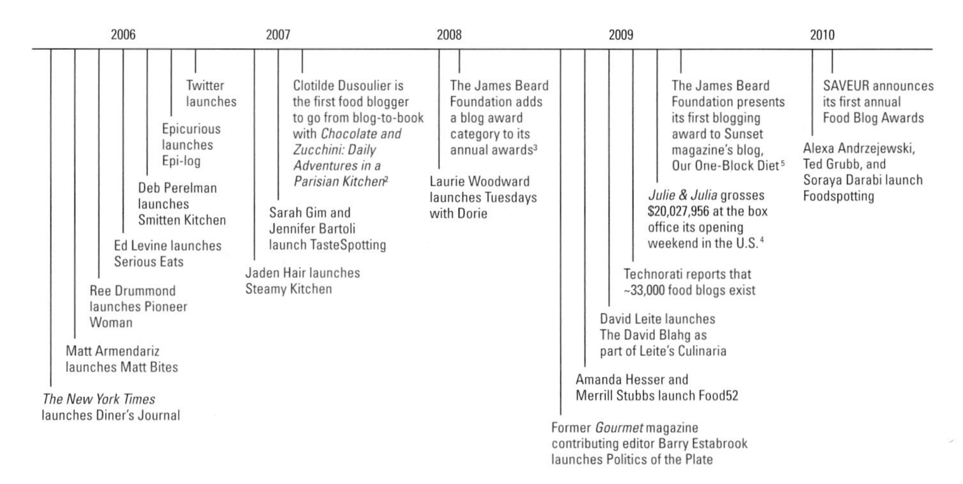

1 www.wordpress.com; *2 Published by Clarkson Potter; 3* http://www.jamesbeard.org/files/2009_JBFAwards_Entry_Press_Release.pdf; *4 The Internet Movie Database* (www.imdb.com); *5* http://www.jamesbeard.org/files/2009_JBF_Award_Winners.pdf

The State of the Food Blogosphere survey produced some surprising and encouraging findings for first-time food bloggers. As the results in Figure 1-2 show, roughly 30 percent of respondents reported launching their food blog less than one year ago. Translation: You did not miss the boom. You're living (and eating) in it!

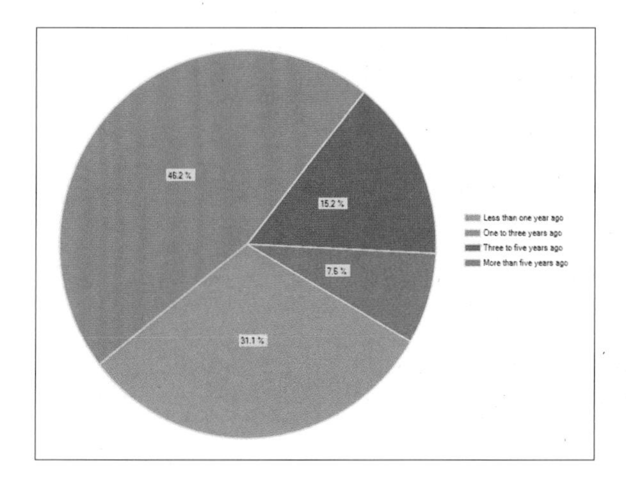

Figure 1-2: Roughly one-third of survey respondents reported launching their blog in the past year.

Beginner bloggers often face barriers with the technical aspects of setting up a blog. But lucky for you, this book walks you through the technical requirements that could block the path to publishing success. But there is one intangible roadblock with the potential to leave you more frozen than a Lean Cuisine: perfection.

Countless food bloggers with talents in recipe development, food writing, photography, food styling, and beyond wow me on a daily basis. And most of them have no formal training in their craft. Their work is inspiring, but I also realize it can be paralyzing, which is why you have to approach the start of your food blogging journey with the following mindset: Your blog does not have to be perfect on the day you launch.

There's no day like today to dive into the necessary prep work required prior to launching your blog. Like all new endeavors, there will always be elements to adjust days, months, and even years after you launch. That's what blogging is all about — growing, evolving, and constantly improving.

Understanding the Varied Roles of Food Bloggers

Maintaining a food blog is very similar to owning and running a restaurant. Countless tasks require attention each day to ensure your haute hangout stays up and running and customers stay satisfied. But imagine if you are the only person responsible for every task at your restaurant. You take on the roles of owner, chef, waiter, manager, accountant, bartender, and yes, even dishwasher. Welcome to the realistic life of a multi-tasking food blogger.

Regardless of your blog's niche, every food blogger has duties extending beyond the basics of cooking and writing. Here is a list of 13 possible roles tied to the creation and maintenance of an average food blog. Your blog may not require you to take on the entire dozen, but it's important to understand running a food blog involves much more than simply cooking, writing, and consuming calories:

- **Cook:** Shopping for ingredients and preparing dishes featured on your blog
- **Recipe developer:** Creating original recipes by drawing inspiration from the people and places surrounding you
- **Recipe tester:** Verifying the accuracy and reproducibility of recipes to ensure your readers will have success in the kitchen
- **Food stylist:** Plating and styling food so it's visually appealing and an accurate representation of the accompanying recipe
- **Prop stylist:** Selecting the appropriate props to create a mood and establish a space around your food
- **Photographer/videographer:** Taking photos and/or video of your culinary creations and finishing any required touch-ups with a few tweaks using photo-editing software

- **Writer:** Writing succinct copy that is inspiring, entertaining, and engaging
- **Editor:** Editing the copy you write to ensure it's free of spelling and grammatical errors and follows your established style guide
- **Managing editor:** Creating an editorial calendar to ensure consistency and frequency in your posting and managing all business-related decisions
- **Technical director:** Overlooking the technical maintenance of your blog, whether that means you troubleshoot issues yourself or you find (and possibly pay) the right expert to make the fix for you
- **Chief Financial Officer:** Overseeing all financial decisions and requirements tied to your blog, such as purchasing groceries, paying for restaurant meals, and exploring options for earning revenue from your blog
- **Social media strategist:** Establishing and maintaining a presence in all social media platforms tied to your blog
- **Publicist:** Promoting your content online and offline

Although this list of roles is geared more toward bloggers who are cooking and styling recipes at home, a majority of the roles still apply to bloggers who are reviewing restaurants or writing about their culinary travels. All food bloggers take on the roles of photographer, writer, editor, managing editor, technical director, Chief Financial Officer, social media strategist, and publicist — regardless of what topic they're blogging about.

It may seem like a tall order to take on the responsibilities of 12 roles, but believe me, it can be done. Just take Marla Meridith from Family Fresh Cooking, as shown in Figure 1-3, for example.

Figure 1-3: Marla Meridith of Family Fresh Cooking takes on multiple roles to maintain a successful blog.

Marla is a one-woman team (with a few pint-sized taste testers) that develops original recipes, tests those recipes, styles food, provides suggestions for tabletop setups and décor, photographs food, writes inspiring posts, publishes inspiring posts, *and* runs a robust social media campaign. So she may admit to waking up at 4 a.m. every day, but still, Marla is a prime example of a food blogger who successfully wears many toques to maintain the flourishing community centered on her popular blog.

Marla is a prime example of how food bloggers in the current digital age have to be willing and able to take on multiple roles, from creating content to engaging with the larger food community and beyond. By planning ahead and instituting a few tips for time-management success, you'll be wearing multiple toques in no time flat. (See Chapter 5 for more on devising a strategy to keep up with your blog.)

Meeting Your Fellow Food Bloggers

They've been blogging for days, weeks, months, or years. They're professionally trained chefs, amateur cooks, award-winning authors, and spell check-averse writers. They blog for a living, and they blog without earning a dollar. Regardless of their skills, experience, and goals, every food blogger serves as inspiration to one another, helping an already thriving community continue to produce and share food-centric content tied to every topic and every medium.

Why get to know them? Because your fellow food bloggers are skilled advisors on every topic from blog-hosting software and food styling to social media marketing and photo editing. Turn to them for guidance, and if you're lucky, you may even find a lifelong mentor. But even if you aren't in the market for advice, you'll still have the chance to cultivate new friendships online as you bond over your mutual love of doughnuts, tartar sauce, fried ravioli, and any other foods that light your fire.

As you tour the current food blogosphere, notice a handful of common characteristics apparent on many of the more well-known blogs:

- A passion for their defined niche
- A unique voice in text and visuals
- An ability to inspire through words and photos
- A presence in social media
- An active community on their blogs

A closer look at three popular food blogs reveals these five characteristics in addition to countless other identifying elements that not only make their food blogs successful, but also make them uniquely theirs.

Kalyn Denny launched Kalyn's Kitchen, as shown in Figure 1-4, in 2005 to chronicle her healthy, lower-glycemic approach to cooking and eating after she lost 40 pounds on the South Beach Diet. By streamlining her passion into the healthy cooking niche, Kalyn has built her blog into a reliable online destination for food lovers in search of lighter recipes, practical cooking tips, and personal advice about weight loss and diets. Her blog is packed with lightened up versions of comforting classics, such as ham and cauliflower casserole au gratin, grilled zucchini pizza slices, and pesto pasta salad, all of which are paired with colorful step-by-step photos. Kalyn's vast recipe archives and honest approach to healthy eating has attracted more than 10,000 fans on Facebook and has led to an active and engaged blog community in which readers post comments, pose questions, and find support among fellow healthy food advocates.

Figure 1-4: Kalyn Denny's passion for healthy, lower-glycemic cuisine shines through on her popular blog.

Two years after Kalyn joined the food blogging community, Annie M. launched Annie's Eats, as shown in Figure 1-5. Food lovers flock to her blog's drool-worthy photographs, engaging text, and creative recipes that aim to encourage readers to stick to the homemade take on everything from baby food and barbecue sauce to chocolate ice cream and Ranch dressing. Detailed explanations on cooking techniques and ingredients help readers remain fearless in the kitchen as Annie guides them to step outside their culinary comfort zones. A self-taught cook and photographer, Annie's DIY approach to food has gained her a strong, 20,000-plus following on Facebook, where she attracts fans with humorous cooking anecdotes, fun food finds, and endearing photos of her children helping out in the kitchen.

Figure 1-5: Annie M. built a strong community of DIY'ers around her popular blog Annie's Eats.

In 2008, Kevin and Amanda Bottoms joined the online community of food lovers with their blog, Kevin & Amanda, as shown in Figure 1-6. In the three short years since their launch, their blog has become a rich resource for in-depth food photography tutorials that cover every topic from the best lens for your digital single-lens reflex (dSLR) camera to basic and advanced tips for editing images. In addition to instructive how-to's for photo buffs, Kevin & Amanda is also home to the couple's collection of free custom fonts, a majority of which are hand-drawn replicas of text samples submitted by their blog readers.

The talented duo shares their skills and their love of food through informative, easy-to-read posts complete with stunning images, which can be clicked to reveal technical information about the photo, such as the type of camera used, the lens, and the aperture and focal length. Amanda's personal reflections on weight loss and health have also attracted a devoted following not only on Facebook and Twitter, but on the blog itself, where her heartfelt post about losing 30 pounds has more than 330 comments from readers.

Kalyn's Kitchen, Annie's Eats, and Kevin & Amanda are all popular blogs with dedicated followings as a result of not only their abilities to produce and share original, inspiring, and informative content, but also their willingness to encourage and promote others in the surrounding community. This give and take of knowledge and resources is what makes the food blogosphere such a prosperous place for generating ideas and friendships.

Figure 1-6: Kevin and Amanda share their tips for cooking, photography, scrapbooking, and more.

Setting Yourself Up for Success

Achieving success in the world of food blogging requires a strong blend of passion, creativity, determination, and patience as you find your place in the melting pot of online talents ranging from self-taught cooks to full-time photographers and every skill level in between.

Looking to your fellow food bloggers and dreaming of all that's in store may serve as motivation to fire up the burners and get your blog in motion, but your best chance for success is to first lay down a strong foundation consisting of your streamlined interests and original voice.

Finding your niche

The food blogosphere is just like an all-you-can-eat buffet in that the sheer quantity of blogs means the online audience has options with what they put on their plates. Streamlining your blog's niche sets you up for the best chance of success because by publishing content in a more specialized area, you satisfy the specific cravings of your readers as a go-to expert in a designated field. The goal is to be the Jack of all tasks, master of one niche.

Finding your niche involves a careful mix of homing in on your passions while identifying your weaknesses and strengths related to culinary and technical skills. Regardless of where your individual interests and abilities lie, to be successful in your niche, your first step is to get in touch with your inner detail-oriented self by embracing the specifics and narrowing the focus of your blog.

For example, rather than launch a blog centered on original recipes, dig a bit deeper into what topics really make you tick by further zooming in on your niche. Your blog's original recipes could be tied to specific dietary considerations, such as vegan or gluten-free, or they could all utilize the same cooking technique, such as braising or stir-frying.

In Chapter 2, I provide tips for streamlining your interests and inspirations, and in Chapter 5, I help you determine your full content menu. However, why not seize this moment to kick off your culinary brainstorm? Make a list of your food-centric passions, as well as the types of posts — reviews, top-ten lists, and interviews are just a few — you're interested in writing.

You may already know what your niche is, or you may just be starting the search for your true food passions. Zone in on your interests by scanning the blogosphere for inspiration from your fellow food bloggers. For example, Heidi Swanson, creator of 101 Cookbooks (see Figure 1-7), has clearly and effectively established her blog as an authoritative resource on cooking with natural ingredients and on vegetarian and vegan cuisine.

Figure 1-7: Heidi Swanson zoned in on her passion and niche by launching a blog focused on cooking with natural ingredients.

Heidi has parlayed her popular blog into three successful cookbooks, and her work as a photographer and writer has appeared in *Food & Wine, Glamour,* and *The Washington Post.*

Another example of a food blogger who's carved out a well-defined niche is Adam Roberts, creator of The Amateur Gourmet, as shown in Figure 1-8. Adam launched his blog in 2004 and quickly shot to food blog fame after his recipe post about cupcakes resembling Janet Jackson's infamous Super Bowl "wardrobe malfunction" landed him on CNN. Adam has since developed his blog into a witty, resource-packed online destination for food lovers of every skill level. His personality and knowledge shine through every post, making for easy reading and inspiration for stress-free feasting.

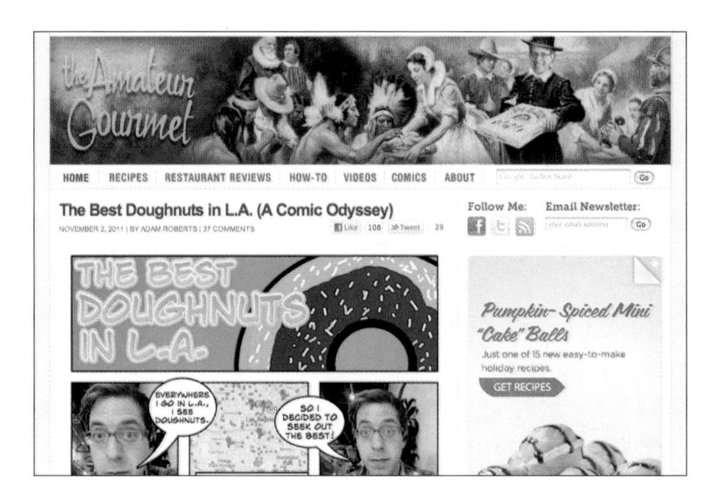

Figure 1-8: The Amateur Gourmet has attracted a devoted following of beginner and advanced cooks.

Owning your voice

After you decide the niche for your blog, the next step before setting up your online space is to focus on your voice, both in text and in visuals. Every food blogger starts their journey at a different place. You may be a passionate foodie keen on polishing your photography skills, or you may be a professional photographer looking to strengthen your skills as an artist of words. No matter where you start, you will grow and evolve in every role you play in your food blogging journey.

Developing your voice: Words

Finding and fine tuning your voice as a food writer involves developing your personal style and tone, both of which help make your voice uniquely yours. Your style addresses elements such as punctuation and length; your tone relays your feelings about a given topic. Although blogging is much more casual and conversational in style than other forms of published work (think newspapers and magazines), the same rules for proper grammar, spelling, and punctuation still apply. (See Chapter 6 for more on establishing your own style guide.)

The more you write, the more you will home in on the defining elements of your voice. Authenticity is critical. Looking to fellow food bloggers is a great way to get inspired, but you don't want to sound like anyone but yourself. If you try to tweak your tone or shape your style based on another writer, you lose the element that makes your voice uniquely your own. In Chapter 4, you'll discover that the best way to remain authentic is to allow your current mood to steer your tone, whether it be playful or pensive, humorous or serious.

Take, for example, Monica Bhide of A Life of Spice (shown in Figure 1-9), who has spent years cultivating a strong, authentic voice to share her passion for Indian cuisine. Monica's blog features recipes for dishes such as hot curry leaf potatoes and saffron salmon bites, but it is in her longer posts about the intersection of her Indian heritage and food that she shines in the role of storyteller.

Figure 1-9: Monica Bhide writes about the intersection of her Indian heritage and food on A Life of Spice.

In one of her most popular posts, Monica asks the question, "Does a recipe need to be complicated to be good?" Her answer that follows is a passionate, personal response detailing the importance of simplicity in ingredients and in preparation. Her style is direct, and her tone is opinionated, yet intimate, as she recalls her parents teaching her to cook with a focus on the freshness and purity of foods. The heartfelt, authentic writing earned her a nomination for Best Culinary Essay in the 2011 SAVEUR Food Blog Awards.

Developing your voice: Photos

Just as you develop your voice as a writer, you'll also develop your visual voice as a photographer. It's no secret that photographs are one of the leading elements of a successful food blog. Without a single written word, an image of piping hot artichoke and Parmesan cheese dip slathered atop toasted baguette slices can invigorate an appetite (and an attraction).

Turn to your fellow bloggers for inspiration and to gain a sense of the variety of visual approaches to food. Take, for example, Béatrice Peltre of La Tartine Gourmand, as shown in Figure 1-10. Her photography style is light, effortless, and almost angelic in tone. Her work reinforces the fact that lighting is the most important element of shaping your photography style and your visual identity.

Figure 1-10: Developing your visual style as a photographer is just as critical as developing your voice as a food writer.

Every food blogger has a different style and approach to the visual representation of food. Some prefer a simple setup focusing solely on the food, whereas others prefer an extravagant spread highlighting an entire meal within the context of a scene.

Six tips for sweet success

Finding your niche and owning your voice puts you well on your way to finding success in food blogging, no matter how you measure it. From reaching your goal for monthly unique visitors to mastering the art of making puff pastry, you can evaluate the success of your blog in countless ways.

Regardless of how you define success, give yourself the best chance for it by remembering these six tips as you get your first taste of the world of food blogging:

- **Set goals:** Now is the perfect time to set a goal for where you want your blog to be in one week, in one month, and in one year. Seize the fact that you're fresh to the scene by setting realistic aspirations for every element of your blog, such as unique visitors, ad revenue, or total number of posts. (See Chapter 2 where I discuss defining your interests, setting goals, and taking the plunge into the food blogosphere.)
- **Embrace technology:** Technology can be your best friend or biggest enemy. Regardless of how comfortable you are with setting up and running your blog, vow to stay calm through any technological storms that pass. (See Chapter 3 for assembling the mechanics of your blog.)
- **Contemplate design:** Give some serious thought to the layout and design of your blog. Although the digital format means changes can be made in seconds, save yourself the back-and-forth struggle by setting a definitive strategy for the look and feel of your blog before you start publishing posts. (See Chapter 7 for strategizing your blog's design and layout.)
- **Socialize:** It's never too soon to start getting involved in the social media spheres by claiming your blog's Twitter handle, setting up a Facebook brand page, and electronically introducing yourself to your fellow food lovers. (See Chapter 3 for getting a handle on your social media space.)
- **Commit:** Keep the dozen roles of a food blogger in mind as you contemplate the amount of time you can realistically dedicate to your blog. Commit to a routine posting frequency to start establishing consistency on your blog. (See Chapter 6 for devising a strategy to keep up with your blog.)
- **Get hungry:** Literally.

2

Finding Your Niche

In This Chapter

- Streamlining your interests and inspirations
- Becoming a member of the food blogging community
- Getting to know your audience
- Defining success through different perspectives
- Brainstorming the perfect blog title

Cake decorating disasters. Teenage restaurant critics. Recipes for triathletes. Vegan *sous-vide* desserts. You name the topic, there's likely a food blog dedicated to it.

But just because every ingredient, concept, technique, and cuisine seems like it's being covered by 2 or 2,000 food blogs doesn't mean you can't join the conversation. In fact, it doesn't even mean you can't eventually become an expert voice within the conversation. It just means you need to identify your *niche* — that unique angle that's going to make you and your blog stick out among the rest.

In this chapter, I lead you on a path of discovery to identify where your true food passion lies so that you can determine where your blog will live within the food blog digital neighborhood. I also have you set some goals as you create your own recipe for success — no matter how you measure it. Your niche-finding journey begins with a spark, and ends with one of the most important decisions you'll ever make: your food blog's name.

Starting with a Spark

Every person has that moment. That moment when you decide you're going to start a food blog. For some, the impulse strikes in an instant; for others, it grows slowly over time. Regardless of when and how the fire ignites, what matters is how you fan the motivations and inspirations to keep it burning.

As I discuss in Chapter 1, The State of the Food Blogosphere survey I conducted provided invaluable information about food bloggers' behaviors in the current blogging environment. The questions I feature in the survey were based not only on the topics stemming from what every blogger should know prior to launching a blog (which I cover in Chapter 15), but also the topics everyone wants to know about — such as ad revenue, pageviews, and effective marketing strategies — but might not feel comfortable asking or answering in a non-anonymous setting.

One of the most important questions in The State of the Food Blogosphere survey I conducted was, "Why did you initially start your food blog?" Bloggers were given an option of four choices — To Create an Online Legacy, To Become a Better Cook, To Express My Opinions about Food, To Connect with Other Food Lovers — and could select multiple answers, or include their own response.

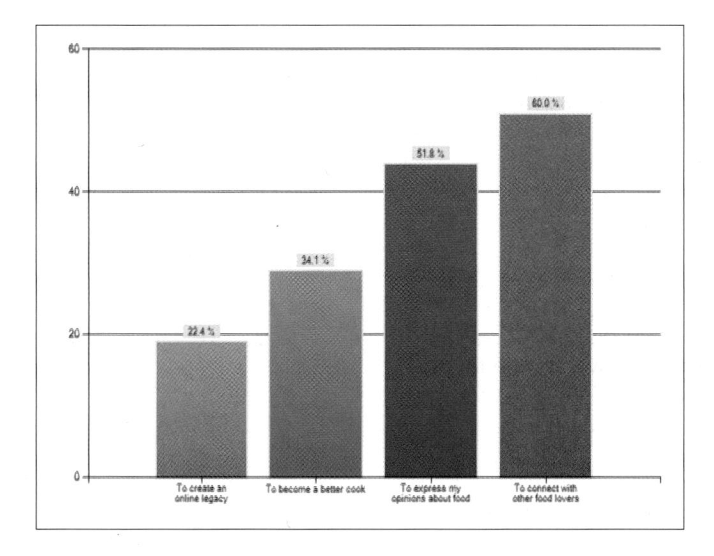

Figure 2-1: Survey results indicating the reasons why food bloggers choose to start a blog.

As the results in Figure 2-1 show, 60 percent of respondents chose To Connect with Other Food Lovers as a strong motivating factor, followed by 50 percent who responded with To Express My Opinions about Food.

Tied to the theme of connecting with others, 45 percent of responses detailed in the Other category centered on sharing recipes with family members and friends. This concept of exchanging information, whether through recipes or food anecdotes, was a leading force behind the launch of many of the most popular food blogs in existence, including Smitten Kitchen, Homesick Texan, and Simply Recipes.

The motivations for starting a food blog can be vast and varied. And although the survey provides a broader view of the reasoning process, your own factors of inspiration are most important. Why are *you* starting a food blog? Discovering the answer to this question is the first step toward homing in on your niche within the greater food blogosphere.

Streamlining your foodie interests

Most blogs in existence can be categorized into a *niche,* or an underlying concept that groups the blog's content under a general theme. These themes could be blogs about politics, fashion, parenting, sports, finances, and pretty much every other category imaginable. And the good news is that in deciding to write a food-centric blog, you've already picked your overall niche. But you're not done just yet!

Time to dig into the details by streamlining your passions into an even more specific niche within food. Why not just blog about anything and everything food-related that peaks your interest? Because in doing so, you establish yourself as knowledgeable in everything, but masterful in nothing. Specifying the topic of your food blog gives you the best chance of not only becoming an authority in your area of interest, but also of attracting a consistent audience based on the content you publish as an information provider.

This advice comes with an important caveat: Not everyone may want to become an expert, have an expansive following, or be a crowded stop on the Internet information highway. Your food blogging goals are as unique as you are, and how you define success is based simply on that: your definition. I dive into creating your own recipe for success later in this chapter, but for now, keep in mind that your first steps toward homing in on your blog's topic are about identifying your interests rather than joining the ranks of the trendiest topic *du jour.*

From Indian food restaurant reviews to quick-fix recipes starring all things cheese, your blog's focus is a direct indication of you and your personal interests. Although food blogs can cover countless concepts, a few of the more common topics include blogs dedicated to

- Original recipes with an underlying theme
- Baking and dessert recipes
- Restaurant reviews

Don't panic if you don't see your interest in the preceding short list. Finding a focal point — popular or not — by focusing on your specific interests is exactly what will make your blog unique to you. If essays on food politics or haikus about ham get you fired up, by all means ignite those burners and let the flames burn bright. As you begin to pinpoint your motivating factors, consider the following questions related to your potential food blogging niche:

- **Are you passionate enough about the topic that you could write about it every single day if you had to?** Your should feel driven to want to read about, talk about, research, and stay current on the niche you select.
- **Is your blog's concept broad enough to merit an infinite number of posts?** Specificity is crucial, but too specific will leave you in a brainstorming bind.
- **Are you aware of any blogs with a similar, if not identical, focus?** Do your research to determine what other blogs currently share your space. If similar blogs are already in existence, aim to approach the niche from a different (and hopefully unique) angle.

The answers to these questions may not be entirely evident at this early stage of your planning, but it's a good idea to keep these questions in mind as you continue to narrow your interests.

Although the entire goal of finding your niche is to focus on a specific angle, remember the need for sustainability before you settle on a topic. You may decide to start a food blog featuring only recipes that incorporate sea urchin roe and bubblegum foam. And although you'd fit right into the category of eclectic food combinations, the reality is, you likely can't consistently post recipes featuring two such specific ingredients (dare I say even stomach *eating* such a combo week after week).

It's impossible to define exactly what makes a niche too narrow or too broad, so don't go crazy trying to find a topic that's a perfect balance between the two. Instead, dedicate your time to seriously contemplating what it is within the food world that excites you. Like a good pork belly brine, let the concept for your blog marinate at least overnight to give yourself ample time to see whether it's a topic worth pursuing.

You should be able to summarize your blog's niche in one sentence. Table 2-1 features a list of food blogs and how they can be categorized according to their specific angle. This short list alone highlights the varying degrees of specificity within the larger food blogging niche.

Table 2-1 Examples of Food Blogs and Their Niches

Food Blog	*Niche*
Panini Happy	Recipes created with a Panini maker
EatingAsia	Culinary travels throughout Asia
Celiac Teen	Gluten-free recipes
$5 Dinners	Recipes and tips for cooking $5 meals
Veggie Belly	Vegetarian and vegan recipes

From individual cooking techniques to dietary preferences, there's no limit to the passions and interests of the online food community. But the unifying factor among all these blogs is that each author chose a topic they were passionate about and then they stuck to it.

It is this consistency that allows readers to identify their blogs as more than just food blogs, but rather as distinctive, topic-driven sites regularly dedicated to a particular interest. That's not to say you have to have the same focal point for all your blogging eternity because it's only natural that your interests will change. But for now, zero in on the topic that inspires you the most and then let your writing, photos, recipes, or reviews do the talking.

Identifying what makes you different from other food bloggers

Special. Unique. Distinguished. Unconventional. How you label your individuality doesn't matter, what matters is how you make the most of it. Before you can make your uniqueness work to your advantage, you first have to answer the essential, albeit cliché, question: "What defines you?"

I know what you're thinking, "Food blogging tips *and* unsolicited psychological advice? This book's a bargain!" But stick with me here, and I promise you'll reap the rewards of a bit of (coerced) self-reflection.

Not every path to self-discovery has to wind up on Dr. Phil's stage. In an attempt to avoid getting overly philosophical, I find it best to make a list of the top three qualities that you'd use to describe yourself to a stranger. Go on, grab a pen, and jot them down — in the margin, in a notebook, on a napkin, anywhere. This is no time for humility, so go on and toot that horn.

Next to your list of qualities, make a list of the top three food-related topics that interest you the most (see Table 2-2 for a sample exercise). For a helpful nudge, I list a few options here, but this list is by no means all-inclusive:

- Trying new restaurants
- Making staple foods from scratch
- Cooking with only organic ingredients
- Discovering the scientific side of food
- Teaching your family or friends how to cook
- Traveling to new culinary destinations

As you stare down both lists, mix and match your various qualities with your interests. Are you an attentive person who enjoys taking photos of every meal you eat? Or perhaps you're more inquisitive and inspired by eco-friendly fare. Whatever qualities and interests you possess, these short lists serve as a quick reference for targeting your niche while also ensuring that the topic you choose is one that truly interests you.

Table 2-2 Targeting Your Niche

Top Three Qualities about Yourself	*Top Three Food-Related Topics of Interest*
Inquisitive	Molecular gastronomy
Analytical	Fusion cuisine
Detail-oriented	Food history

The biggest mistake you can make when deciding on a blog topic is settling on one purely because it's trendy or already has a large audience. I hate to be the bearer of bad news, but trends die. And they die fast.

More importantly, not connecting with your subject out of pure passion or interest will be easily spotted through your writing. So don't just jump on the cake-pop bandwagon because it seems like the cool thing to do. Jump on the cake-pop bandwagon because you legitimately enjoy baking bite-sized treats and eating sweets from a stick.

Building your food blog skills

What interests you and what you're good at could be two very different things. When I first decided to start a food blog, my biggest inspiration was food photos — large, striking, taste-it-through-your-screen food photos. But all I had was a point-and-shoot camera, and the likes of Matt Bites and Smitten Kitchen for inspiration.

Unprepared and admittedly untalented, I started snapping photos and publishing them with my recipe posts. Figure 2-2 depicts one of the first photos I ever published on my blog, which featured a recipe for spinach salad with cherry tomatoes and warm bacon dressing.

Horrific, right? I achieved the impossible juxtaposition of creating a photo that was both overexposed, and yet somehow also underexposed. The fluorescent lighting and lack of balance in the frame are the two crowning cherries atop a cake that nobody wants to eat.

But I proudly claim this photo as my own and have yet to delete it from my blog for a very important reason: It demonstrates the evolution of my skill set. No one said you have to be Diane Cu and Todd Porter, of famed food photography blog White on Rice Couple, the first time you publish a photo.

Figure 2-2: A photo of spinach salad is overexposed, unbalanced, and unappetizing.

The truth is, everyone has to start somewhere. So whether your interest is in photography, recipe development, writing, or reviews, don't shy away from it simply because you don't feel talented enough to blog about the topic from the get-go. For most, you need time to become an expert and develop your talents.

You also don't want your blog to turn into a massive labor of love — *labor* being the key word there. Doing things you aren't as skilled at is more difficult and requires more time, so although you should push yourself and set goals related to your interests, be aware of and take advantage of the strengths you already possess. Those strengths could very well be the main factors that make you unique.

Joining the Food Blogging Community

When you launch your blog, you instantly become a part of the online food community; a community thriving with eclectic palates and calculated diets, masterful prose and incomplete thoughts, award-winning photography and smartphone snapshots. The community is teeming with every degree of the creative, artistic, and linguistic spectrum.

You will find people who are like you and those who are unlike you; those who inspire you and those who aspire to be you; those who build you up, and unfortunately, those who break you down. But it's all a part of the giant pot you dive into that first time you click Publish.

The first food blogger who inspired me was Matt Armendariz of Matt Bites. Three years ago, when I stumbled across his site, his talents had already catapulted him into the upper echelons of the food blogging world. His photography was breathtaking. His honest and witty writing was awe-inspiring. And then one day, just a few months after launching my own food blog, I e-mailed him. I thanked him — for being an inspiration, and for igniting my passion for food. Less than 48 hours later, I got a response:

> Kelly,
>
> Thank you so much for your e-mail. It really touched me.
>
> I might be doing some workshops in the future, so let's definitely keep in touch!
>
> Matt Armendariz

I still have that e-mail in my inbox, more than three years later. Sure, Matt may be the exception. I mean, how many mega-successful bloggers, who receive hundreds of e-mails a day, actually take the time to respond to a total stranger?

But based on my experience as a member of the food blogging community, Matt is, without a doubt, the rule. He, like the greater community, is inviting, welcoming, and supportive. Of course you may meet a food blogger gone astray, the one hell-bent on leaving anonymous soul-crushing comments. But for the most part, the food blogging community functions like a family, pulling together in times of despair and celebrating one another during times of triumph.

When you have a firmer grasp on your blog's focal point, you can familiarize yourself with the community you're joining. The best place to start is by meeting your soon-to-be readers, those very people who will help you transform your site from a one-way dialogue to a two-way conversation.

Knowing Your Audience

I assume you aren't starting your food blog with the goal of keeping it hidden from outside readers. You may adjust your blog's privacy settings or limit who you send your URL to, but ultimately, you aren't hitting Publish with the end goal of having no other soul read what you wrote. This element of putting yourself out into the Internet abyss invites an audience to engage with your content, and in turn, interact with you.

When you first launch your blog, you will likely have only a vague sense of who your audience is. They probably have an interest in food — whether in recipes, cooking anecdotes, restaurant reviews, photographs, or otherwise. Knowing even the most limited insights about your readers is an invaluable guide when it comes not only to what content you display on your blog, but also how you display it and in what context.

Even if your current audience starts with your mom and ends with your grandmother, there are still countless advantages of knowing whose eyeballs grace your page, including helping you

- Connect with your readers to create a more interactive and engaging experience.
- Build a larger audience by understanding effective ways to communicate with them.
- Tailor your content to make it more relevant to your readers' needs, interests, and varying skill levels.

The last advantage may have you stumped. Aren't you supposed to be writing about content that interests *you?* The short answer is "yes," but the marketing answer is "to a degree." (See Chapter 13 for more on marketing your blog.)

If you really want to build your site into a strong, revered destination for your area of interest, it is essential to be aware of who your audience is.

Knowing your audience doesn't mean you literally have to meet them face to face, or have their favorite beverage and movie theatre snack of choice memorized. But you do want to be as tuned in to your blog's demographic as much as possible, which includes being aware of

- How they found your blog
- Why they came to your blog
- How they access the information on your blog (desktop computer or mobile device)
- What type of content they gravitate toward the most
- What type of content they interact with the most

And just how exactly will you find out such critical information? Cancel that appointment with the psychic because all this information can be accessed in a flash and for free.

Countless online resources track your blog's statistics and analytics. I discuss the full benefits of such resources, and how to install them on your blog, in Chapter 13, but it doesn't hurt to be familiar with these popular and user-friendly options:

- **Google Analytics:** Arguably the most popular free web analytics tool, Google Analytics generates detailed statistics about the visitors to your blog, as shown on the Visitors Overview page depicted in Figure 2-3. The tool also provides statistics tied to popular posts, common entry/exit pages, referring sites, and more. (`http://google.com/analytics`)

- **Site Meter:** With both free and paid options, Site Meter adds a web counter to your blog, giving you the option to display the number of visits and to collect specific data about visitors, such as their geographic location by country, their browser, and the duration of their visit to your blog. (http://sitemeter.com)
- **AWStats:** AWStats graphically displays the statistics tied to your blog, generating bar graphs that catalogue a variety of information tied to visitors and referring sites. (http://awstats.sourceforge.net)

Figure 2-3: The Visitors Overview page on Google Analytics highlights basic blog statistics.

There are also more direct means for learning who your audience is and what their interests are. If you're comfortable with being totally out in the open in your search, include questions in your blog posts aimed directly at your readers. You can solicit their advice about what type of content they want to see, or about how and why they arrived at your blog. Another option is to display a poll asking your readers questions about their demographics and areas of interest.

Whether you solicit information, or your readers provide it, remember that you're engaging in an interactive dialogue. Don't go silent after they answer your questions. Pay careful attention to your readers' responses left in the comments section or sent via e-mail. And remember that regardless of how you gather the information, it takes time to fully understand who reads the content on your blog.

Knowing who your audience is also sheds insight into what other sites they read, which gives you a clear view of the other blogs in your niche. Consider them as friendly next-door neighbors rather than the competition, and get to know them as useful resources with like-minded interests. Just like Mom said, there's always room to add another spot to the family table!

Writing Your Own Recipe for Success

After you home in on your niche, you have a better sense of where you're heading and can even start thinking about what your early goals are for your blog. They can include any element along the food blogging spectrum, which for some is publishing their first post, while for others it's publishing their first cookbook. No matter how basic or how lofty, goals serve as further motivation. It's more inspiring when you know you're aiming high, rather than not aiming at all.

I asked bloggers in The State of the Food Blogosphere survey how they measured success on their blog. Respondents could select more than one answer, but as the results in Figure 2-4 indicate, a majority named In Traffic (Uniques/Pageviews) as the predominant marker of success.

Paying attention to unique visitors and pageviews, much less understanding what they are and where they come from, may seem like a tall order before you've even published a single post. Sure, they're the most clear and tangible statistics to relay your blog's quantitative draw. But do your best to not let the numbers affect you during the preliminary stages of your blog. The numbers alone don't serve as a total gauge of your success, and in all honesty, they likely won't be large enough to warrant attention early on.

Put your focus and efforts into creating quality content rather than measuring how many people read it. You can decide when, or if, the numbers really matter because you're the one defining not only your goals, but also what it means for you to be a success in the food blogging world.

You can measure your success in countless ways, which can include tangible and intangible achievements everywhere from within the four walls of your home kitchen to the headlines of national publications. In addition to calculating unique visitors and pageviews, success can also be measured by

- Becoming a better cook
- Mastering food photography or styling
- Meeting people with common culinary interests
- Receiving comments from readers
- Preserving your family's food legacy online
- Making money from your blog
- Garnering offers for speaking engagements, book deals, TV appearances, and career opportunities

Which of the preceding, or other options not listed, do you connect with the most? Jot down your top three and then tuck them away. In one year, you can reread your early goals and see how, or if, your definition of success has changed.

Do you have visions of fortune and fame in the form of a bestselling cookbook? Are you aiming to catalog your great grandmother's 110-year food history? No matter the size or scope, inspiring to reach a goal in any capacity automatically gives you a threshold to measure your success.

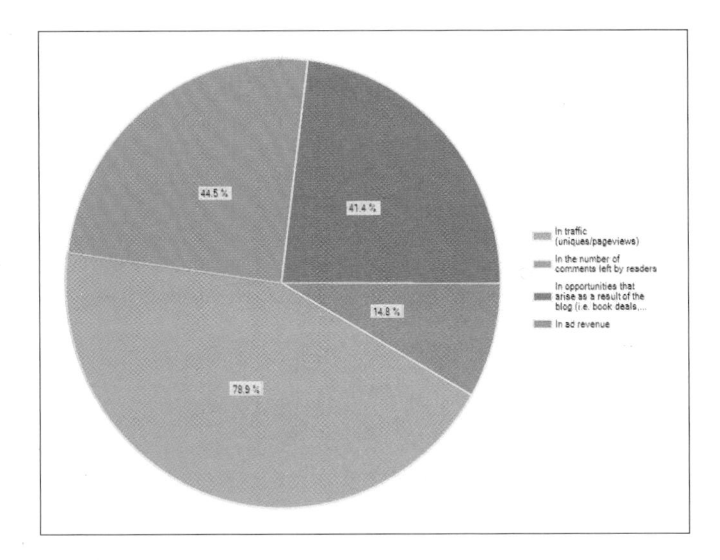

Figure 2-4: Survey results for the question, "How do you measure your food blog's success?"

And at the risk of pushing the corniness threshold (don't worry, I won't be offended if you save your heartfelt tears for dicing onions), remember that what matters most is not how small or large your goals are, but the fact that you have goals set.

The Secret Sauce for Naming Your Blog

You've streamlined your interests and identified your niche. You've outlined your goals and set the bar for success. Now it's time for one of the most important decisions you'll make: your food blog's name.

The name of my blog, Just a Taste, was inspired by a phrase my grandmother has been saying for as long as I can remember. After every meal, she appears with a box of my family's favorite Fannie May chocolate turtles and encourages us all to have "just a taste." No matter how stuffed you think you are, there is always room for "just a taste" of dessert. My mom later adopted the saying, and soon the memorable phrase evolved from my family's food mantra to the title of my blog. It's short, unique, and most important of all, has personal significance without being obscure.

Much like the name of any business, the title of your blog should encompass a careful balance of

- **Personal affinity:** Do you have a connection with the meaning or origin of the name?
- **Creativity:** Does the name peak interest without being too obscure?
- **Originality:** Are there any other food blogs or established businesses with similar names?
- **Relevancy:** Does the name relate to the blog's content and niche?
- **User-friendliness:** Is the name straightforward enough to remember and to spell?
- **Marketability:** Is the name easy to say aloud, translate into text, or depict in a logo?

Each of these naming elements plays a critical role in defining your blog, tying it to its niche, and establishing it as a personal brand. I discuss the concept of transforming your blog from a website to a brand in detail in Chapter 3, but for now, keep in mind that naming your blog is like naming a baby: It's in your best interest to pick a name and stick to it because the bigger it gets, the harder it is to change.

In addition to considering the essential elements for your blog's name, pay particular attention not to fall victim to these common naming downfalls:

- **Acronyms:** Unless you're KFC or T.G.I. Friday's, stay away from using acronyms in your blog's title because they can dilute the recall factor of your blog or be misunderstood.
- **Inside jokes:** You and your friends might get a giggle out of an inside joke for your blog's name, but if your goal is to attract an audience larger than your social circle, think twice about using an otherwise obscure reference.
- **Design disconnect:** Characters, such as ampersands and dashes, don't translate well from the web to print, or vice versa, and they can hamper consistency within your URL.
- **Uncommon extensions:** Aim for a URL that utilizes a `.com` rather than `.net`, `.me`, `.co`, `.us`, or any other uncommon domain extensions. Anything other than `.com` makes it more difficult for readers to remember your URL.
- **Long and laborious:** You're dealing with a blog name, not the title of your grad school thesis, so aim for short and sweet to get maximum recall.
- **Strange spelling:** Phood, whine, phlavor — you get the point. Steer clear of odd spellings or you'll get *krushed* when it comes to search engine optimization (SEO). (See Chapter 13 for more on SEO.)

- **Digital duplicate:** Just like you wouldn't name your search engine Goodle or Wahoo!, avoid giving your blog a similar title to an already established food blog.

I've covered the do's, and I've red-flagged the don'ts, time to enter Blog Naming Boot Camp. Get ready to exercise your mind as you transform a single, inspiring word into a full-fledged brand name to call your own.

Brainstorming your way to a name

With all the crucial and adverse-naming elements in mind, begin the brainstorming process by making a list of food blogs whose names you gravitate toward. Consider the similarities among those sites. Do they all have short names? Do they use puns? Are they more practical than creative? Do they make you laugh? Do they have the elusive wish-you-thought-of-that factor?

The blogs that leave you wishing you'd thought of that are often the ones you connect with or are inspired by the most. The following list outlines my personal favorites for food blog names that are original, memorable, and adhere to the short and sweet rule by sticking to four words or fewer:

- **Poor Man's Feast:** Simple, authentic recipes for everyday life
- **Bake or Break:** Dessert recipes from an amateur baker
- **Cookin' Canuck:** Family-friendly recipes from a Canadian-born blogger
- **We Are Not Martha:** Martha Stewart-inspired recipes and entertaining tips
- **Tokyo Terrace:** Recipes and culinary musings from an American living in Japan

Regardless of what food blog names inspire you, it is critical to tie your blog's title to its niche because doing so solidifies its placement within a particular category rather than filing it away in the generic food blog pile.

To tie your blog to its niche, pick five to ten keywords that you associate with your blog's focal point. For example, if you're a working mother who is creating a blog centered on dinner recipes for families with dietary considerations, your keywords might include

- Family-friendly
- Gluten-free
- Make-ahead
- Quick-fix
- Approachable

Now take your list of keywords, along with your list of inspiring blog names, and write down any and every blog title that comes to mind. Forget filtering your ideas at this point and just get as many options down as possible — include the cutesy, the obscure, the random, the obvious, and so on. Take that list and put it out of sight.

After a day has passed, reread the list and select the top three names that grab your attention. Before moving on to the next step of the naming process, make the quickest cut in your process of elimination by checking whether the URLs for your top three contenders are still available. Nothing kills a blog name faster than a URL that's already been spoken for!

With your three favorites in hand, ask yourself the following set of questions for each proposed name:

- **Does the name already exist online in any capacity?** If your proposed blog name is also the name of a bakery in San Francisco or a popular coffee shop in New York City, stop right there and consider an alternative before reading on. And if you want to safeguard a step further, double-check Twitter and Facebook for handles or pages already claimed.
- **Can your friends spell the name after hearing it once?** The last thing you want to do is hand out a pop quiz when you share your blog's name. Keep it simple enough so that no dictionaries (or studying) are required.
- **Is the name timeless?** Avoid names with timestamps, such as including your current age, grade in school, or number of children. You never know how long your blog will last or how far it will take you, so it's best to ensure that the name doesn't hold you to a distinctive point in your life.

Hopefully at least one of your three options has made it this far through Blog Naming Boot Camp. But before you can claim your URL and get your blog's backend into motion, your proposed title has to make it past one more obstacle: The Friends, Family, and an Acquaintance test.

Gauging instant reactions

You've spent days, maybe even weeks, settling on the perfect name for your food blog. The name you came up with is original, creative, marketable, available, and most importantly, resonates with you and your blogging niche. So why does anyone else need to give you the go-ahead?

No matter how in love you are with your blog's title, run it by another set of eyes and ears, not so much to validate its worth, but to solidify its appeal to an outside audience. The last thing you want is to have claimed your URL, set up your software, and started publishing posts only to share your blog's URL and get met with a chorus of "Huh?" "I don't get it." "How do you spell that?" "Wait, what was that?"

Such reactions will douse your excitement faster than a gallon of extinguishing foam on a fondue flame. So before you become fully invested, pass all three of your potential blog names through The Friends, Family, and an Acquaintance test by asking each person to weigh in. First gauge their instant reactions and then ask them for further feedback. Was it immediately obvious that your blog is a food blog? Did they have to think twice about how to spell it? Do they have an idea of what the blog is about?

After you collect their feedback and weigh it with your preferences, make the final cut from three stellar options to one standout selection.

3

Setting Up Shop

In This Chapter

- Registering and hosting a blog
- Choosing between a hosted and self-hosted blog
- Picking the right web host
- Selecting blogging software
- Getting a handle on your social media space

Whether you're a total tech nerd or a self-confessed technophobe, there are several important decisions to be made when assembling the mechanics of your food blog.

Should you choose a hosted platform or a non-hosted platform? Will you enter the world of WordPress or go Google? Is it better to join Twitter now, later, or never? Do you smile in excitement or cringe in horror at the phrase "backend of your blog?"

If you've been dreading the tech stuff, time to leave behind those fears. This chapter breaks it all down one simple step at a time, ensuring that you build your blog with a strong foundation that fits your needs, while also taking into account your wants.

Figure out how to mix and match your way to the best combination of a hosting site and blogging platform, and get ready to turn your vision into a full-blown food blog reality.

Registering and Hosting Your Blog

After you narrow in on your food blogging niche and decide on a name for your blog, two topics I cover in Chapter 2, you're faced with decisions and tasks related to all things technical. The first two decisions are whether to use a hosted or self-hosted blog solution and which blogging software to use.

From there, the tasks include registering your domain and picking a web host (if you choose the self-hosted option) and possibly installing the blogging software.

First you must understand the difference between hosted and self-hosted blogging solutions. A *hosted* blogging solution is one in which a company houses and maintains your blog on its servers. This solution frees you from the stress of managing backups, updating your software, and paying for a web host, which means more time for cooking, photographing, writing, and taking on the variety of other food blogging tasks I cover throughout the book. Examples of hosted blogging platforms include

- **WordPress.com:** It's important to note that the popular blogging platform WordPress exists as two options — WordPress.com and WordPress.org. WordPress.com is the free hosted version, which features an easy setup process involving minimal technical knowledge; however, ads are generally not allowed and plugins cannot be used. A WordPress.com blog will generally include the platform name in the URL, such as `www.iloveblogging.wordpress.com`.
- **Google Blogger:** Blogger is Google's foray into free hosted blogging platforms. Blogger is a quick and simple way to get your blog up and running while leaving the technical stuff to the pros. Much like WordPress.com, a Blogger blog will not allow ads or the use of plugins, and `.blogspot` appears in the hosted blog's domain name, such as `www.iloveblogging.blogspot.com`.
- **TypePad:** TypePad is a hosted blogging platform that is available for purchase. Although TypePad isn't free, the tradeoff is that you have total control over your blog, which means ads of any shape or size are permitted, as well as the use of plugins.
- **Other:** Additional hosted platforms include Tumblr and Posterous Spaces, which are considered microblogging platforms in that they feature shorter forms of content. Both platforms are free and are two of the fastest and easiest ways to get your content on the web.

Throughout the book, I focus primarily on WordPress and Blogger because they're the most commonly used platforms in the current blogosphere, and for good reason. Both platforms are known for their ease of use, design customization, and expansive online resources for troubleshooting technical issues.

A self-hosted blogging solution is much like it sounds in that you maintain total control of your site. You decide on one of the self-hosted blogging platforms, which provides its software, which you then download and install using your selected web host. Sound like a lot of work? The reality is that self-hosting your blog is a big undertaking, and one in which you will be responsible for making every decision tied to the technical and aesthetic elements of your blog. You'll not only set up the blogging software, but you'll also maintain it and create backups, all while shelling out the cash for the rights to use a custom domain and implement ads and run plugins. If you're willing to take on the responsibilities, along with the rewards, of having total control, self-hosting is the best bet for your blog.

Popular self-hosted platforms include

- **WordPress.org:** Although the WordPress.org hosting software itself is free to use, it costs money to run your blog on WordPress.org because you're paying to register your domain and use a web host. But these purchases come with the added benefit of you having total control over your blog, including the use of a custom domain name, the option for running ads, and using the wide variety of available plugins. But the control also extends to technical setup and maintenance, which you oversee.
- **ExpressionEngine:** ExpressionEngine requires you to purchase a license to utilize its blogging platform, but after you do, you have complete control over your blog. Although time and money must be spent to get your blog up and running, the good news is you'll have a custom domain name and the ability to display ads.

The long and short of it is this: A hosted solution best suits someone looking to get his blog up and running in ten minutes or less and is uneasy at the thought of dealing with the technical ins and outs of self-hosting. A hosted blogging platform, on the other hand, is cheap, quick to set up, simple to use, and easy to maintain because software updates and backups are left in the trusting hands of your host. A hosted platform is a stress-free way to blog. Tables 3-1 and 3-2 outline the unique sets of pros and cons for each option.

Table 3-1 Pros and Cons of Hosted Blog Solutions

Pros	*Cons*
Either very cheap or free to use	Limited design options
No setup or advanced technological knowledge required	No plug-ins available
Takes care of backups, software updates, and spam protection	Possible restraints to running ads and monetizing your blog
Don't have to register or pay for your domain	Domain may be a sub-domain of your host

Table 3-2 Pros and Cons of Self-Hosted Blog Solutions

Pros	*Cons*
Total control over your blog	Requires paying for a web host, and in most cases, paying to register your domain
Endless customizations	Requires installing blogging software
Plug-ins available	Requires maintenance for software updates, spam protection, and back-ups
Custom domain	Requires setup and advanced technical knowledge

Many bloggers will tell you to bypass the hosted option and head straight for self-hosting, regardless of how much or how little confidence you have in your technical prowess. Why advise a technophobe to dive into the digital deep end? Because a self-hosted solution may cost you more setup time (and a bit of cash) in the short run, but it will give you endless options in the long run. And the first option is one of the most critical: having a custom domain. Hosted blogs are generally restricted to a URL that's a sub-domain of the host's domain, such as `www.foodblogfan.wordpress.com`, rather than simply `www.foodblogfan.com`.

This distinction has implications that stretch far beyond the difference in URL character count. A custom domain is valuable for several reasons:

- It's more professional in appearance and serves as your first, and often most utilized, marketing tool.
- It's easier to remember because it's shorter than having a sub-domain of your blogging platform.
- It reinforces brand alignment by making the name of your blog the exact same as your domain name.

You can forward a custom domain name to a hosted blog (thus eliminating the `.wordpress` or `.blogspot` from your domain), but it requires paying to register your domain. And because domain registration is the first step in setting up a self-hosted blog, you might as well skip the finagling and enjoy the perks by going custom from day one.

If you go the hosted route, the good news is you can bypass these next few pages and head straight to the "Choosing a Blogging Platform" section, as setting up a hosted blog is as simple as picking a blogging platform and signing up. For all those who've mastered baking cupcakes and are ready to tackle the task of making perfect soufflés, read on to get a taste of sweet, self-hosted (and perfectly puffed) success.

Registering your domain

If you're reading this, you have chosen the longer, windier road to creating your food blog. Bravo. Don't let the length or the windiness get you down because, although you've chosen a more complex journey, you will be rewarded for your efforts. Not only will you enjoy total control over the look and feel of your blog, but you'll also have access to installing a variety of plug-ins to further enhance the appeal and functionality of your site. (See Chapter 9 for more on plug-ins.)

In Chapter 2, I discuss the many elements that encompass an ideal blog name, one of which was making sure the domain name isn't taken already. Your custom domain name is used to identify the specific Internet Protocol (IP) address of where your blog is located. *IP addresses* are strings of numbers, such as 69.167.175.14, and they're unique to every site on the web.

But imagine how difficult it would be if every site was known by a string of random numbers! A domain name is, therefore, registered to refer to its corresponding IP address, making it much easier to remember the location of a site. So rather than tell someone my blog is located at 69.167.175.14, I tell them it's located at `www.justataste.com`.

Countless companies offer domain registration services, web-hosting services, or both. Keep in mind the critical difference between a *domain registrar* and a *web host*:

- **Domain registrar:** A company that facilitates the process of you claiming sole ownership for a given domain name.
- **Web host:** A company that gives you space on its server to house all your blog's information, such as software files, photos, e-mail addresses, site backups, and so on.

The following lists details the pros and cons to using one company for registering your domain and hosting your site, or using a separate company for each. If you use the same company for both tasks:

- You create only one account.
- It can be cheaper because many web hosts offer free domain registration.
- All your site information is in one place, so you know exactly where to go to troubleshoot an issue.
- If anything at all happens to that one company (be it technical problems, financial problems, or otherwise), both your registration and your hosting are held captive.

This last point is a perfect example of why you should always back up your blog on a routine basis, and also store those backups in multiple places, including your computer's desktop as well as a flash drive.

If you use a different company for each task:

- You have to set up two accounts.
- You have to go through an extra step of transferring the domain to your web host.
- If anything goes astray with your host, you still control the domain, so you can switch to a different host and vice versa with the registration.

Don't give in to the temptation of one-stop shopping by using the same company for both registering your domain and hosting your blog. It might be the easier option, but it's also the most risky. If you're counting on one company to handle both duties, one failure on its behalf means two gigantic headaches for you.

So what company is best for which duty? That depends on what functionality you're in need of and what price you're willing to pay. At the most basic level, a domain registrar needs to

- Provide thorough customer service.
- Offer the option to create an e-mail address specific to your domain, such as `kelly@justataste.com`.
- Feature an intuitive user interface for stress-free domain maintenance.

Table 3-3 lists a few of the more popular and respected domain registrars, along with their pricing for a one-year `.com` registration. Individual benefits to each registrar can be viewed on their respective sites, and extensive consumer research, statistics, and ratings for each registrar can be found on WebHosting.Info (`www.webhosting.info/registrars`).

Table 3-3 Domain Registrars and Pricing

Registrar	*URL*	*Price (.com)*
Moniker	`www.moniker.com`	$8.99/yr
Namecheap	`www.namecheap.com`	$9.98/yr
Go Daddy	`www.godaddy.com`	$11.99/yr
Gandi.net	`www.gandi.net`	$15/yr
Network Solutions	`www.networksolutions.com`	$34.99/yr

Going beyond .com

Aim for a domain name that uses the suffix `.com` (short for *commercial*) because it's the most widely used and recognized suffix online. Because of its popularity, web users have become conditioned to assume that a site lives at a `.com` address, rather than a different suffix, such as `.net` (network), `.org` (organization), or `.biz` (business).

Although your food blog's `.com` address is a critical domain to own, consider registering additional suffixes to protect the ownership of your blog's brand. Owning additional suffixes is also important if your blog happens to be an actual business or organization, in which case the `.biz` and `.org` domain names are thematically relevant.

After you decide on a domain registrar, follow the steps on the specific company's site to complete the registration process. For example, if you're using Go Daddy, first create an account by pointing your web browser to `www.godaddy.com`, clicking the Create Account link, and completing the process. When you have an account, you can register your domain by following these steps:

1. **Go to `www.godaddy.com` and select Domain Name Registration from the Domains drop-down list, as shown in Figure 3-1.**

   The Domain Search Name page appears.

2. **Type your food blog's name into the Start Your Domain Search Here text box.**

Domains

REGISTER OR TRANSFER

Domain Name Registration
Own your corner of the Web.

Transfer Domain
Includes a FREE 1-year extension.

Bulk Domain Name Registration
Save when you register 6 or more domains.

Bulk Domain Transfers
Transfer up to 1,000 domains at once.

Internationalized Domain Names (IDN)
Speak to your audience in their language.

Discount Domain Club
Enjoy the industry's lowest domain prices.

Domain Buy Service
We'll help get the domain you want.

EARN MONEY

CashParking®
Use your parked domains to earn cash.

Go Daddy Auctions®
Buy, bid, and sell existing domain names.

ADD-ONS

Private Registration
Protect your personal information.

Business Registration
Increase your traffic and visibility.

Deluxe Registration
Promote your site and keep your privacy.

Protected Registration
The most secure domain ownership protection.

Certified Domain
Gain your visitors' trust and confidence.

Premium Listing
Sell your domain where millions shop.

Premium DNS
Powerful, easy-to-use DNS management tools.

Domain Backordering
Get a domain as soon as it's available.

MANAGEMENT

Domain Management
Organize, renew and upgrade your domains.

Figure 3-1: Register your domain name via the Domains drop-down list on Go Daddy.

3. **Select the domain suffix, such as `.com`, from the drop-down list and click Go.**

   Go Daddy returns a page with all available domains and suffixes, as shown in Figure 3-2.

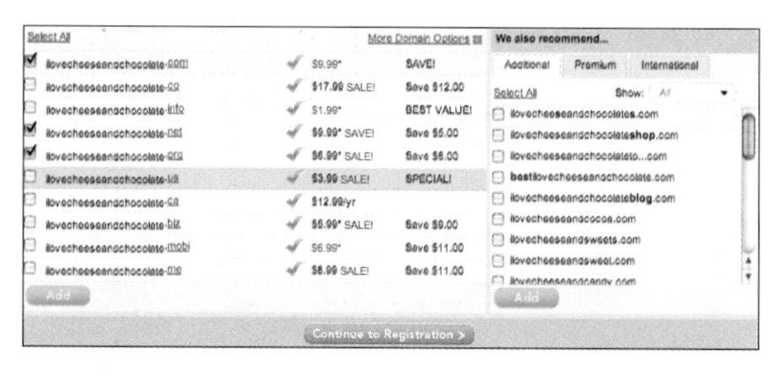

Figure 3-2: Select from the available domains and suffixes related to your desired URL.

4. **Pick the domain you want to purchase by selecting the check box next to your desired choice.**

   You can opt to register more than one suffix for your domain, such as `.net` or `.biz`. (For more information about additional suffixes, see the "Going beyond .com" sidebar.)

5. **Click the Continue to Registration button to be directed to the Your Domain Settings page, where you can choose the duration of your registration.**

6. **Click the Next button to be directed to the Your Privacy and Domain Protection page, where you can choose your desired level of privacy.**

   You can select the Standard Registration, which is included, or pay an additional amount for extended privacy.

7. **Click the Next button to be directed to the Add Email page, where you can choose how many e-mail addresses you want to register with your URL and what type of hosting plan you want to use.**

   The e-mail addresses you purchase are specific to your URL, such as `kelly@foodblogfan.com`, and the hosting package prices vary according to the amount of space and bandwidth.

8. **Click the Next button to be directed to the Review Your Shopping Cart page.**

9. **If you are satisfied with your selections as they appear, click the Continue to Checkout button, where you enter your credit card information and place your order.**

Selecting a web host

Deciding which web host will be home to your blog requires crafting a balanced blend of the features that you want with the features that you need. If you're new to the realm of web-hosting, chances are you'll want a user-friendly interface for ease of use when maintaining your blog. You may also be focused on the price, or even be lured by the promises of free domain registrations, unlimited e-mail forwarding, or custom spam protection.

Although such features are worth noting, the following four elements are the essentials for your list of web-hosting needs. Regardless of which host you select, it needs to provide

- **Reliability:** Is the host a trusted company? If you don't have tech-savvy friends to answer that question, consider my suggestions for reputable web hosts later in this section. Research the frequency of each company's server disruptions, which can result in your blog being inaccessible for minutes, hours, or (gulp) days.
- **Sufficient capacity:** You may just be starting out, but that doesn't mean you shouldn't consider the future size and scope of your blog. Take note of the *drive space* (the amount of content you can store on the server) and *bandwidth* (the amount of data that can be transmitted) offered by your potential host.
- **Security:** Review what measures your host takes to secure its servers and what sort of spam protection packages are included versus offered as an upgrade.
- **Customer service:** This is especially important for new bloggers who may need assistance 24/7 when first setting up their site. No matter what unforeseen pickle you happen to get yourself into, using a host with a proven track record for solid customer service is the fastest way to peace of mind.

Begin your search for the best host to fit your wants and needs by polling your fellow blogging buddies, performing a quick search online, or getting a feel for three of the most popular and reputable hosting companies summarized in the following list. And for more in-depth information about considerations for choosing a web host, check out *Blogging For Dummies* by Susannah Gardner and Shane Birley.

Here are the most popular hosting companies:

- **Bluehost:** Bluehost has been in the web-hosting business since 1996 and provides unlimited drive storage along with outstanding customer service by web or by phone 24/7. Bluehost also features WordPress Auto-Install, which sets up the WordPress.org blogging software on your site in just a few clicks. The basic Bluehost package starts at around $6.95 a month. (`www.bluehost.com`)
- **DreamHost:** DreamHost is a popular web host known for its user-friendly interface and solid customer service. Among many features, it offers unlimited bandwidth and simple and fast auto-installation of WordPress software. The DreamHost basic hosting package starts at around $8.95 a month and you can option for a two-week trial period. (`www.dreamhost.com`)

- **iPage:** iPage is an established web host that prides itself on offering a user-friendly interface with unlimited drive space and bandwidth. The company ranked top in Consumer Reports 2011 for web hosts customer service, which is provided 24/7 via phone, e-mail, or online chat. You also get extensive features for hosting packages that start at around $3.50 a month. (`www.ipage.com`)

Choosing a Blogging Platform

From uploading photos and publishing posts to moderating comments and installing widgets, your blogging platform is responsible for all the day-to-day functions that allow you to create, edit, publish, and share your content. So no pressure here, but you might want to give this decision some serious thought!

Regardless whether you chose the hosted or self-hosted paths, everyone has to decide which blogging platform suits them and their blog the best. Before diving into the details of all your options, consider your approach to the decision-making process by answering these questions:

- **How dedicated are you?** If you're just looking to give this whole food blogging business a quick test drive before making a purchase, stick to a less involved (read: cheap and quick) platform until you determine your level of commitment to the craft. But keep in mind that the self-hosted route is best in the long run, and switching from hosted to self-hosted will cost you time and require advanced technical knowledge for a seamless transition.
- **Will you ever want to monetize your blog?** Hopefully this decision was made in the first few pages of this chapter when you were picking between a hosted and a self-hosted blogging solution, but if not, remember that hosted platforms *generally* don't allow you to run ads and monetize your blog while self-hosted platforms do.
- **What's your budget?** From free and cheap to doable and exorbitant, building and maintaining a blog can be a frugal affair or a costly enterprise. Cash enters the equation when it comes to domain registration, web hosting, site design, upkeep, and even technical support, which can be worth its weight in white truffles.
- **Are you a tech nerd or a technophobe?** Your technical aptitude will determine the level of importance you give to the platform's user-friendliness, particularly its *dashboard,* or central command area. Figures 3-3 and 3-4 depict the differences in dashboards between two popular platforms, WordPress.com and Google Blogger.

What's simple and affordable for one person can be complex and costly for another, so choosing a blogging platform is a personal decision (despite what all the cool kids might be doing). With your own goals and budget in mind, you're ready to test-drive the options to determine which blogging software will be best for you and your blog.

Knowing your blogging software options

You don't want to blindly follow the cool kids, but knowing which platforms are being widely used by current food bloggers provides a dependable place to start your search.

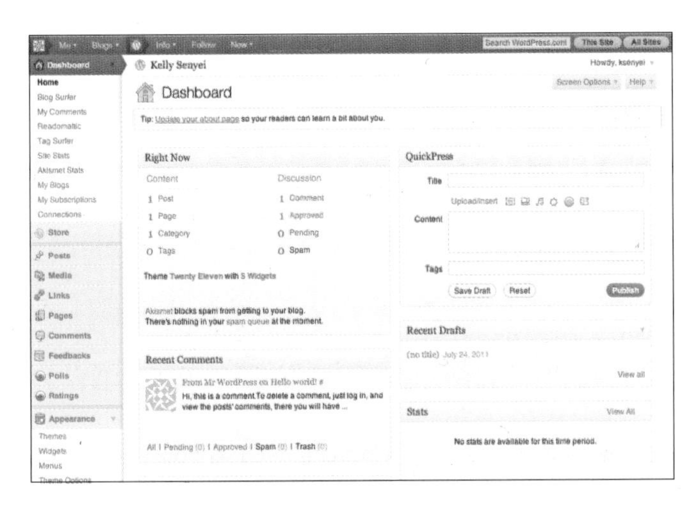

Figure 3-3: The Dashboard of the WordPress.com blogging platform.

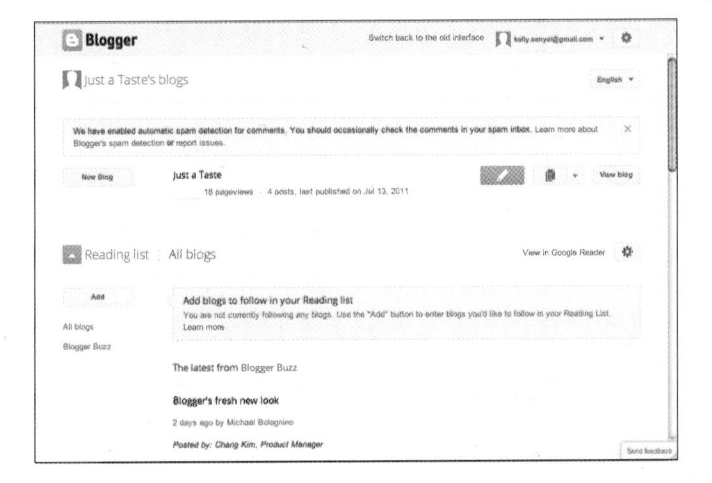

Figure 3-4: The Dashboard of the Google Blogger blogging platform.

As the results of The State of the Food Blogosphere survey indicate in Figure 3-5, when it comes to blogging software, WordPress is the platform of choice. Sixty-two percent of respondents reported using WordPress, which includes either its hosted `.com` version or its self-hosted `.org` version — a distinction I cover later in this section. And in second place? Google's Blogger platform, which garnered a third of the votes at 31 percent.

WordPress is a popular choice among bloggers, and for good reason. It holds a stake both in the hosted and self-hosted realms — a point worth noting when it comes to the fairness factor of competing with other platforms. First introduced in 2003, WordPress quickly grew to what it is today: a home to more than 56 million blogs worldwide. Roughly half of those blogs are hosted by WordPress, whereas the other half are self-hosted blogs utilizing outside web hosts to house their files.

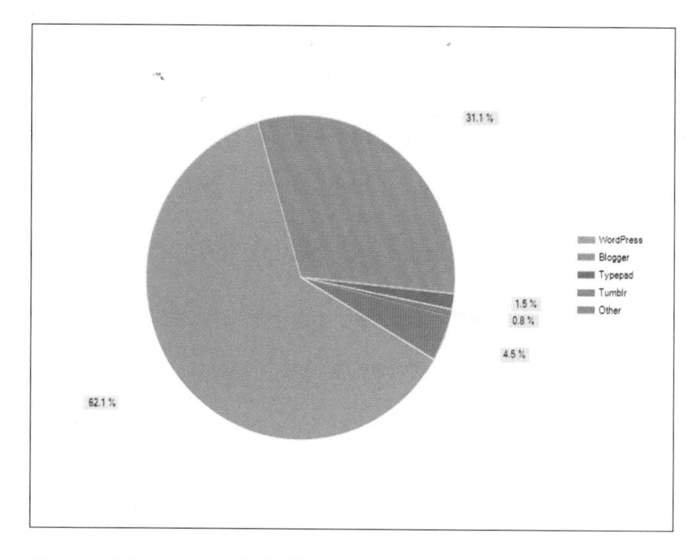

Figure 3-5: Survey results indicate a majority of food bloggers use WordPress.

A taste of Tumblr

Tumblr (`www.tumblr.com`) is a popular *microblogging* platform, which is an abbreviated version of a blog that features shorter updates in the form of text, photos, videos, quotes, music, and more. Founded in 2007, Tumblr is currently host to more than 27 million blogs and provides users with the fastest, cheapest way to get their musings onto the web. You can be the owner of a Tumblr blog, complete with customizable themes and color palettes, in 30 seconds or less. A focus is placed on ease of use, which means FTP, installation, and technical support never even enter the equation. Tumblr is the perfect option for both technophobes and commitment-phobes alike because it's a great way to test out the food blogging waters before deciding whether to take the plunge.

This is where the confusion often lies because WordPress exists both as WordPress.com and WordPress.org. Don't let that tiny difference in suffix throw you for a loop! WordPress.com is a hosted blogging platform, whereas WordPress.org is a self-hosted blogging platform. The technical differences can get tricky because customer support doesn't necessarily translate from one option to the other. (If you need a refresher in hosted versus self-hosted platforms, re-visit the earlier section "Registering and Hosting Your Blog.")

And with that final cautionary flag, time to test-drive all your available options, beginning with three of the most popular hosted platforms currently on the market. As you read through the blogging software options, think about your needs, wants, and budget to determine which of the hosted or self-hosted blogging options best fits your food blogging endeavors. Don't be afraid to further explore each option with additional on-site research, and then if one of the hosted options is most enticing, head over to the platform's site to get yourself up and running.

WordPress.com

WordPress.com (`www.wordpress.com`) is one of the easiest, fastest, and cheapest ways to get your blog up and running. Because WordPress.com is a hosted platform, very little technical knowledge is needed to create and manage a WordPress.com blog. With that benefit also comes restraints in the form of design and domain names.

Here's a breakdown of the identifying elements of the WordPress.com platform:

- **Setup and maintenance:** Setup consists of a ten-second signup process to register your blog, and all maintenance in the form of backups, software updates, and spam protection is handled by WordPress.
- **Domain name:** Your domain is a sub-domain of WordPress, such as `www.iloveparmesancheese.wordpress.com`. You can map a custom domain, but it comes at a cost.
- **Design:** Customization is limited in that you must use any of the provided 125 design templates and can't build your blog from scratch. You also can't utilize plug-ins. (See Chapter 9 for more on plug-ins.)
- **Ads:** You can only run ads on your blog under very specific circumstances, such as having a large amount of traffic or managing your installation. WordPress also maintains the right to run Google AdSense ads on your blog. There is an upgrade to opt out of the ads, but it costs $29.97 a year.
- **Cost:** WordPress.com is free.

Google Blogger

Blogger (`www.blogger.com`) is Google's take on hosted blogging software. Much like WordPress.com, Blogger is a fast, easy, and cheap way to launch your blog. An interface overhaul in August 2011 updated the user-friendliness of the *Post editor* (the area in which you write, format, and publish posts). The new layout, as shown in Figure 3-6, is sleek and intuitive for creating content.

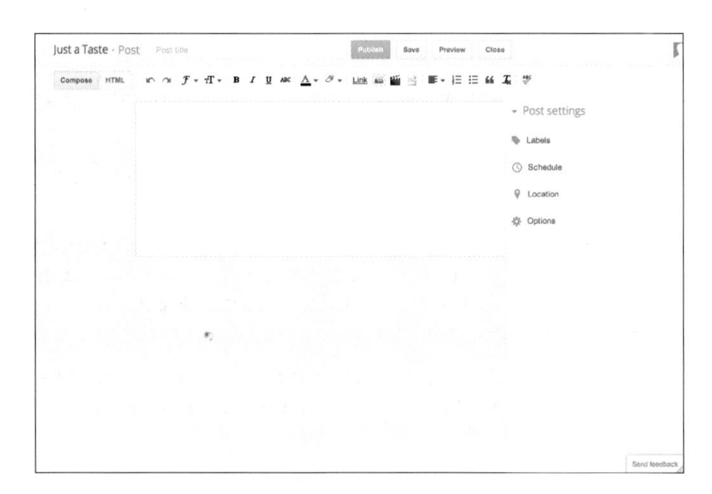

Figure 3-6: Blogger's Post editor interface received a welcome makeover in August 2011.

Here are the identifying factors of a Blogger blog:

- **Setup and maintenance:** Setting up your blog simply requires registering it at `www.blogger.com`. All maintenance in the form of software updates and backups are taken care of by Blogger.
- **Domain name:** Your URL contains the Blogger domain `.blogpost`, however, you can upgrade to a custom domain for an annual fee.
- **Design:** Blogger features design templates that are customizable to a degree, but don't give you total control over the look and feel of your site. You can use widgets, which extend the functionality and appearance of your blog. (See Chapter 9 for more about widgets.)
- **Ads:** Blogger allows you to monetize your blog with Google AdSense ads. (See Chapter 14 for more on ads.)
- **Cost:** Blogger is free.

If what you're reading peaks your interest and you want to find out more about the Blogger platform, check out *Google Blogger For Dummies* by Susan Gunelis.

TypePad

TypePad (`www.typepad.com`), although technically a hosted blogging solution, blurs the lines when it comes to strictly adhering to the common elements of hosted platforms. TypePad is a great choice for bloggers who are willing to pay for a hosted platform but are too wary of the technical requirements associated with self-hosting their site.

Here's a breakdown of the specific elements of the TypePad platform:

- **Setup and maintenance:** Setup is a simple registration process, and TypePad takes care of all technical maintenance, including upgrades, backups, and spam protection.
- **Domain name:** A custom domain can be created using TypePad's Domain Mapping feature.
- **Design:** You have total control over the look and feel of your blog, allowing you the flexibility to either create a custom site or choose from the hundreds of available themes. The use of widgets further extends your blog's functionality and feel.
- **Ads:** Any and all ads are allowed on TypePad blogs, including the option to implement a *tip jar* where readers can show their support (by showing you the money).
- **Cost:** You have your choice of three package options: Plus ($8.95/month), Unlimited ($14.95/month), or Premium ($29.95/month), each of which offers a variety of basic and/or enhanced features.

If you're opting for the hosted solution, WordPress.com, Blogger, and TypePad are three outstanding options to choose from. And for all those who are heading down the DIY route, read on for a trio of options from the world of self-hosted software.

WordPress.org

WordPress.org (`www.wordpress.org`) is one of the leading options for self-hosted blogging platforms. WordPress.org is an ideal choice for bloggers who want to customize the look and feel of their blog and have the tech chops (or desire to learn the tech chops) for running a self-hosted site. WordPress.org differs drastically when compared to the features and functions of its `.com` cousin.

Here are the distinguishing elements of the WordPress.org platform:

- **Setup and maintenance:** Setup is required and includes registering your domain, signing up with a web host, and downloading and installing the WordPress.org software. You're also responsible for maintaining blog backups and software updates.
- **Domain name:** Your blog has a custom domain name.
- **Design:** You can fully customize the look and feel of your site by tweaking existing design templates or by building an entirely unique design. You also can use plug-ins to extend the appearance and functionality of your blog.

- **Ads:** Ads of any kind are allowed on WordPress.org blogs.
- **Cost:** The WordPress.org software is free to download, however, it costs money to register your domain and utilize a web host.

ExpressionEngine

ExpressionEngine (www.expressionengine.com) is a powerful self-hosted blogging platform that provides total control and flexibility when constructing your blog. ExpressionEngine is for the serious food blogger who's looking to control all aspects of her site.

Here are the distinguishing elements of the ExpressionsEngine platform:

- **Setup and maintenance:** ExpressionEngine requires registering your domain, signing up with a web host, and then installing the platform's software. You're also responsible for all site maintenance.
- **Domain name:** Your blog has a custom domain name.
- **Design:** You have total control over your blog's design and can customize its look and feel to any degree.
- **Ads:** Ads of any kind are allowed on ExpressionEngine blogs.
- **Cost:** ExpressionEngine offers three licenses for the software download: Freelance ($99.95), Non-Commercial ($149.95), and Commercial ($299.95).

Installing your blogging software

After you choose a self-hosted blogging platform, download the software and install it. Every blogging platform requires a different process for installation, so unfortunately there's no one road that gets you from Point A to Point B. That being said, most platforms include detailed setup guides for taking their software from a download link on their site to your blog's File Transfer Protocol (FTP).

Here are links to the installation guides for each of the three major self-hosted platforms I discuss earlier, which also include information related to the technical requirements for installation:

- **WordPress.org Installation Guide:** http://codex.wordpress.org/Installing_WordPress
- **ExpressionEngine Installation Guide:** http://expressionengine.com/user_guide/installation/installation.html

If you check out either of the guides, you'll likely glance over words like *MySQL database, cgi-bin directory,* or *console-based tools.* Not exactly light reading for the technologically faint of heart. But the good news is you have a few options when it comes to the "who" and "how" of your installation.

First decide who is going to install the software. If you're ready to jump from baking cupcakes to mastering soufflés, go for it. But I would warn that you need to be really eager to *more than dabble* in the technical side of blogging. This is serious stuff that requires serious understanding and implementing. My advice is to save yourself the migraine of getting lost among the uncompressing of `.zip` files and find an expert (who also comes with a price tag), such as

- **Your hosting company,** which will likely charge you extra to install the software.
- **A web designer,** who will provide an installation quote. (Remember to get quotes from multiple designers.) I used a web designer and successfully saved myself an unthinkable amount of time and stress.
- **An FTP-savvy friend,** who will hopefully accept payment in the form of two dozen chocolate chip cookies.

The "how" of installation also lends itself to a few options. Many web hosts offer *one-click installation,* which essentially provides a hand to hold through the setup process. You want to have made some BFFs in the technical support department, and even then it could still come with a price.

WordPress.org boasts a Famous 5-Minute Install (as shown in Figure 3-7) that breaks it down into six simpl*er* (not *simple*) steps. And if the technical jargon in those steps still makes you cringe, your best bet is to hand over the reins to a trusted professional and subsist on ramen noodles for a few days, if need be.

Famous 5-Minute Install

Here's the quick version of the instructions, for those that are already comfortable with performing such installations. More detailed instructions follow.

If you are not comfortable with renaming files, Steps 3 and 4 are optional and you can skip them as the install program will create wp-config.php file.

1. Download and unzip the WordPress package, if you haven't already.
2. Create a database for WordPress on your web server, as well as a MySQL user who has all privileges for accessing and modifying it.
3. Rename the `wp-config-sample.php` file to `wp-config.php`.
4. Open `wp-config.php` in a text editor and fill in your database details as explained in Editing wp-config.php to generate and use your secret key password.
5. Upload the WordPress files in the desired location on your web server:
   - If you want to integrate WordPress into the root of your domain (e.g. `http://example.com/`), move or upload all contents of the unzipped WordPress directory (but excluding the directory itself) into the root directory of your web server.
   - If you want to have your WordPress installation in its own subdirectory on your web site (e.g. `http://example.com/blog/`), rename the directory `wordpress` to the name you'd like the subdirectory to have and move or upload it to your web server. For example if you want the WordPress installation in a subdirectory called "blog", you should rename the directory called "wordpress" to "blog" and upload it to the root directory of your web server.

   Hint: If your FTP transfer is too slow read how to avoid FTPing at : Step 1: Download and Extract.
6. Run the WordPress installation script by accessing `wp-admin/install.php` in a web browser.
   - If you installed WordPress in the root directory, you should visit: `http://example.com/wp-admin/install.php`
   - If you installed WordPress in its own subdirectory called `blog`, for example, you should visit: `http://example.com/blog/wp-admin/install.php`

That's it! WordPress should now be installed.

Figure 3-7: The six-step setup process for installing WordPress.org blogging software.

Claiming Your Social Media Space

From Facebook to foursquare, Twitter to Flickr, new social media platforms pop up faster across the web than Chipotle locations across the U.S. They're everywhere. And they allow you to be everywhere and to connect with people from all over the globe from the comfort of your couch.

Users are flocking to social media platforms — in record numbers to Facebook and Twitter, in particular — and whether you care who's folding laundry at 2 a.m. or who just had their cast signed by `@justinbieber` outside Wendy's, you need to look past the inherently inane nature of social media to realize its primary purpose to you as a food blogger: to better connect you with your audience.

Benefiting from social media

Participating in the social media scene as a food blogger has many benefits:

- **Joining a community:** You become a part of a massive online society that's overflowing with enthusiasts on every subject. The community provides a sense of tight-knit camaraderie and interactivity in an online world that can at times seem so big you feel out of touch.
- **Sharing your voice:** You have access to a platform from which to express your thoughts outside of your blog. This in turn puts you in contact with people who may not otherwise find your blog, which extends your reach across the web by quickly alerting an even broader audience about the fresh and exciting content you're creating.
- **Getting inspired:** You become privy to countless ideas for inspiration on your blog and in everyday life. The more experiences you have with food bloggers, the more opportunities there are to make lifelong friends and meet mentors that can guide you in your efforts.
- **Finding resources:** You can solicit help, find resources, and learn from others in your area of interest. Communicating with fellow bloggers in your blog's comment section limits your interactions to strictly your readers. By branching out into social media, you expose yourself to a much broader array of bloggers, which translates to many more opportunities for learning and growing.
- **Staying in touch:** You can stay connected to friends and fellow bloggers who you may know only through interactions in the digital space. Social media sustains cross-country friendships and doesn't limit your interactions to strictly the bloggers in your zip code.

With so many advantages, it's hard to imagine how anyone can have a successful blog and not be a part of the social communities taking shape online. I show you how to let readers know you're in the social media world in Chapter 9, but first you need to decide the most practical approach to jumping onto the fast moving social media treadmill.

Strategizing your social media approach

Are there really any rules to this crazed maze of tweets and check-ins and tags and photo swaps? It's hard to say. Some bloggers will tell you that there's no such thing as a social media strategy — to just "let it happen" and organically grow your audience outside your blog. Still others will produce a ten-step plan for going from unknown to a trending topic in three months or less. The truth is, the answer lies somewhere between both approaches.

Nearly every food blogger who participated in The State of the Food Blogosphere survey reported using social media to promote their blog. When asked which platform they use the most, the results in Figure 3-8 indicate that 48 percent of respondents use Twitter as their go-to source for spreading the word about their blog, followed by Facebook, and then a combination of the two.

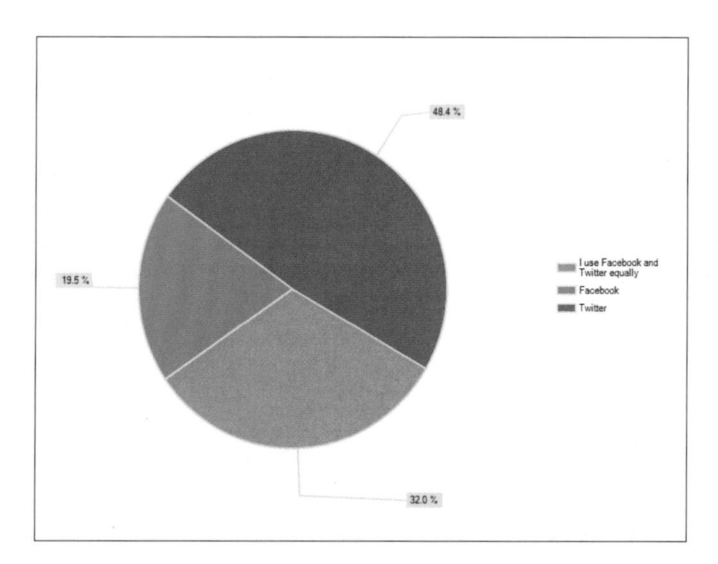

Figure 3-8: Survey results indicate Twitter is the most widely used social media platform.

How you choose to enter, or even re-invent yourself in, the social media space is a personal decision based on your level of comfort. My advice for the most basic level of involvement is

- **Register your Twitter handle.** Hopefully the name of your blog is still an available Twitter handle. If so, grab it! If not, use your own name instead.
- **Create a Facebook brand page for your blog.** This page is separate from a personal profile page and can be created by visiting `www.facebook.com/pages/create.php`.

If you feel like taking it a step further, consider other platforms listed here that are designed to fuel networking and connect you with an even bigger audience outside your blog:

- **Flickr:** Upload photos and share albums while viewing content created by fellow users. Opt to engage by leaving comments or adding others' photos to your list of favorites.
- **LinkedIn:** Create a professional space for yourself on the web by utilizing this well-known professional version of Facebook.
- **Video sites:** Go viral with your culinary videos or sample channels created by users with similar interests by sharing them on YouTube, Vimeo, or Dailymotion.

As you establish your social media presence online, keep in mind a few important don'ts when it comes to effectively utilizing social media:

- **Don't be contrived in your messaging.** It's best to be authentic rather than come across like you have an agenda.
- **Don't get too sucked into the scene.** Chapter 8 details tips for being present without letting social media take over your life.
- **Don't auto-follow people on Twitter.** Setting up your Twitter account so that you automatically follow anyone who follows you is too impersonal and doesn't show any sort of effort or genuine interest in fellow Twitter users.
- **Don't use only social media to market you or your blog.** Remember there's a give-and-take nature that applies to more than your publicity goals.
- **Don't publicize your blog too soon.** Wait until you're at least ten posts deep into your blog to promote it across the web. This gives readers a better sense of the overall feel, tone, and theme of your blog.
- **Don't force it.** There's no set rule about having to tweet or post on Facebook every day. Avoid participating just for the sake of participating.

Part II
Finding Your Voice

In this part . . .

Photography will have its moment in your blog's spotlight, but just because food porn is all the rage doesn't mean you can push the written word to the backburner. In Part II, you discover the ways of finding and fine-tuning your voice as a writer while you set the full content menu for your blog by paying particular attention to consistency and frequency.

As you begin brainstorming different avenues for original and adapted content, your ideas make the jump from the privacy of your computer to the front page of the World Wide Web. Discover the power of going public, plus get a primer in food blog legalese as you discover that recipe copyright law is anything but black and white (and I'm not talking about the cookies).

4

Is This Thing On?

In This Chapter

- Finding and fine-tuning your voice
- Mastering the basics of good food writing
- Realizing the power of going public
- Publishing your first post on a WordPress or Blogger blog
- Understanding the legal matters of food blogging

Although pictures can be "worth a thousand words" and are certainly important to a food blog, your blog will not be successful unless your text shines, too.

Establishing your voice and setting the tone of your blog is an evolving process, but it starts first and foremost with you — your personality, your style, and your attitude. This chapter leads you on the search to find and fine-tune your voice while helping you build a solid foundation by mastering the basics of good food writing.

As you find out the technical ins and outs of publishing your first post, you also discover the power and implications of being thrust into the public eye. And no foray into online exposure would be complete without a lesson in Food Blog Legalese 101.

Finding Your Voice

It's out there. Somewhere. Your strong, passionate, inspiring, authentic voice. The question is: How do you find it?

If you're a writer by trade or a natural wordsmith, you've likely already homed in on it and are staring down food writing as the next challenge. But for those who weren't born with a dictionary in one hand and a laptop in the other, now is the time to make your voice heard.

Your voice transforms your personality into plain text by conveying your perspective, your thoughts, your reflections, and your experiences to your readers. Your voice is what distinguishes your blog as uniquely yours. And just like no other person has your identical personality, no other blog has your identical voice.

Making a good first impression

With so many food blogs to turn to for information and entertainment, readers will use the voice of your blog as a gauge as to whether they take a quick glance at the menu or sit down for a full meal. Although your blog is all about you, it's also about the reaction it draws from your audience. Does your blog make them laugh? Feel inspired? Get hungry? Shed a tear? Crack a smile?

One of the clearest examples of a well-defined voice is on Gluten-Free Girl and The Chef, written by Shauna James Ahern. This is a short excerpt from a blog post about Shauna discovering the ideal gluten-free pasta:

> *"See that pasta there? It's gluten-free.*
>
> *"You wouldn't guess from the look of it, the way the individual strands stay slightly separated from each other, not clumping together like frightened seventh-grade girls along the walls of the gym at a school dance. It's robust pasta, full of flavor and a real bite. It's not gummy or spongy, not falling apart at the first touch or too tough to chew for longer than a moment.*
>
> *"This is pasta."*

Six sentences are all it takes to identify the soothing, welcoming, nurturing rhythm that defines the Gluten-Free Girl and The Chef blog — through the gluten-free girl's voice. And that voice is uniquely Shauna's and for several reasons. Her voice — as your voice needs to be — is a combination of the language she uses, the style she pursues, and most importantly, the authenticity she demonstrates. In the same vein, your voice wouldn't truly be your voice if it wasn't genuinely *you.* Consider the following tips for fine-tuning your unique and genuine voice:

- **Project confidence:** The worst way to write is with insecurity as your guide. Feeling confident about your writing will take time and practice, but everyone has to start somewhere. Leave the worries behind and focus on putting your voice, and yourself, out there.
- **Choose your words wisely:** Just because you weren't given a word count doesn't mean you should write without length in mind. The general rule for post length is 250 words, but inevitably, some instances require less or demand more. Lengthier posts may define your writer's voice over time, but first aim to master the short-form before attempting longer prose. Regardless of length, make every word on every page count.

- **Avoid mimicking:** Don't hide behind the facade of another writer's voice that you admire; it's way more work to fake authenticity. Save yourself the time and just let you be you.
- **Envision your brand:** Identifying your voice gives your blog a personality, which transforms it into more than just a URL. Your voice makes your blog an online destination with you as the main attraction.
- **Edit, edit, edit:** Writing, and rewriting, is about the process of trying different words until you find a combination that most clearly and concisely relays your message. Although editing is a critical step in the process, know when to stop trimming the fat so that perfect copy doesn't become the enemy of a strong draft.
- **Utilize visuals:** If blogger's block strikes, describe what's shown visually (photos, videos, or graphics). Doing so encourages more descriptive prose and toggles your memory enough to get the juices flowing again.

Setting the tone

If your voice is your personality, your tone is your attitude. Whether you're sassy and sarcastic or quiet and contemplative, the tone of your blog relays how you feel in relation to the topic you're writing about.

Blogging is much more casual and conversational in tone compared to writing that appears in books, online magazines, newspapers, or elsewhere. This is due in part to the shorter length of blog posts and the immediacy of online publishing. Digital equates with instant, on-the-fly, and sometimes, hasty. A simple blog post can be published in five minutes. A single tweet can be sent in seconds. Urgency doesn't leave time for contemplation, so people blog like they talk and write how they think. Regardless of how instantaneous the digital medium is, always take the time to edit your writing.

Unlike your personality (or voice), your attitude (or tone) in your posts changes based on your emotional reactions to the experiences in your everyday life. For example, I portray the sarcastic side of indulging in an unhealthy meal in this excerpt from my post on candied bacon and fried eggs:

> *"Everyone knows if you eat something that's candied while eating something else that's fried, the calories in those two foods just cancel each other out. It's like multiplying two negative numbers to get a positive. Add bacon and eggs to the equation and you'll be buying smaller jeans by the time you finish reading this post."*

The humorous tone I conveyed in this post was a way for me to connect with readers who share my belief that good food is always worth the calories. Rather than warn about the unhealthy nature of the meal, I poked fun at the obvious splurge factor of enjoying not only fried eggs, but fried eggs *and* candied bacon. In this instance, my tone conveyed a lighthearted approach, but it could have just as easily addressed the health factors associated with consuming bacon coated in a sugary syrup or the relationship between egg yolks and cholesterol (yawn).

Regardless of the experience, strive for authenticity by allowing your current mood to govern the tone of your posts. Just as I was in a witty mood when writing about candied bacon, I was feeling more pensive when reviewing food writer and critic Frank Bruni's book, *Born Round: The Secret History of a Full-Time Eater* (Penguin Press), because of the subject matter he addresses. You can sense the more reflective nature and contemplative tone in the post excerpt below:

> *"Bruni's latest release is more than a food novel. It's an intimately exposed diary. And like all diaries, it contains a series of giddy highs and crashing lows dictated in a way that make the reader feel as if they've been leaked access to a man's deepest, darkest secrets. There were the binges, and then the purges. There were the pills, and then the crash diets. It was a never-ending war waged between a man's calorie-obsessed psyche and his ballooning weight."*

Dictate your posts

Jaden Hair of Steamy Kitchen devised one of the best and most practical tips for maintaining a conversational tone on your blog: Dictate your posts. Jaden records her voice and inputs the recording into a speech-recognition software program that automatically transcribes her spoken words into written text. When she writes a blog post (and even her cookbook), she refers back to the transcriptions. The tone of her blog matches her way of speech because the written words literally are her spoken words.

If you're struggling to keep a conversational tone, try the dictation method with either of these software programs:

- **MacSpeech Scribe:** Apple's take on transcription software is one of the best on the market. Upload your audio file, and with a single click, the files are quickly and accurately transcribed into written text. The software ranges from $100 to $150 depending on where you buy it.
- **Dragon NaturallySpeaking 11.5 Home:** The Dragon software program types the words while you speak them, creating a fast and accurate transcription. This specific software, which costs $99.99, is for PCs, although Dragon also makes a similar Mac version.

If spending $100 isn't in your budget, opt for the cheaper, though less efficient, alternative: a digital recorder. Basic recorders are as cheap as $20, although I suggest spending at least $30 because you get what you pay for. The tradeoff is you're the one left to transcribe, which entails listening to the audio files and typing them word, by word . . . by word. If there's zero budget for additional equipment, try the cheapest trick of all: Read your prose out loud to decide whether it sounds natural or stilted.

Clearly conveying your tone through each post is a direct way to connect with readers on an emotional level. As you open up to them through your writing — whether humorous, serious, sarcastic, or even angry — your readers get to better know you as the person and voice behind your blog. Finding and fine-tuning your voice is an evolving process that takes practice, time, and a sturdy foundation in food writing.

Mastering Good Food Writing

Delish. Sinful. Yummy. Scrumptious.

Those are my four biggest offenders when it comes to food writing. Have I been guilty of using those words in the past? You bet. But if and when I have used them, it's been sparingly, as a little "delish" goes a long way. When I'm feeling tempted to use (or re-use) any of my go-to words, I take a moment to consider whether a more descriptive alternative is available. By simply pausing when the "yummy" urge strikes, I force myself to get more creative with my choice in language, which keeps my writing fresh and vibrant rather than stale and dull.

This is not to say you should abandon any desire to strike linguistic-gold with a Rachael Ray-esque buzzword like "yum-o" (love it or hate it, you have to admit it's catchy). I utilize my catchphrases like I salt my steak — you need enough to accentuate the flavor without overdoing it and spoiling the meal.

In the preceding section, I discuss how the tone of blogging differs from everyday writing in that it's more casual and conversational. Don't let this relaxed tone be a ticket to bypass the foundation for exceptional prose.

The fundamentals of good food writing are not unlike the fundamentals of any good writing. Aside from a strong voice and an authentic tone, emphasis is placed on correct grammar, spelling, and punctuation, along with conveying a clear, concise message that leaves an impact on a reader. Food blogging is no different. So in this section, I focus first on some writing fundamentals before moving into details about writing and editing recipes.

Descriptions

Writing about food is a complete sensory experience. You begin with the words you see in a cookbook or menu, followed by the feel of ingredients or utensils. They lead to the sounds you hear from the kitchen — simmering, bubbling, oozing. And then the smell hits you, just as a fork meets your lips for a taste.

The five senses — sight, touch, hearing, smell, and taste — are essential elements to include in the content you write for your blog. They also serve as a reminder for one of the most important characteristics of good food writing: description.

Descriptions exist in all grammatical forms and are the bridge between you, the person having the experience, and your reader, who's left only to rely on your words to be a part of the moment. Start by paying close attention to the adjectives you use to describe food.

Table 4-1 pairs commonly used adjectives with less ambiguous substitutions. Every alternative is not meant as a one-for-one substitute with the originals, as more descriptive words take on a positive or negative slant because they're, you guessed it, more specific.

Table 4-1 Food Writing Adjectives

Commonly Used Words	***Descriptive Substitutions***
Flavorful	Pungent, biting, acerbic
Spicy	Fiery, zesty, flaming
Chewy	Leathery, fibrous, gristly
Sweet	Saccharine, candied, syrupy
Appetizing	Toothsome, piquant, tempting

Do I really think the next post on your blog should feature the sentence, "I was too distracted by the acerbic taste of the key lime pie to notice the piquant aroma of the raspberry coulis?" No way. There is a rare type of person that naturally writes with the vocabulary of a spelling bee champion. If that's you, more power to you. But if I wrote that way, I wouldn't be staying true to the authenticity of my voice.

The whole point in exploring less ambiguous adjectives is not to try to stump your readers with five-syllable words, rather it's to be as descriptive as possible when you write about food and your experiences with it. Transport your readers from their computer screen to your kitchen and make them feel like they're sitting at your table. I guarantee you they'll be back for a second serving.

If description is the grandfather of solid food writing, meet Grandma Show, Don't Tell. The two concepts go hand-in-hand when it comes to breathing life into your writing. Rather than tell your readers what happened — be it in your kitchen, a restaurant, or a faraway destination — show them by placing the five senses within a scene.

Below are two paragraphs describing the same experience I had at the popular The Purple Pig restaurant in Chicago:

> **Example 1**
>
> *I went to The Purple Pig last night and had the pork-fried almonds. They were made with garlic and rosemary. They weren't crunchy and were actually soft in texture. The nuts weren't too salty, and I'd definitely order them again.*
>
> **Example 2**
>
> *The slogan "Cheese, swine, & wine" was enough to lure me into The Purple Pig. I grabbed a corner seat at the communal table and within minutes was snacking on pork-fried almonds. Slicked in pig fat, my fingers picked through the salted nuts in search of the lone roasted garlic clove. In place of the expected crunch was the sticky, tender bite of fresh herbs. The taste of warm pork fat lingered into the next course.*

This is obviously an exaggerated example, but can you tell the difference between the two paragraphs? The first one is direct and concise, and tells you exactly what happened in the scene. The second one is descriptive and clues you into the senses I associated with the experience; it puts you in the moment with me.

The second paragraph is also longer than the first, which often happens when writing with a descriptive flair. You sometimes have to sacrifice word count to effectively show rather than tell a story to your readers, so it's not the perfect approach for every writing scenario. The concept doesn't apply only when writing with a serious, serene tone. You can be witty or sarcastic and still reference the senses within a scene.

The basics

In addition to the importance of descriptions and showing rather than telling through your writing, there are several other tried-and-tested criteria for defining the style and substance of solid food journalism.

Grammar, punctuation, and spelling

In the world of blogging, you are your own editor (and copy editor and fact-checker). Don't let the casual tone of food blogging make you lazy. Pay attention to the grammar and punctuation on your blog and always use spell check. Similarly, never publish a post before viewing it in the preview setting so you can make any necessary corrections before you publish. That being said, you are only human, so a typo here or there won't get you a ticket from the Spelling Police. Readers often serve as accidental copy editors by pointing out errors. Being a language nerd, I am both thankful for and made physically ill by the "there's a typo in your recipe" e-mails I receive. You, too, will have typos. And somehow, life will go on. (See Chapter 6 for more on grammar and your blog's style guide.)

Trustworthy reviews

There's an art to writing a good restaurant review. There are also countless considerations with regards to free meals in exchange for positive reviews. If your niche is critiquing, the number one rule to live by is honesty. Be transparent, be candid, and be enlightening in your reviews. The same standards for good food writing also apply to writing restaurant reviews, especially when it comes to incorporating the five senses.

Enticing headnotes

Headnotes are the short paragraphs that lead into recipes. They can include information about the inspiration behind the dish, the source of the recipe, or the ingredient or technique that makes it unique. The goal of a headnote is to inform and entice, so figure out what it is that makes your recipe for macaroni and cheese different from the other nine million on the web and then make that the focus of your writing.

The Power of Going Public

The whole point of launching your food blog is to share your thoughts and inspirations with others. After all, this isn't *Keeping a Diary For Dummies,* so get comfortable with the idea that the second you click Publish, you're opening yourself up to the entire online universe — that includes your mom, plus two billion other people.

Don't let the numbers scare you: It's a brave feat for you to put yourself out there, to suscept your personal opinions to other's feedback, and to expose your talents to an audience of strangers. How much you choose to share is entirely your decision. You might not be comfortable divulging personal details at the launch of your blog, and it may take time for you to find the right balance as to how much of you and your everyday life shines through.

Although everyone hopes for a positive response and constructive criticism, the truth is the Internet is not a safe haven from negativity. In fact, the Internet sometimes breeds negativity. But by taking the good with the bad, you'll discover the advantages outweigh the disadvantages when it comes to the power of going public.

Ranting and raving

If something's online, it's eternal, making it more important than ever to be conscious of the content you publish on your blog, on other blogs, and on social media platforms. The ability to take a screengrab of a post, a photo, or a Tweet means that even if you delete published content, someone, somewhere could have immortalized your thought with the click of a button. This isn't meant to scare you, but rather to remind you: Think twice, post once.

Countless occasions may merit an online rant, whether it's as benign as a lousy meal at a local sushi restaurant or as offensive as a blog comment turned personal attack. And although you have every right to voice your opinion, the real finesse comes in how you reply.

There is a difference between bashing and critiquing. If the sashimi made you sick and you feel like sharing your experience (sans the graphic details), by all means, let the public know. If someone left a blog comment that your Mom's famous meatballs weren't even edible by their dog's standards, take a deep breath and think twice before (or if) you respond. Curse words are curse words, even if they're in another language.

If you wouldn't be comfortable with your boss or grandmother reading what you publish, chances are you shouldn't publish it. The bottom line: Going on a rant is like getting a tattoo. Don't do it unless you're 100 percent comfortable living with it for the rest of your life.

Publishing your first blog post

After all the brainstorming, reflecting, strategizing, organizing, uploading, and downloading, the time has finally come to publish your very first post.

You've maybe dabbled in your Dashboard a bit or tinkered with your settings, but now you're going to officially launch your blog and make that first byline a reality. An inaugural post is not an art form; however, it is your digital first impression, so you might as well start off strong! Consider the following topics:

- **An introduction to you:** Greet your newfound fellow food bloggers and give them a taste of what or who inspired you to join the community.
- **An introduction to your blog:** Provide information about what you intend to blog about, topics that inspire you, or goals for you and your blog.
- **Content for your niche:** Whether you're blogging about recipes, reviews, photography, or some combination of the three, launch your blog with a compelling post that relays your niche and clues readers in to your interests.

With a clear vision of what to post, move on to the "how." I'm going to take you through the ins and outs of publishing your first post on either WordPress or Blogger, and I give you a taste of fancier formatting with tips and tricks for getting the most out of your Post editor, which is the tool that allows you to create and publish posts.

WordPress and Blogger provide two editing views, via tabs at the top of the body text boxes, for their respective Post editors. For WordPress, these views are Visual and HTML; for Blogger, they're Compose and HTML. When you edit in the Visual tab for WordPress or the Compose tab for Blogger, you're editing in a WYSIWYG (What You See Is What You Get) interface. When you edit in the HTML tab for either platform, you're editing in the coding interface that translates specific HTML code into the WYSIWYG format.

For example, rather than applying the HTML code to make text appear bold, you simply highlight your desired text then click the Bold button in the text editor and it does it for you. The WYSIWYG interface allows you to format your text without you knowing a single HTML element. To keep things easy, new bloggers should always stay in the WYSIWYG tab. And then after you're comfortable (or interested), start dabbling in the HTML view to get a better sense of the formatting being applied to your text and to further customize your posts.

Publishing your first post in WordPress

Regardless whether you use the WordPress.com or WordPress.org blogging software, the Post editor is the same and features identical functionalities. First log in to your blog's Dashboard by entering your username and password. After you're logged in, follow these steps for creating and publishing your first post:

1. **On the left sidebar of your Dashboard, click the Posts category and in the drop-down list that appears, choose Add a New Post.**

   The Add New Post page appears, which displays the Post editor, as shown in Figure 4-1.

2. **Enter the title of your post in the top text box and then enter the text of your post into the body text box.**

   Use any of the formatting buttons to change the look of your text or to add hyperlinks or photos. (See Chapter 6 for inserting photos.)

3. **Click the Save Draft button in the Publish editor.**

   Although WordPress auto-saves your changes every two minutes, get in the habit of frequently saving your work by clicking the Save Draft button. Saving your draft doesn't publish it, but rather preserves the latest changes you've made in the Post editor.

4. **Categorize and tag your post via the Categories and Post Tags editors in the right sidebar.**

   Categories and tags help organize your posts. (See Chapter 5 for more on categories.)

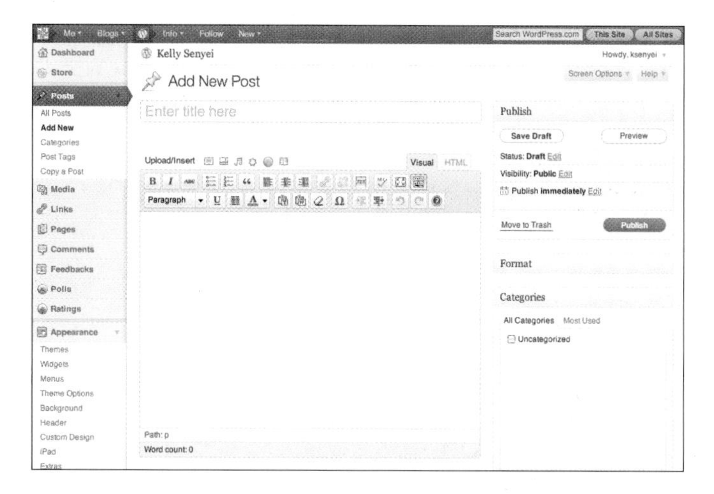

Figure 4-1: WordPress.com and WordPress.org blogs feature the same Post editor.

5. **Click Preview in the Publish editor in the right sidebar.**

   A new window opens with a preview of exactly how your post will appear when published. Use the Preview window to proof your post for spelling, grammar, punctuation, and formatting.

6. **Return to the Post editor window to make any necessary changes, and then when you're satisfied with the final preview, click the Publish button.**

With the basics of your Post editor under control, explore additional formatting functionalities found in the toolbar, as shown in Figure 4-2.

Scroll over the various buttons in the toolbar to view what each icon represents. A few of the options include

- **Unlink:** Removes a hyperlink.
- **Insert More Tag:** Splits a post so that only the portion above where you insert a More tag (which appears as a link) is viewable on the home page. Clicking the More link takes you to the full post on a separate page.
- **Show/Hide:** Reveals or hides the additional formatting toolbars that contain the Paragraph through the Help functions
- **Remove Formatting:** Deletes any formatting that's been applied to text or that impacts layout.
- **Insert Custom Character:** Inserts special characters and symbols, such as © and ¼.

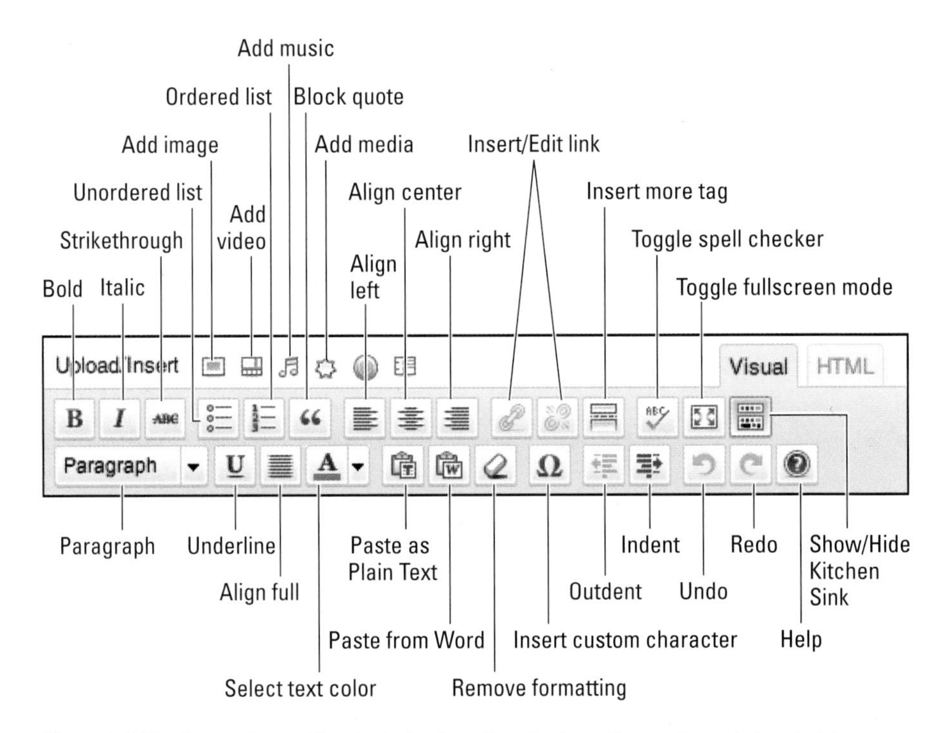

Figure 4-2: The formatting toolbar includes functions for inserting audio and visuals into your post as well as changing the appearance of your text.

The WordPress Post editor is a user-friendly tool that allows you to easily and quickly transform your ideas from text in a Word document to fully formatted blog posts. If you ever get lost, simply scroll over the individual icons to discover the function of each button.

Publishing your first post in Blogger

Alternately, if you're using Blogger, first log in to your blog's Dashboard and then follow these steps to create and publish a post:

1. **Click the orange pencil button on your Dashboard.**

   The Post editor page appears. Confirm you're in the Compose view (rather than the HTML view), which features the Blogger formatting toolbar, as shown in Figure 4-3.

2. **Enter the title of your post in the top text box and then enter the text of your post into the body text box.**

   Use any of the formatting buttons to change the look of your text or to add hyperlinks or photos. (See Chapter 6 for inserting photos.)

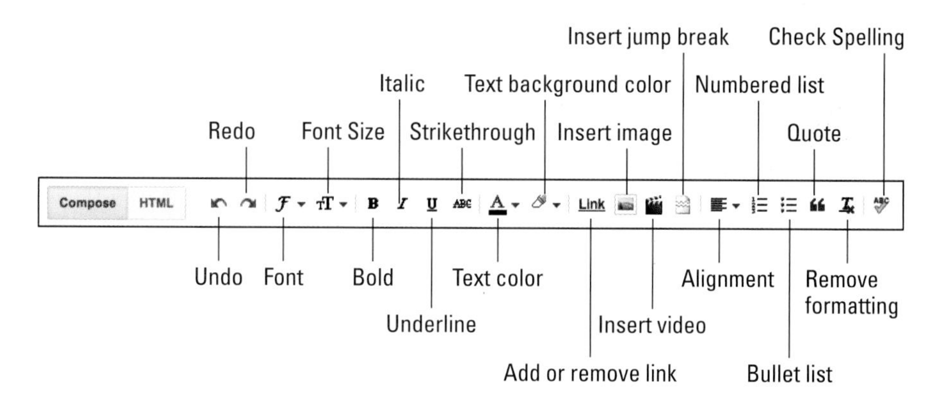

Figure 4-3: The toolbar includes a variety of functions for editing and formatting your post.

3. **Click the Save button at the top of the page.**
4. **Add labels to categorize your post via the Post Settings editor in the right sidebar, as shown in Figure 4-4.**

   Labels function similarly to Categories and help organize your posts. (See Chapter 5 for more on labels.)

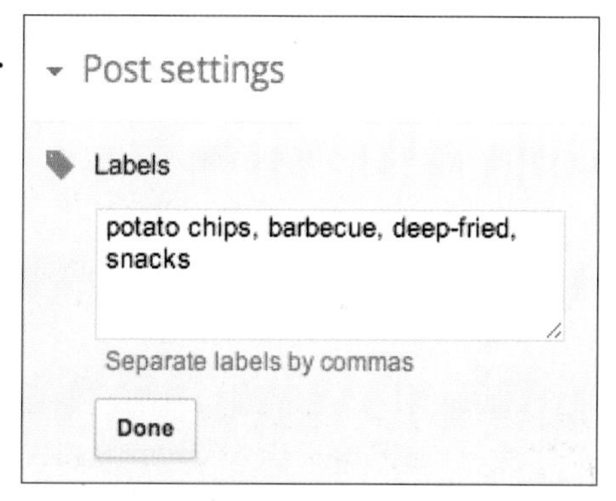

Figure 4-4: The Post Settings editor allows you to add labels to organize your posts.

5. **Click the Preview button at the top of the page.**

   A new window opens with a preview of exactly how your post will appear when published. Proofread your post for spelling, grammar, punctuation, and formatting.
6. **Return to the Post editor window to make any necessary changes, and then when you're satisfied with the final preview, click the Publish button.**

Food Blog Legalese 101

Before I provide an ounce of insight on the legal matters relating to food blogging, I want to preface this section with the following: I am not a lawyer and this is not intended as legal advice for your blog. The information in this section is meant to provide background and context for better understanding food blog legalese. When in doubt, consult a lawyer.

There are countless questions swirled into the icing atop the sticky cinnamon roll of a topic that is food blogging copyright and credit. And every blogger has their own views on what's right or wrong, fair or unjust, honorable or egregious. Before delving into the ethical considerations associated with all things attribution, I first want to clear the air by answering the most frequently asked question: Can you secure copyright protection in a recipe?

The safest and most accurate way for me to answer this question is to send you straight to the language provided by the U.S. Copyright Office at `www.copyright.gov/fls/fl122.html`. I'll wait here while you read that.

Although I'm not a legal expert, I can give you a quick and plain English translation: You cannot protect a list of ingredients, but you can protect a method of preparation.

Originality also plays a role because only original works are protected by copyright. The U.S. Copyright law identifies an *original* work as one an author produced "by his or her own intellectual effort instead of copying it from an existing work." So regardless whether you publish an entire cookbook in print or a single recipe post online, if it's original, you own the copyright.

A lesser known fact is that by the sheer act of publishing your original recipe online, you automatically own the copyright to it. The second it hits the web, it's yours. The only time you have to register for copyright is if you want to sue someone over copyright infringement.

Protecting your content

You don't have to jump through a thousand hoops to secure copyright protection on your blog. In fact, registration isn't even required to do so, meaning that anyone and everyone can place the copyright symbol (©) on their blog. The law doesn't require a copyright notice, but it does help to let people know you own it. The copyright symbol serves as a red flag by warning everyone you're the owner of the content. Of course, notice alone doesn't actually prevent somebody from stealing the content. At most, and at best, it serves as a deterrent — but it's a deterrent worth putting in plain sight.

Other technical precautions can be taken when it comes to your blog's photos, such as adding a watermark (usually the name of your blog) to reiterate your ownership. Beyond the Plate's watermark, as shown in Figure 4-5, is a subtle reminder to readers that her photos are her property.

To be even more direct with your readers, include a Terms of Use page outlining how your content can and cannot be used, or feature a short disclaimer on the sidebar, footer, or About page of your blog.

Use a watermark to help protect your photos.

Figure 4-5: Beyond the Plate adds a watermark to photos to reiterate ownership.

Garrett McCord of Vanilla Garlic includes a legal disclaimer at the footer of his blog, as shown in Figure 4-6, which displays the copyright symbol along with a link to the Creative Commons license page that details how his content can be used — if it's attributed, not used for commercial purposes, and not altered in any way.

© 2006-2011 Garrett McCord. This blog is for personal use only. Please respect my own work, essays and recipes and do not copy them without permission. Anything on this site should never be used for someone else's financial gain. Otherwise you might be guilty of copyright infringement, under the Creative Commons Attribution-Noncommercial-No Derivative Works 3.0 United States License under which some rights are preserved.

Figure 4-6: Vanilla Garlic displays a legal disclaimer warning of copyright infringement.

Specifying exactly how your content should be used avoids leaving readers guessing and lets them know that you're serious about any infringement of your rights. To read more about Creative Commons licensing and to get its badge, visit `http://creativecommons.org/licenses`.

Determining what's appropriate usage is a personal decision. For example, you might be comfortable with another blogger publishing your photo, as long as she includes a link back to your original post, or you might indicate that photos can't be republished or reused without your prior consent. If you're leaning toward a more strict usage policy, just remember that it's not a bad thing for other bloggers to occasionally re-post your content (with proper attribution). And in fact, re-posted content can actually have a positive impact by bringing a whole new audience to your blog and increasing your traffic.

If, despite all deterrents, you come across a blog that wrongly uses your content, contact them directly and ask them to either remove the content or to correctly source it. Sometimes new bloggers are unaware they're infringing on your copyright, and still others do it blatantly and knowingly. Regardless, keep your cool when contacting people who avertedly or inadvertently steal from you and save those four-letter words for when you char the Thanksgiving turkey.

A final measure to help protect yourself is to form a *Limited Liability Company (LLC),* which is a type of business entity that combines the tax benefits of a partnership and the limited liability of a corporation. The basic take-away: When properly structured, an LLC generally protects you and your personal assets from any legal action in connection with your blog.

For example, if I post a recipe that contains nuts and someone with a nut allergy makes, eats, and gets sick from the recipe, she can generally sue only my LLC and not me personally, which means my personal assets are protected. However, here are three disadvantages to forming an LLC:

- **It costs money to file for and form an LLC.** Every state has specific filing instructions, regulations, and costs.
- **LLCs do not always protect the owner from being sued, and therefore, do not always protect the owner's assets.** On rare occasions, a plaintiff may be able to "pierce the corporate veil," and an owner can still be sued in his individual capacity, despite having formed an LLC. (There could be a whole other book on this subject, so I'm going to just leave it at that and suggest that if "piercing the corporate veil" peaked your interest, talk to an attorney!)
- **Formal paperwork is required to form an LLC.** Seek assistance from an attorney to file in your desired state.

Being credible, not a copycat

The natural follow-up question about recipe copyright is whether changing a few ingredients in a recipe while using the same method of preparation is enough to call the recipe your own. And this is where the Sangria starts to get cloudy.

No law that says changing *X* number of ingredients in someone else's recipe means you can't post it on your blog, claim it as your original creation, and not have to credit them. For example, if I make Kalyn's Kitchen's recipe for Stuffed Green Peppers with Brown Rice, Italian Sausage, and Parmesan, but use red peppers, brown rice, Italian sausage, and pecorino cheese, could I post that recipe as my own on my blog without giving Kalyn any credit?

Sure. But would I? No. Kalyn worked hard to fine-tune the recipe's method of preparation, and for me to swap a few ingredients and slap my own name on it would be taking credit for something I didn't originally create. Instead, I would post the recipe on my blog along with the phrase "This recipe was adapted from Kalyn's Kitchen," and link back to Kalyn's original post. This type of attribution has become the respected community standard among food bloggers when crediting someone else's work.

Other than "adapted from," you're most likely to use the phrase "inspired by" for providing attribution. Although similar in nature, the two phrases have different meanings:

- **Adapted from:** An adapted recipe originates from another recipe and you've made minor modifications to the ingredient list or method of preparation.
- **Inspired by:** You create a recipe based upon another recipe, dish, or technique that inspired you. Rather than make a few minor substitutions, you use different ingredients and a different method of preparation from the originating work.

Attributing recipes, or any other content, comes down to a question of ethics. The web makes it incredibly easy to claim someone else's ideas as your own. But at the end of the day, remember that you're part of the larger food blogging community — a community that's thriving with creative, inspiring, hardworking, and talented folks from every corner of the globe. Everyone wants to keep the standards high and give credit where credit is due. I know that I want my content properly attributed, and I'm guessing you do, too.

Classic recipes, such as chocolate chip cookies or Caesar salad dressing, fall in the gray area because they have standard ingredient lists and methods of preparation. The International Association of Culinary Professionals' (IACP) Ethical Guidelines state it is not necessary to credit a *classic recipe* (defined as a dish with ten or more traditional versions) as long as you've added your own unique twist to it, such as incorporating dried cherries or white chocolate chips into the cookie dough batter.

So although you could bake a fellow food blogger's peanut butter brownies with chunky peanut butter instead of smooth and call it your own recipe, the question lingers: Why do it? You are no less of a talented baker by utilizing someone else's recipe and giving them credit — especially if you pair it with a drool-worthy photo and your comments for how you made the method even better.

If you're unsure as to whether you can use another blogger's content, send him an e-mail and ask. And when in doubt, utilize these best practices for providing proper attribution:

- **Recipes:** Include "adapted from" or "inspired by" along with the original creator's name or blog. Then link to the original blog, or if it's from a cookbook, a site that sells the book.
- **Photos:** Include the photographer's name and link back to her blog.

Refer to any of the following online resources for more about intellectual property law as it pertains to food blogging as well as food blogger's rights and a code of ethics:

- **The Blogger's Legal Guide by the Electronic Frontier Foundation:** `www.eff.org/issues/bloggers/legal/liability/IP`
- **The Food Blog Code of Ethics by Brooke Burton and Leah Greenstein:** `http://foodethics.wordpress.com/the-code`
- **Recipe Copyright by The U.S. Copyright Office:** `www.copyright.gov/fls/fl122.html`

5

Setting Your Content Menu

In This Chapter

- Brainstorming blog post concepts
- Developing, writing, and creating recipes
- Organizing your content into categories

Strip your blog of every bell, whistle, horn, siren, gong, and cymbal, and you're left with the core of your site: the content.

What you publish — be it photos, reviews, recipes, videos, or essays — is the value you provide to the online world, and in turn what attracts readers to your blog. Engage and inspire, and you'll find a loyal fan base; distract and disappoint, and you'll be a one-click wonder. So do you offer a flavor for every palate? Or should you stick to a single dish and do it right?

In this chapter, you find inspiration for setting your menu by mixing and matching from a variety of post concepts. Some serve to entertain whereas others strive to inform, but they all require dedicated time and effort to ensure that quality prevails over quantity. With your menu set, discover how to get the most out of your content through creating categories, and discover a strategy to keep your blog active without feeling imprisoned by the demands of what can be a 24/7 endeavor.

Defining the Content on Your Blog

The two primary types of blog content are content that services and content that entertains. Both add value by creating and enriching the experience you construct for your audience, whether that means providing inspiration for tonight's dinner or prompting a laugh after a long day. Many posts feature the best of both worlds by teaching while also entertaining.

Some readers may stumble upon your blog by chance, whereas others are led straight to your home page in their hunt for information. Regardless of how they find your blog, what matters is how you're going to keep readers' attention in an online space jam-packed with tens of thousands of other informative and entertaining destinations. And this is where quality and variety rule.

If content is king, quality is queen. In Chapter 6, I cover the importance of consistency and frequency in blogging, but post quantity doesn't become a factor until after you master the art of creating superior content. With your niche defined, the next step is to focus on the specific topics and ideas you want to pursue in your blog posts.

As the results of The State of the Food Blogosphere survey indicate in Figure 5-1, 66 percent of food bloggers reported recipes make up the majority of content on their blog. "Photos and text" was a distant second at just less than 18 percent.

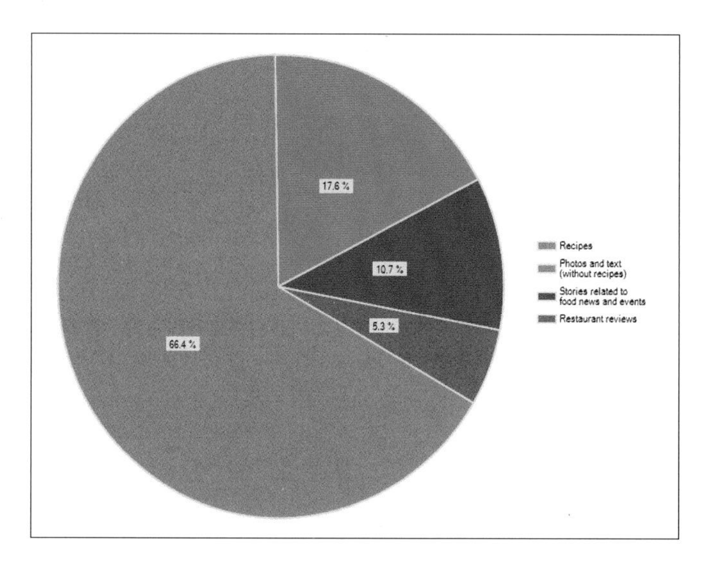

Figure 5-1: Survey results indicate the immense popularity among writers of recipes as a content focus.

Don't panic at the sight of these statistics if you don't plan to feature recipes. Recipes are the most popular content category, but definitely not the only content category. The best way to engage an audience is to provide variety, whether that variety is as general as types of posts or as specific as types of recipes. Defer to your niche and your passions for inspiration and kick-start your creative juices in the next sections with just a few (or 17) of my post suggestions.

Brainstorming blog post ideas

From interviews and podcasts to slide shows and giveaways, you're not limited to the variety of posts to feature on your blog. You might spend hours flinging flour in the kitchen creating dessert recipes, or you may never step foot into your own kitchen and instead woo your readers with worldly travels. Regardless of the angle of your blog, remember that an assortment of content will appeal to a broader audience.

Although satisfying a larger audience's preferences is important, mass appeal shouldn't be the inspiration behind your posts. If you aim for audience size, you'll end up going the generic route to please every palate. Instead, let your high-quality, informative, entertaining — and most of all, authentic — content do the luring. Begin by considering the following post concepts for your blog.

Reviews

Share your experiences and insights about restaurants, cookbooks, kitchen gadgets, and food brands to provide your audience with tried and tested suggestions for expanding their culinary repertoire.

How to's

Go back to the basics by featuring simple technique posts tied to your area of expertise, such as How to Sharpen a Knife, How to Pipe Rosettes, or How to Order from a Restaurant Wine List. This concept also applies to providing step-by-step photos to illustrate the process of preparing longer recipes. Angie Dudley of Bakerella (www.bakerella.com) provides clusters of photos (shown in Figure 5-2) to guide readers with visual clues.

www.bakerella.com

Figure 5-2: Bakerella features step-by-step photos guiding readers through a recipe.

Series

Create a themed series for your blog by dedicating an entire day, week, or month to a specific ingredient or topic. For example, dedicate the first week of December to foods that make great holiday gifts, post only about ice cream for the month of July, or join the established popular online series Meatless Mondays (a meat-free post every Monday) or Wordless Wednesdays (a photo-only post every Wednesday).

Virtual recipe events

No matter the time of year, you'll always find food bloggers declaring a day in which anyone and everyone posts a recipe featuring the same ingredient. These virtual recipe festivals are attended by anywhere from 20 to 2,000 food bloggers and can help expand your blog's community while increasing traffic by virtue of *linkbacks* (links to your blog from other sites) from other participating blogs.

Food news

Timely posts about the latest happenings in the food world give you a chance to inform your readers and to also weigh in with your opinion. Food news posts create awareness and establish your blog as an "it" destination for the latest culinary updates.

Videos

Videos enhance the multimedia component of your blog, but they also take time and require technical ability and a budget. However, you can create video content without extreme equipment and deep pockets. John Mitzewich of Food Wishes (`http://foodwishes.blogspot.com`; shown in Figure 5-3) is the mastermind behind more than 500 instructional cooking videos and has attracted more than 132,000 followers by posting his videos on YouTube. They're simple, straightforward, and incredibly user-friendly.

Figure 5-3: Food Wishes displays rich content in the form of instructional cooking videos.

Podcasts

A *podcast* is a series of audio files you record and post on your blog in a single segment or in multiple episodes. You drive the course of the content; but unlike videos, podcasts require less time, money, and technical ability to create. Listing your blog's podcasts on YouTube is also an effective way of bolstering readership.

Slide shows

Slide shows are a compelling platform for increasing the visual appeal of your blog. You implement a slide show either by installing a plug-in (if you are self-hosting your blog) or by utilizing a *photo-sharing site,* as shown in Figure 5-4. Photo-sharing sites allow you to create slide shows and embed the code into your posts without knowing a single HTML element. Here are three of the most popular photo-sharing sites:

- **Flickr:** `www.flickr.com`
- **Photobucket:** `www.photobucket.com`
- **Snapfish:** `www.snapfish.com`

Aim to use 8 to 12 photos per slide show; if you use more, your audience will lose interest.

Figure 5-4: Use a photo-sharing site to easily embed a slide show code into your posts.

Top-ten lists

Top-ten lists are one of the best ways to make content go viral. My highly scientific reasoning behind this is that people in general just really like lists. They simplify information by breaking down topics into more digestible parts, and in an era of overstimulation in real life and online, short and simple rules over long and complicated. Topics can range from your Top Ten Sweet and Salty Combos to your Top Ten Go-To Kitchen Gadgets. Publish your list and invite your readers to comment by weighing in with their own top-tens.

Taste tests

If you're a ketchup connoisseur or a grapefruit juice guru, create a taste test in which you evaluate various brands of a product. Ranking your choices adds the ever popular "list" element to taste tests, so publish your post and then steer clear of the impending stampede. Serious Eats (`www.seriouseats.com`), one of the most popular large-scale food blogs, posts results from monthly taste tests (shown in Figure 5-5) and ranks the results while asking readers to share their preferences.

Interviews

Post a simple and straightforward interview with a notable food name or fellow blogger that's both informative and entertaining. Address trendy topics, such as their top five favorite restaurants or what foods are always in their fridge — the more insider tips and anecdotes you can provide, the better. Promoting your culinary comrades enhances the online community centered around your blog, is a great way to meet new people, and introduces your audience to new faces.

www.seriouseats.com

Figure 5-5: A Taste Test post on Serious Eats evaluates various brands of dill pickles.

Kitchen failures

When in doubt, embrace the humor in culinary failures. Everyone has had a recipe gone awry or been exposed to a catastrophe in the kitchen. A great example of humor done right is the blog Cake Wrecks, as shown in Figure 5-6, which pairs professional cake-decorating errors with hilarious commentary. The authors created an entire blog using the concepts of failure and humor, so a single post is definitely doable.

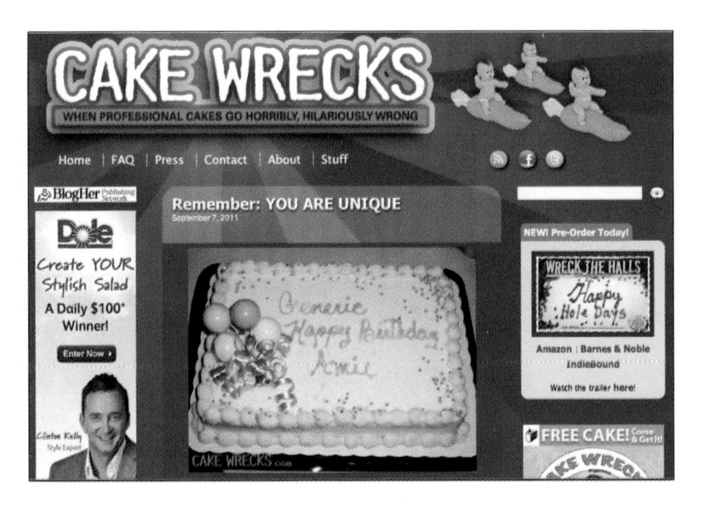

Figure 5-6: Cake Wrecks approaches cake decorating disasters with a humorous tone.

Engaging your audience

Although every post on your blog should be aimed at engaging your audience, certain posts elicit more of a response than others. The heavy hitting bloggers post a recipe and get more comments than a blooming onion has calories. Being a heavy hitter when you haven't even stepped on the field yet can be hard, though. Opt for any of these five types of posts that are guaranteed to ignite the burners and stir up a conversation.

Link roundups

Not to be confused with link exchanges, which are a big no-no (see Chapter 13), *link roundups* highlight the blogs and sites you're reading or simply want to share. They're a themed post, such as seven recipes for fried chicken from across the web, or they're a generic shout-out to an interesting post or a job well done.

Behind-the-scenes

Everyone loves a glimpse of the reality behind your blog, whether that be a view of your photography setup or a shot of your kitchen pre- and post-remodel. Behind-the-scenes photos satisfy curiosity cravings and prove existence of a real human behind your blog. Two Peas and Their Pod posted a reveal of their newly remodeled kitchen, as shown in Figure 5-7, and received 356 comments (and counting).

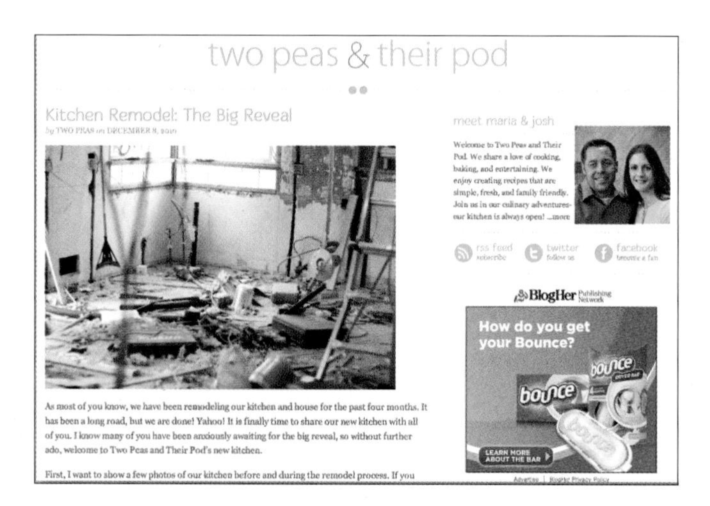

Figure 5-7: A behind-the-scenes post on Two Peas and Their Pod received more than 350 comments.

Guest posts

Inviting another blogger to publish a post on your blog (hopefully, you can do the same for them) is an effective way to introduce a new voice, and thus attract a new audience. Guest posts foster your online community by bringing together two distinct readerships under the common roof of your comments section. They have the added bonus of giving you a breather in the posting process, making a blog-free vacation a reality.

Polls

Polling your readers has two big benefits: You gain valuable insight about their preferences and desires, and they're encouraged to have a voice (and be heard) outside the comments field. Polls cover every topic imaginable, including favorite foods, recipe requests, restaurant recommendations, and any other topic you want to explore. Simply ask a question in your post and collect responses in your comment field, or use any of these popular polling tools:

- **Bloggeries:** `www.bloggeries.com/blog-polls/build`
- **Blog Polls:** `www.blogpolls.com`
- **WP-Polls:** `www.wordpress.org/extend/plugins/wp-polls`

Giveaways

Giveaways consist of you asking your readers to answer a question, to like your Facebook page, or to tweet a message for a chance to win a prize. Giveaways exist in the gray area of food blogging ethics in that some bloggers swear by them for engaging an audience, whereas others don't indulge in the temptation to solicit readership.

Giveaways involve legal requirements pertaining to the value of the prize, how you solicit entries, and whether your post even qualifies as a giveaway versus a lottery, sweepstakes, or contest. Although comments will flood your blog at the mention of a giveaway, know upfront what legal strings are attached before joining The Prize Patrol. (See Chapter 14 for more on giveaways.)

Writing and Creating Recipes

The task of developing, writing, and editing recipes deserves an entire book of its own. Later in this section, I address the best practices for recipe development, but first I want to focus on the primary considerations for writing your own recipes.

The following pointers help you to accurately and efficiently transfer your original culinary creations from your dinner plate to a published recipe on your blog:

- **Consider skill levels:** Knowing who your audience is helps you better write to their varying skill levels. Provide details about basic techniques in the first few months of recipe posts, and then wean your readers onto more direct and concise methods of preparation as they become more accustomed to your recipe style. Take, for example, an ingredient listed as "1 cup pecans, toasted." Do your readers know how to toast pecans? Or should you include the directions to preheat your oven to 350°F, place the pecans on a cookie sheet lined with parchment paper, and roast them for 10 to 15 minutes or until fragrant? This is ultimately your decision, but I don't think there's such a thing as being too obvious when writing recipes. I'd rather provide too much instruction than not enough.
- **Know your measurements:** Pay particular attention to measurements with regard to weight or volume. Certain ingredients, such as flour, are more accurately depicted as weights (ounces) rather than volume (cups). Everyone measures flour differently, so my one cup might not be the same as your one cup. But if you weigh 11 ounces, you know you have the same amount of flour as your audience. A quality digital kitchen scale isn't hard to find and is definitely worth the $15 investment.
- **Organize ingredient lists:** List the ingredients in the order in which they're used in the recipe.
- **Always proofread:** Even after you finalize your recipe, pass it along to a friend. A second, fresh set of eyes is more likely to catch errors or discover common stumbling points within a recipe you've written yourself and read countless times.

- **Pay attention to details:** Be mindful of the impact a single word can have on a recipe. Listing an ingredient as "3 tablespoons chopped parsley" is not the same as "3 tablespoons parsley, chopped." Similarly, when specifying cooking times such as "sear the chicken breasts for about three to five minutes on each side," you're including two estimations: "about" and "three to five." The range in minutes is already an estimation, so "about" is repetitive.

Writing recipes is one thing, but developing and testing them is an entirely separate skill. Creating a recipe from scratch involves a process that begins with conceptualization and ends with a satiated reader. In this section, I specifically address recipe development, rather than creating flavor profiles and mastering cooking techniques.

Recipe development involves the same basic steps whether you're making a puff pastry from scratch or adapting an already tasty dessert to be gluten-free or vegan-friendly. Regardless of your approach, all recipe development results in an edible outcome (with some requiring a few more tweaks and cross-tests than others).

- **Know your audience.** To meet the needs and wants of your audience, you might need to consider these restrictions and requirements:
  - *Dietary:* Is a gluten-free, vegetarian, or vegan option needed? Are there any food allergies to highlight?
  - *Budget:* Should you aim to feed a family of four for $30 or less? Or should you make the recipe worth a splurge?
  - *Ability:* Are your readers comfortable slicing and dicing or fearful of losing their fingers? How specific do instructions need to be?
  - *Accessibility:* Can your readers locate all the recipe ingredients at their local grocery stores?
- **Generate an idea.** You can do this completely from scratch or from inspiration drawn from cookbooks, magazines, friends, other food blogs, restaurant dishes, or travels.
- **Pay attention to seasons and holidays.** Not many people look for a pumpkin pie recipe in July, and you probably won't have the best-tasting tomato salad in December. Take advantage of the freshest flavors by using produce when it's at its seasonal peak; then begin conceptualizing your recipe by writing it down so you have something tangible to edit. After you decide on a concept and draft the recipe, the testing process begins.
- **Test your recipe. Then test it again. And again.** What could be more frustrating than going to the grocery store, buying ingredients, spending time cooking a recipe, and feeling the anxious anticipation of that first bite, only to discover it's under-cooked, over-salted, or otherwise

essentially inedible? Recipe testing is a critical component of the development process. Big-name brands put recipes through a rigorous testing process, with different cross-testers making each recipe five, six, or even seven times, before publishing them.

Countless elements must be addressed in the testing process, and each element must be specified for a recipe to work as it is intended:

- The exact size of pots, pans, baking dishes, and sheet trays
- The exact tool, be it a wooden or metal spoon, a heavy-bottomed pot, or a nonstick pan
- The exact condition of ingredients, such as peeled or unpeeled, drained or undrained, and so on
- The exact cooking time, including visual references such as "cook until the consistency of custard," or "bake until a toothpick inserted comes out clean"

- **Log your culinary journey.** Jot down notes while you test your recipe so you don't forget any necessary edits in the process. Better yet, snap step-by-step photos along the way to provide yourself (and eventually your readers) with visual cues tied to the color or consistency of foods in different stages of preparation.
- **Confirm your edits and finalize the recipe on paper.** Make sure your recipe is final before you start typing.
- **Write your post containing the recipe.** Include any information regarding recipe requirements. For example, note whether the recipe can be made for $20 or less, whether it's vegetarian, or whether fresh tomatoes are preferable to the canned variety.

  Take your time when typing the recipe into your Post editor because simple mistakes, such as using "tablespoon" instead of "teaspoon," can make all the difference (and usually not in a good way). If you aren't the best typist, first type your post into Word or another word-processing software, and then copy and paste it into your Post editor. This also provides you with a backup of all your recipes and posts in the event your blog has a major technical glitch.
- **Proofread and publish.** After you proofread your post and insert any images, click Publish, and then dig in.

Organizing Your Content

After you become tuned in to the smorgasbord of posting options, you can start planning how to present your content to your readers. A search bar is a critical element of your blog's layout, which I cover in detail in Chapter 8, but to make search effective, organize your posts so readers can easily find and sort through all available content. From creating categories to adding tags, the internal navigation on your blog is critical for getting the most from every post you publish.

Creating categories and subcategories

The most effective way to guide readers through your blog is to create categories and subcategories that allow them to easily and quickly browse through your content. Think of categories as filing cabinets, and subcategories as files within each cabinet. Both organize your content and make it easily accessible and searchable by your readers.

If your blog is home to a variety of recipes, for example, create categories and subcategories that organize your creations based on course, ingredient, or method of preparation. For example, the Breakfast category (which is a course) could include the following subcategories:

- Doughnuts
- Egg Dishes
- Jams
- Muffins
- Smoothies

Creating categories and subcategories on WordPress.com and WordPress.org blogs is done via the Dashboard, and the same method is used for both versions of the blogging software. To create a new category on a WordPress blog, log in to your Dashboard and follow these steps:

1. **Choose Posts⇨Categories on the left side of the page.**

   The Categories page appears.

2. **Enter the name of your category in the Name text box, as shown in Figure 5-8.**

3. **Click Add New Category.**

   Your new category is added to the list of categories on the right side of the page, which is where you manage all your categories and can edit them at any time.

4. **Further organize your posts by creating subcategories.**

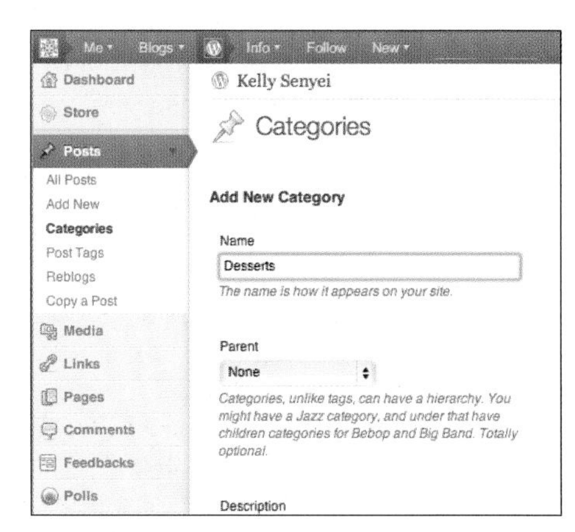

Figure 5-8: Enter the name of your new category in the top text edit box.

On the same Categories page, create a subcategory, and then choose which category it will live under from the Parent drop-down list, as shown in Figure 5-9. Adding the Parent field turns a category into a subcategory.

Figure 5-9: Choose an option from the Parent drop-down field to create a subcategory.

Categories on a Blogger blog are Labels. To apply a new or existing label to your post, click Post Settings in the Post editor and either select from the previously used labels (which auto-populate) or type a new one.

A more efficient way to add labels to Blogger posts is via the Posts page, as shown in Figure 5-10, which allows you to select multiple posts and apply labels to them all at the same time.

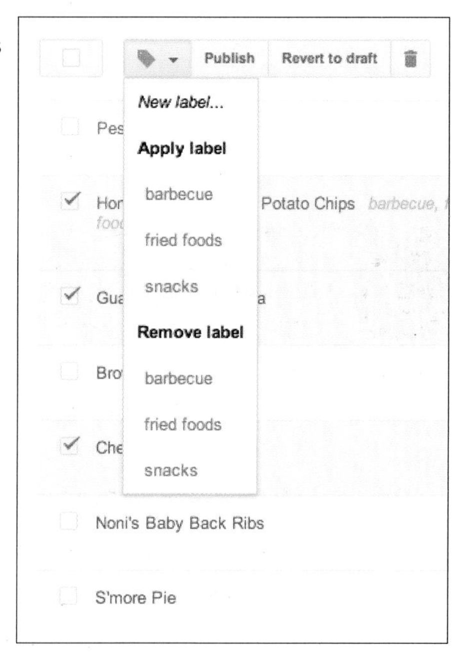

Figure 5-10: Add a label to multiple posts at once via the Posts page.

Blogger doesn't offer the option to create sub-labels, so the labels you create — no matter how general or specific — will all appear on your blog. There are technical workarounds for creating sub-labels, but they require a certain comfort level with HTML and JavaScript. (JavaScript has nothing to do with coffee, just in case you're feeling tempted.) I encourage you to save yourself the HTML-induced headache and stick to the basic labels.

Pay attention to how many categories or labels you create. Although there is no magic number, you don't want your sidebar to become a never-ending list of links. To avoid this, steer clear of getting too specific with overall category or subcategory names, and keep in mind that their basic purpose is to be filing cabinets and folders. If you have only one or two recipes in different categories, consider consolidating them into a combination, such as Soups and Salads. Although your number of categories may be limited, readers can still see every post assigned to a specific category when they click the category link.

WordPress also provides the option to tag your posts, which involves adding keywords to identify your posts beyond their categorizations. Tags, categories, and labels all play an important role in search engine optimization (SEO) and maximizing where your posts rank in online searches. (See Chapter 13 for more on SEO as it relates to organizing posts.)

Understanding pages versus posts

With such a strong emphasis placed on the content that lives in your posts, don't overlook the other areas on your blog that are rich with information. Posts are the foundation of your site, but the pages you create are also essential editorial elements for context and navigation.

Posts appear in chronological order on your home page, allowing you to decide via your template settings how many appear before getting bumped onto the second page. Unlike posts, *pages* are static in that they never get pushed onto another page. The permanent nature of pages makes them a prime destination for content tied to identifying yourself, explaining your blog's purpose, providing contact information, and so on. (See Chapter 8 for more on the navigational importance of pages.)

Creating pages is a separate process from creating posts, which varies according to your blogging software. To create a page on a WordPress.com or WordPress.org blog, log in to your Dashboard and follow these steps:

1. **Choose Pages⇨Add New on the left side of the page.**

   The Post editor for a new page appears.

2. **Enter the name of your page in the Enter Title Here text box and then enter your content in the Text editor.**

   Text, photos, videos, and links can be added to a page just as they are added to a post.

3. **Enter the numerical order of the page in the Order field of the Page Attributes editor on the right side of the page, as shown in Figure 5-11.**

Figure 5-11: Ordering pages on a WordPress blog is done via the Page Attributes editor.

Assigning number 1 positions the page on the top (or far left) of your list of pages. Number 2 is second (or second from the left), and so on. Update the order at any time as you add new pages. You can also add a Parent page to your new page. Choose an option from the Parent drop-down field, or leave the default "(no parent)" as the selection.

4. **Click Preview to proofread your new page.**

   A new window appears displaying how your page will look after it's published on your blog, as shown in Figure 5-12.

5. **When you're satisfied with the preview, click Publish.**

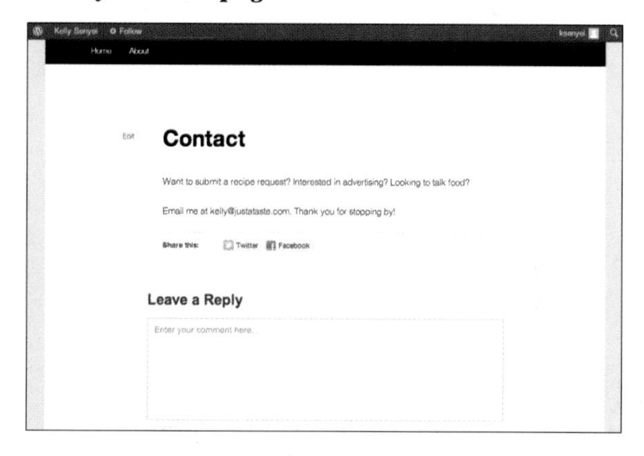

Figure 5-12: The preview window appears with a view of how your published page will look.

To create a new page on a Blogger blog, log in to your Dashboard and follow these steps.

1. **Click the Go to Post List button drop-down list, as shown in Figure 5-13, and select Pages.**

   The Pages page appears.

2. **Click the New Page button at the top left of the page and choose Blank Page from the drop-down list.**

   The Pages editor, which functions the same as the Post editor, appears.

3. **Enter the name of your page in the Page Title text box at the top of the page and then enter your content in the Text editor, as shown in Figure 5-14.**

   Text, photos, videos, and links can be added to a page just as they are added to a post.

Figure 5-13: Click the Pages link to create a new static page on a Blogger blog.

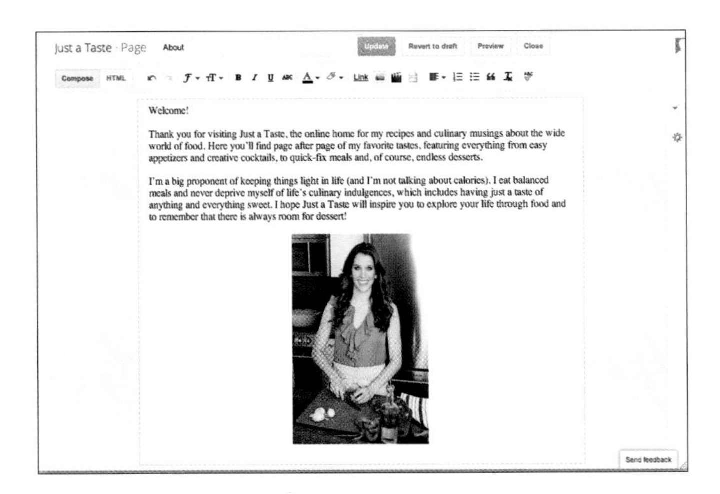

Figure 5-14: Add text and visuals to your new page in the Text editor.

4. **Click Save and then click Preview to proofread your new page.**

   A new window appears displaying how your page will look after it's published on your blog.

5. **When you're satisfied with the preview, click Publish.**

To change the order of your pages, go to the Pages page to access your created pages, which are listed in blue and white text boxes, as shown in Figure 5-15. Drag and drop the boxes into your desired order and then click the Save Arrangement button in the top-right section of the page. From this page, you can also change the placement of your page links by choosing from the drop-down list of the Side Links button.

Gauging content and time commitments

Depending on the type of content, a blog post can take minutes, hours, or even days to complete. After your first post hits the web, though, the blogging restaurant has officially opened for business. Now you can either hide behind the stove and let potential customers go hungry, or you can fire up the flames and let the cooking and eating begin.

One of the biggest misconceptions new bloggers have about the world of food blogging is that it's effortless and easy to become a big success with hundreds of thousands of daily pageviews and the ad revenue to match. Publish a few recipe posts, take a few stellar photos, write some reviews that go viral, and *bam!* you're an instant success. In your (and my) dreams.

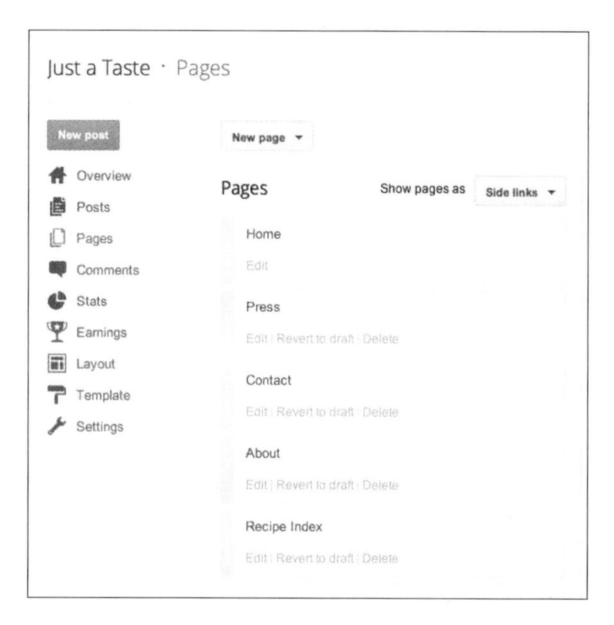

Figure 5-15: Rearrange the order of your pages by dragging and dropping the text boxes.

A quality food blog, like everything in life, demands time and effort to be a success. Blogs, by definition, are updated on a regular basis. Add the 24/7 nature of social media to the equation, and you might as well invest in a sweatband because you're about to burn some serious calories (and likely ingest some serious calories, too). Seem like a scary thought?

My goal isn't to alarm you, but rather to inform you that if you want more traffic than midtown Manhattan, you have to be willing to put in the work. If the numbers don't phase you, a posting strategy to stay sane isn't needed. However, if you're interested in routinely engaging your audience, prompting 100-comment posts, and attracting the attention of the greater digital food world, a posting strategy, which I cover in Chapter 6, is essential to avoid getting sucked into the black hole of blogging.

As you set your blog's content menu, keep in mind the following post-specific tasks that demand more attention and time than you might initially anticipate:

- **Original recipe posts:** *It's a simple risotto recipe, how long could it possibly take?* Those just might be your famous last words. No matter how skilled a chef you are, recipe development requires immense dedication. Each of the following tasks eats up time on the clock.

  - *Cooking:* Plain and simple, cooking takes time. And so does the grocery shopping and preparation prior to cooking. How much time will depend on the type of recipe, but anything involving pre-heating, reducing, braising, and/or chilling likely won't fall under the "quick" category.
  - *Cross-testing:* There is no way to avoid the time commitment and dedication required to test and re-test a recipe. The sheer fact of having to make the same recipe multiple times means cross-testing can be a lengthy process.
  - *Cleaning:* I often forget (or perhaps block out) that dirty dishes come hand in hand with cooking, especially if you don't have the good fortune of a taste tester to tackle the load in the sink.

- **Step-by-step recipe photo posts:** Regardless whether you're assembling a cold cuts-only sandwich or braising short ribs for three hours, stopping every three minutes to capture the next recipe step with a photo adds time to the clock. This is especially true if you're using natural light outside your kitchen, which means hauling your creation back and forth as you photograph the changing color of the caramel or evolving consistency of the red wine sauce.
- **Video posts:** Chances are if you're doing video posts, you're the host, videographer, sound person, producer, director, and editor. A quality video takes time to film and edit, with more time often spent on post-production than on the filming itself. There are ways to cut back on the time, such as doing a single take (no edits or transitions), but the high-tech aspect of videos makes them more time-consuming than the average text-only post.

6

Branding Your Blog through Consistency and Frequency

In This Chapter

- Envisioning your blog as a brand
- Establishing a style guide
- Standardizing recipe formatting
- Inserting visuals into your posts
- Deciding when and how often to post

Quality content and consistency go together like a cheeseburger and fries. Separately they're great, but together they're even better.

Like any burger joint looking to attract a loyal fan base, how much and how often you dish out content will directly impact your success in building your blog into a brand with a strong presence in the digital space, and perhaps beyond.

The amount of time you dedicate to feeding your audience depends on your own comfort level and commitment. But here's a hint: Satisfy their consistency cravings, and they'll become regular customers.

In this chapter, I identify the key elements for shaping your blog into a reliable online destination, which includes everything from envisioning your blog as a brand and formatting recipes, to adding photo captions and decoding the best days to post. Consistency across every sector of your blog is your best bet for attracting and captivating an audience, which gives you the greatest possible chance for sustained success.

Envisioning You and Your Blog as a Brand

Your first thought at the mention of brands might be of the logo on your Kellogg's cereal box or the classic Coca-Cola trademark on your soda can. But brands exist in every form, and in the online world, your brand — by virtue of your blog — is you.

That's a heavy concept for anyone who's just getting their first taste of food blogging. As soon as you begin to look at yourself and your blog from a branding perspective, the easier it is to understand the importance of consistency in relaying your distinctive message and unique identity online.

Your food blog brand exists as a mix of a *logo* (a simple mark or icon that identifies your blog) and an *identity,* which is defined by your blog's unique personality. I cover the essential elements of an effective logo in Chapter 7, but before you can dream up the ultimate design, you have to lay a sturdy foundation for consistency and frequency.

Creating consistency

If I walk into any Starbucks in the world and order an iced grande half-caff skim latte, I know it will taste pretty much the same — in San Diego, in New York City, in Seville, in Budapest. Knowing what I'll get every time I order is what brings me back to Starbucks time and time again.

If consistency has such pull with a simple coffee order, imagine its potential impact on your blog. People crave predictability and regularity in every aspect of their daily routines, which are just that — consistent. I want to know I can rely on Starbucks to provide the same tasting coffee time after time, just like readers want to know they can rely on your blog for the same quality content post after post. Predictability in posting frequency and quality is critical, but keep in mind you want your *actual* content to be anything but predictable so readers are intrigued enough to come back for more.

Consistency isn't only a question of the quality of your content. It also plays a role in how your content looks, how it reads, and how often it appears. All these elements and more contribute to the long list of reasons as to why consistency is such a crucial characteristic of a successful blog:

- **Audience loyalty:** The more reliable you are regarding what and how often you post, the more attractive your blog is to an online audience. Providing an uninterrupted stream of quality content is the best way to grow your readership.

- **Impact on search engine optimization (SEO):** Regularly updating your blog not only attracts readers, but it also attracts search engine spiders to index your pages based on your keywords, links, post title tags, and a variety of other factors that I cover in Chapter 13. The more often your blog is indexed, the higher it is likely to rank in online searches because search engines like Google, Yahoo!, and Bing are all about the latest and greatest content to provide the best search results for readers.
- **Credibility:** Every stylistic element of your blog — including spelling, grammar, and punctuation — affects how your site is perceived by your readers. Consistency in style and tone makes your blog appear more professional, which ups your credibility factor. Readers are much less likely to trust a blog rife with spelling errors and formatting inconsistencies.
- **Brand identity:** The more posts you publish tied to your niche, the more you expose your expertise to readers. Eventually, your readers will associate a specific type and a certain quality of content with your site, which will establish your blog as more than just an online destination for information: Your blog will be viewed as a brand with an underlying focus.

Branding your blog

If you want to be on the fast track to success (defined by traffic, ad revenue, business opportunities, or a mix of all three), you have to envision your food blog as more than just a URL, more than just a recipe database, more than just an online portfolio. You have to envision your food blog as your brand.

One of the best examples of a food-blogger-turned-brand — and in this case, mega brand — is Ree Drummond of The Pioneer Woman blog, who transcended digital to print, and even print to the big-screen. In five years, Drummond transformed her food blog into an empire consisting of a cookbook; a children's book; a novel; an upcoming movie (starring Reese Witherspoon); and most recently, her own show on the Food Network.

As much of a vehicle as The Pioneer Woman blog has been for providing opportunities, the real brand isn't the blog: The real brand is Drummond. Readers fall in love with the loveable, affable, candid charm that exudes from every post she publishes. Ree has had that same allure since her first few posts in 2006. She's always been real, and her story has always been one of everyday life on an Oklahoma farm. It's not hard to feel drawn to someone who acknowledges her flaws, finds the humor in any situation, and is comfortable and confident enough to live her life (with all its ups and downs) in the scrutiny of the public eye.

Is Drummond representative of the average food blogger as a brand? I bet you already know the answer to that question. Despite being new to the blogging scene, you still have just as good of a chance as anyone to transform yourself into a full-fledged success story.

In Chapter 7, you find everything you need to know about branding from a design perspective, followed by every aspect of brand extension in Chapter 13. Before you can design and extend your brand, though, you need to establish it. You can see how to take the first step in Chapter 3 by homing in on your niche, but now it's time to focus on every element of consistency, from quality to quantity, substance to style. Creating standards for each of these elements strengthens your blog's identity, which helps you build a more cohesive brand.

Establishing Your Style Guide

Take a look at Figure 6-1, which depicts the ingredient list for my homemade artichoke spread.

Figure 6-1: A recipe post features the list of ingredients for homemade artichoke spread.

So what's wrong with this list of ingredients? (Hint for all you health fiends: It's not the half-cup of mayonnaise or the eight ounces of cream cheese.)

Look a bit closer. Can you spot the inconsistencies? The recipe calls for 8 oz. canned artichoke hearts, but 8 ounces cream cheese; 1/2 cup sour cream, but 1/2 c. mayonnaise; one cup Parmesan cheese, but 1 jalapeño. I might as well just go for the whole enchilada: Title it "Artechoke Spread" and aggravate every spelling, punctuation, and grammar enthusiast on the planet.

This ingredient list is a perfect example of why every blog should adhere to a *style guide* (or an established set of standards) that outlines the blog's identity as it relates to the consistency of formatting and appearance. Your style guide will be unique to your blog and will convey your personal preferences and tastes when it comes to formatting and frequency.

Deemed "the journalist's Bible," the *Associated Press Stylebook* (Basic Books) is the best place to begin when creating your own style guide. It's especially useful if you don't identify with my fellow grammar nerds but still want to get a grasp on where the pros (that is, national newspapers, magazines, and online publications) turn for industry-wide accepted usage. And the 2011 edition includes an updated section dedicated entirely to food. You can pick up a copy for about $20.

I think the $20 is well spent if you want to adhere strictly to AP style on your blog. Alternatively, do some research on your own to discover what stylistic elements you prefer. Keep reading to see every element of food blogging style you ever dreamed (or not dreamed) of knowing.

Although a style guide is unique to every blog, every style guide should specify the standards for six key elements:

- Post length
- Attribution
- Links
- Images
- Recipes
- General grammar and spelling

These basics address your personal style as it relates to consistency across your site. However, your style is also reflected in the tone of your writing (see Chapter 4) and the look and feel of your site (see Chapter 7). With this overall view of a style guide in mind, dive into the details by outlining the specifics of each element.

Post length

The length of your posts depends on the type of content. Recipe *headnotes* (or brief introductory paragraphs) may require fewer words than a restaurant review, and a podcast may feature a shorter introduction than a taste test with lots of bullet points. In general, every post should abide by the 250-words-or-less rule. But like all rules, there are certain exceptions. Some popular food blogs, such as Orangette or Serious Eats, have made their mark in part to longer posts. Unless you're completely comfortable in the craft of food writing, I suggest starting off by adhering to the 250-word rule and then adapting your post length as your style evolves.

To get a quick idea of what 250 words looks like in print, take a look at the next four paragraphs, which together are about 250 words.

The "250 rule" has become the standard simply because publishing anything much longer risks readers losing interest. A large block of text is unappealing when compared with the massive amount of multimedia material available online. So grab your reader's attention by making every single one of those 250 words count. The goal is to be powerful and poignant, yet brief.

Attribution

How you credit publishing content that isn't yours — whether recipes, text, photos, or videos — relates to the ethical component of blogging. Chapter 4 addresses the accepted community standard for recipes (*Adapted from* or *Inspired by,* plus a link), but sourcing content extends far beyond ingredient lists and methods of preparation.

If you ever want to use text, images, or videos from another source, ask the creator of the content. If or when you do feature another person's work, include his name or affiliation as the source and also provide a link to the original. Note the language and the use of a link in Figure 6-2, which displays an example of accepted attribution when the Kitchen Generation blog republished photos from a cookbook.

All images reprinted with permission from Super Natural Every Day: Well-Loved Recipes from My Natural Foods Kitchen by Heidi Swanson, copyright © 2011. Published by Ten Speed Press, a division of Random House, Inc.

Figure 6-2: Cite your sources.

Although everyone loves to get paid every time our work is featured on another blog or site, the reality is that linking has become an acceptable form of online currency. Payment isn't out of the question, but it's just not the norm. However, a link back is a great way to garner more (and often new) readers for your blog.

Images

Establishing a standard size for horizontal and vertical images creates visual consistency across your blog. How large or how small they are depends on the prominence of photos versus text or other media. In addition to considering size, pay attention to the frequency and placement of images in your posts. I discuss the technical how-two for changing image sizes within a post in the "Inserting Visuals into Posts" section later in this chapter.

If you're publishing recipes, the top image should always be the completed dish (for SEO reasons), followed by step-by-step process shots or additional photos, each of which should also be tagged with its appropriate description to make the most of image SEO. Although the size of your images is a personal style decision, I prefer that my images be the predominant focus on the page, but not be so large that it's impossible to view them in their entirety without cutting off a portion when you scroll.

Links

Links, a critical component of every blog, come in two forms: internal and external:

- **Internal links:** Refer from one page of your blog to another.
- **External links:** Refer to an incoming link to your blog from another site or an outgoing link from your blog to another site.

Best practices for standardizing internal and external links show which words and phrases are consistently hyperlinked. For example, you may specify in your style guide that any mention of a cookbook is always linked to that book's Amazon page.

Linking plays a critical role in SEO, especially with regards to *keywords,* which are the words that best reflect the topic of your content. (See Chapter 13 for more on the relationship among links, keywords, and SEO.) Inserting links in a WordPress or Blogger blog is done via the Link button in the Post editor.

To insert a link in a WordPress.com or WordPress.org blog, log in to your Dashboard, access the post containing the word or phrase you want to link, and then follow these steps:

1. **In the Post editor, select the word or phrase you want to hyperlink by highlighting it, as shown in Figure 6-3.**
2. **Click the Link button on the top level of the formatting toolbar.**

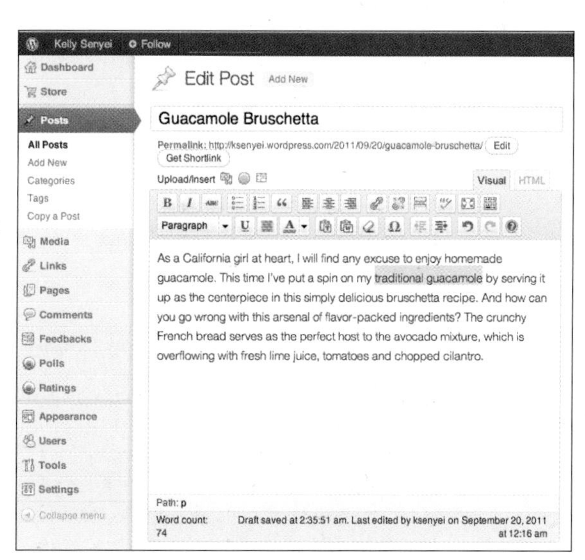

Figure 6-3: Highlight the text that you want to hyperlink.

An Insert/Edit Link pop-up window appears, as shown in Figure 6-4.

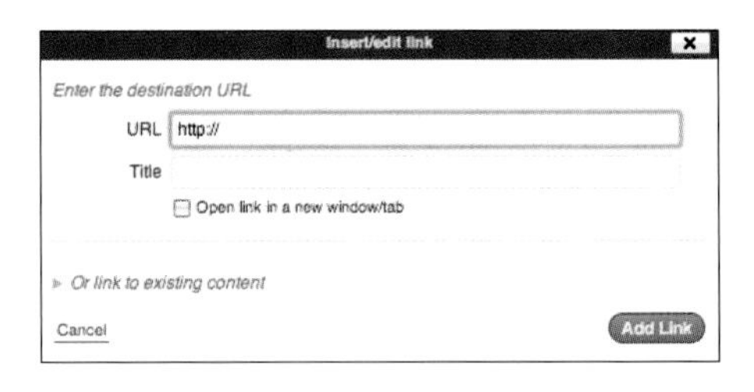

Figure 6-4: A pop-up window appears in the WordPress Text editor for inserting links.

3. **Copy and paste your link into the URL text box.**
4. **Type the name of your link into the Title text box.**
5. **(Optional) Select the Open Link in a New Window/Tab box.**

   There is no definitive rule as to whether links should open in the current window or in a new window. My preference is to have internal links open in the current window and external links open in a new window.

6. **Click the Add Link button.**

   The word or phrase you highlighted is hyperlinked to the URL you specified. Linked words or phrases are identified by a difference in style, such as underlining, bolding, or applying a color.

To insert a link in a Blogger blog, log in to your Dashboard, access the post containing the word or phrase you want to link, and follow these steps:

1. **Select the word or phrase you want to hyperlink by highlighting it, as shown in Figure 6-5.**

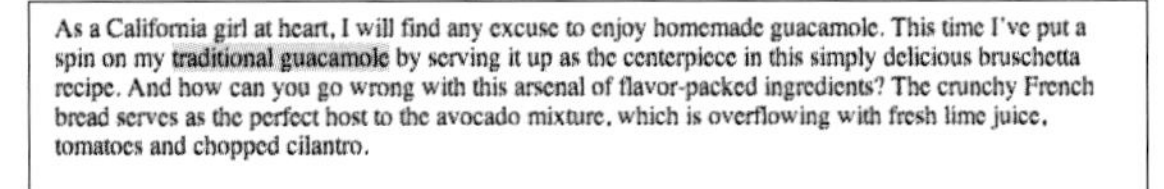

As a California girl at heart, I will find any excuse to enjoy homemade guacamole. This time I've put a spin on my traditional guacamole by serving it up as the centerpiece in this simply delicious bruschetta recipe. And how can you go wrong with this arsenal of flavor-packed ingredients? The crunchy French bread serves as the perfect host to the avocado mixture, which is overflowing with fresh lime juice, tomatoes and chopped cilantro.

Figure 6-5: Highlight the text in the Post editor that you want to hyperlink.

2. **Click the Link button on the formatting toolbar.**

   You see the Edit Link pop-up window shown in Figure 6-6.

3. **Confirm that the word or phrase in the Text to Display field is correct, and then copy and paste your URL into the Web Address field, as shown in Figure 6-6.**
4. **(Optional) Select the Open This Link in a New Window check box, or leave it deselected if you want the link to open in the same window.**

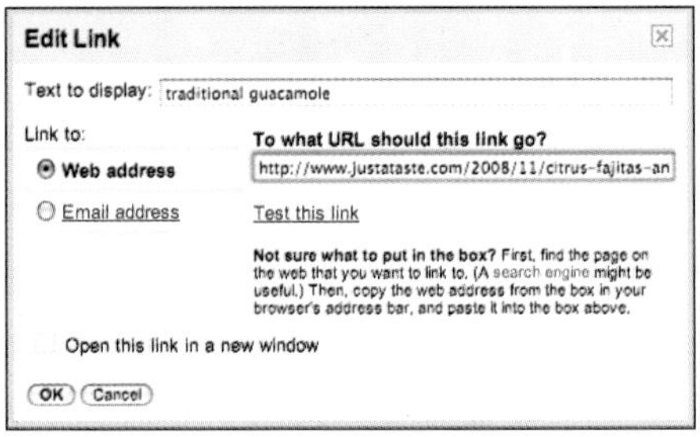

Edit Link
Text to display: traditional guacamole
Link to: To what URL should this link go?
Web address http://www.justataste.com/2008/11/citrus-fajitas-an
Email address Test this link
Not sure what to put in the box? First, find the page on the web that you want to link to. (A search engine might be useful.) Then, copy the web address from the box in your browser's address bar, and paste it into the box above.
Open this link in a new window
OK Cancel

Figure 6-6: A pop-up window appears in the Blogger Text editor for inserting links.

5. **Click OK to insert the hyperlinked word or phrase into your post.**

   The word or phrase you highlighted is now hyperlinked to the URL you specified. Linked words or phrases are identified by a difference in style, such as underlining, bolding, or applying a color.

6. **Edit the link at any time by clicking it and selecting from the Go to Link, Change, and Remove options, as shown in Figure 6-7.**

   The Go to Link option simply takes you to the URL.

Click to go to the link.
Click to delete the link.
Click to edit the link.

Figure 6-7: Click the link in your Post editor to view, change, or remove it.

Recipes

Consistency in tone and structure is especially critical when publishing recipes because they involve measurements and a series of steps — accuracy is essential. When you establish your standard style for recipes, decisions have to be made regarding how to specify amounts, as well as whether you number the steps in the method of preparation.

Table 6-1 displays common measurements, along with options of abbreviated mentions. Pick one style and stick to it so that readers aren't confused by varying abbreviations. Consistency in recipe style is also a strong indicator of credibility and professionalism.

Table 6-1 Abbreviating Recipe Measurements

Measurement	Abbreviations
teaspoon	t, t., tsp, tspn.
tablespoon	T, T., Tbsp, tblsp, tblspn.
ounce	oz, oz., fl. oz.
pound	lb, lb., #
cup	c, c., C, C.

I prefer not to abbreviate measurements because I often find it visually difficult to decipher between "T" and "t" when viewing recipe content on smaller smartphone screens. Although it's your choice as to how you indicate measurements, follow certain web-wide stylistic rules for recipes:

- **Ingredient amounts:** Numbers should be represented as figures, such as "2 tablespoons soy sauce," rather than "two tablespoons soy sauce."
- **Weighted ingredients:** Spell out the quantity of an ingredient when its weight is specified. For example, if a recipe calls for two chickens that are four pounds each, the ingredient should be listed as "two (4-pound) chickens."
- **Cooking times:** Cooking times should be specified as figures, such as "30 to 35 minutes" or "2 hours."

The method of preparation is displayed as either a numbered or un-numbered series of steps — or, in some rare cases, as a paragraph. Regardless of which style you choose, remember to not group too many instructions into one step. Spreading out longer processes makes a recipe more user-friendly.

General grammar and spelling

As I mention earlier, readers are much less likely to trust a blog rife with spelling errors and stylistic inconsistencies. Established style guides offer differing advice, but they all generally abide by basic rules. Paying attention to even the smallest grammatical details demonstrates your professionalism and credibility to your audience:

- **Commas:** Decide whether to use a concluding serial comma, which is the optional comma preceding "and" or "or" in a more-than-two-item series: for example, the comma following "cumin" in "cayenne, cumin, and red pepper flakes." I have always adhered to AP style, which does not use the concluding serial comma, but it's entirely a personal decision as to whether you use it on your own blog.
- **Italics:** AP style specifies that the names of books, TV shows, and movies should be italicized. Whether you follow these guidelines or not, remember to stay consistent with how you reference media. Also consider italicizing foreign language words, such as *Jamón ibérico* and other vocabulary not assimilated in the English language.
- **Capitalization:** Foods that are named after a location are generally capitalized, such as Brie cheese (named after the French region of Brie) and Champagne (named after the French region of Champagne, where it's produced). Foods that are not specific to a location, such as cheddar cheese and french fries (referring to a "french" cut, not the country, according to the *AP Stylebook*), should not be capitalized.
- **Multiple spellings:** Certain food words have multiple spellings. For example, you've probably seen "barbecue" as BBQ, Bar-B-Que, or barbeque. Pick one spelling and stick to it.

Your blog isn't an academic paper, a national newspaper, or a research thesis. Although proper spelling and grammar are important, be flexible in your approach to your style guide. Just because the *AP Stylebook* or *The New York Times* follows a specific style doesn't mean that you have to adhere to it on your blog. A style guide is meant to encourage consistency, but that consistency is based entirely on your preferences.

Inserting Visuals into Posts

A blog without visuals is like a pizza without toppings. Sure, plain cheese tastes fine, but think of all the flavor that's added by piling on pepperoni, fresh basil, green peppers, mushrooms, and olives. A pizza looks better with all that color, and the same goes for your blog. Visuals play a critical role in strengthening your blog as a brand because photos and videos provide ample opportunity to strictly define your unique visual voice and style. The strongest food blog brands can be identified by their photography alone.

Visuals make your blog more appealing to your audience and enhance the quality of your content — a fact that's especially true for recipes. A recipe post featuring Nona's famous fried spaghetti is much more enticing when paired with a colorful photo of the dish, which provides a visual cue and an end goal for readers to strive for. And recipe or no recipe, what's not to love about some quality food porn?

Photos and videos are inserted via the Post editor in your blogging platform, which is also where you adjust photo sizes and add captions. For WordPress.com and WordPress.org blogs, log in to your Dashboard, click the post you want to insert an image into, place your cursor in the location where you want the image to appear, and follow these steps:

1. **Click the Add an Image button located to the right of the Upload/ Insert text above the formatting toolbar.**

   A pop-up window, as shown in Figure 6-8, appears with these tab options for retrieving an image:

   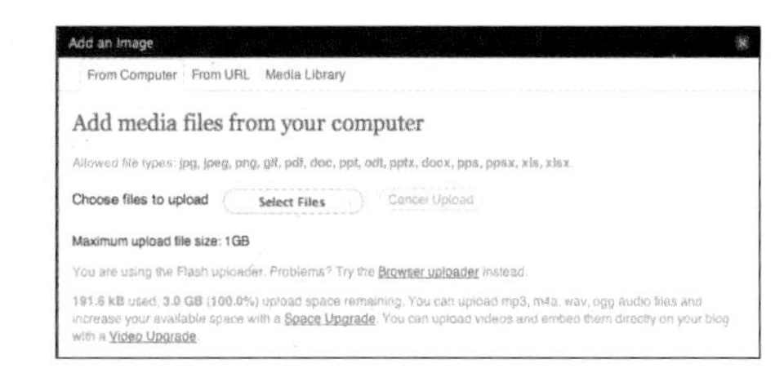

   Figure 6-8: Choose the location of your image from the tabs in the Add an Image window.

   - *From Computer:* Select an image that is saved on your computer.
   - *From URL:* Select an image that appears on another website.

   - *Media Library:* Select an image that has already been uploaded to your blogging platform, but not necessarily published.

2. **If the image is saved on your computer, click the From Computer tab and then click Select Files.**

   A pop-up window appears, giving you access to select the image from where it's saved on your computer.

3. **Select the photo and click Open.**

   WordPress uploads the image file and displays it in the Add an Image window.

4. **Insert the Title, Alternate Text, and (optionally) a caption in the text fields. Then specify the alignment and size by selecting from the options shown in Figure 6-9.**

   Alternate Text should be the same as the Title and is important for SEO purposes.

5. **Click Insert into Post.**

   The image appears in your post.

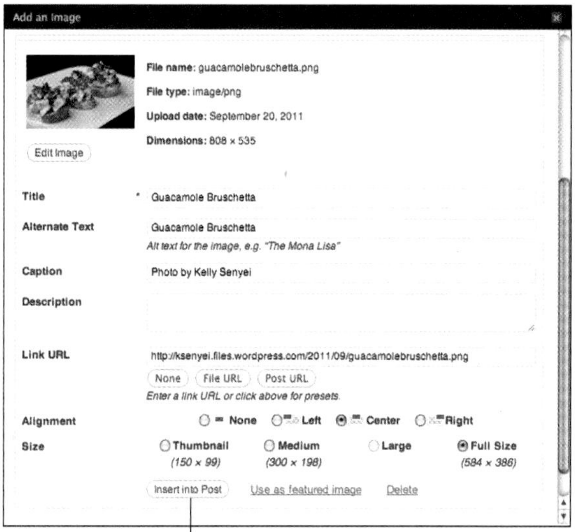

Click to place an image.

Figure 6-9: Select the alignment and size of an image in the Add an Image window.

If you're using Blogger, log in to your Dashboard, click the post you want to insert an image into, and place your cursor where you want the image to appear. Confirm that you're in the Compose Post editor (verified by clicking the gray Compose button in the top-left corner), and then follow these steps:

1. **Click the Insert Image button located on the formatting toolbar.**

   A pop-up window, as shown in Figure 6-10, appears with options for where to get the image.

2. **If the image is saved on your computer, click Choose Files.**

   A pop-up window appears, giving you access to select the image from your computer.

3. **Select the photo and click Open.**

   Blogger uploads the image file to your blog.

4. **Click Add Selected.**

   The image appears in your post.

5. **Click the image after it's in your post to edit its size, alignment, and caption, as shown in Figure 6-11.**

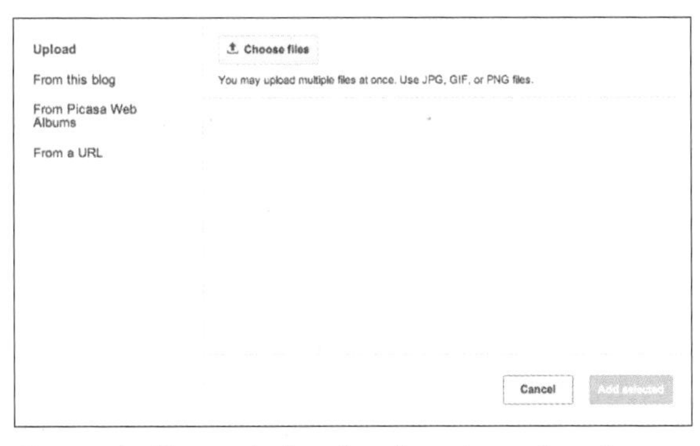

Figure 6-10: Choose the location of your image from the pop-up Image editor.

Figure 6-11: Click the inserted image to edit its size, alignment, and caption.

Here are two methods for inserting videos into a WordPress or Blogger post. Which method you use depends on where the original video file lives:

- **Hosted videos:** Videos that already live online, such as on YouTube, Vimeo, or another video platform, are inserted into a blog post via the embed code generally found below the video, as shown on top in Figure 6-12. Copy the code and paste it into the HTML tab of your Post editor, as shown in a Blogger post at the bottom of Figure 6-12. The video won't appear if you paste the embed code in the Compose tab.
- **Nonhosted videos:** If your video exists as a file on your computer, insert it into your post by clicking the Video icon (located next to the Image icon) and following the same process as adding images.

Figure 6-12: Paste the embed code on the HTML tab.

Focusing on Frequency

Twice a week. At least once a month. Every day. As often as you can. Whenever the mood strikes.

Ask any blogger how often you should post on your blog, and you'll get more answers than Ben & Jerry's has ice cream flavors. The entire industry is split on what the right answer is, including the food bloggers who participated in The State of the Food Blogosphere survey.

As the results in Figure 6-13 show, when asked how often they post on their blog, almost 32 percent of food bloggers indicated "at least once a week," while the rest of the field was relatively evenly divided between "twice a month or less," "at least twice a week," and "more than twice a week."

So which one is right? The answer lies somewhere in the mix of what your blogging goals are and just how much time you have to dedicate to the craft. And, of course, blended into that mix is consistency.

There is consistency, and there is frequency, and then there is the consistency of your frequency. Confused yet? *Frequency,* from a publishing standpoint, refers to how often you post content on your blog. Stay consistent in your frequency because your readers will come to expect new content based on the routine posting schedule you establish. The more reliable you can be in your frequency, the more trusted of a brand your blog will become.

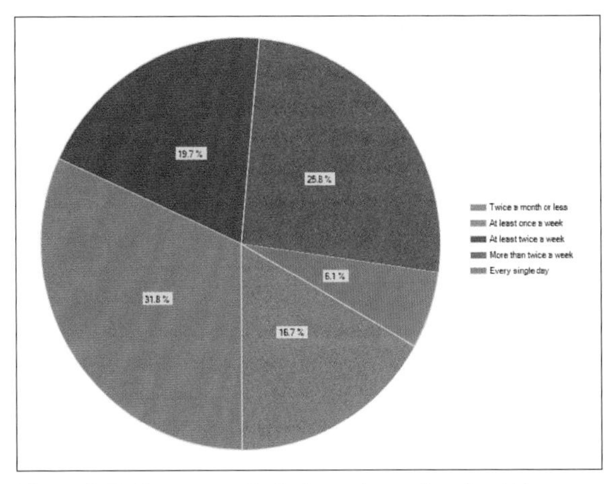

Figure 6-13: Survey results indicate how often food bloggers post on their blogs.

Implementing a posting schedule

Begin by assessing your goals from a traffic standpoint. How many people do you want visiting your blog? And how many times per day do you want those same people stopping by?

If your goal is a mountain of traffic, you need to post once daily, at minimum. Consider the big-name food blogs like Serious Eats, The Kitchn, Epicurious, and Food52, which post anywhere from 3 to 25 times a day. But (and this is a big "but") they're also staffed by multiple bloggers who dedicate their time and their bylines to creating countless posts per day as paid employees. That's a far different scenario than a beginner food blogger with a staff of one.

You, most likely, are what I like to call a *one-person band.* You cook the food. You develop the recipe. You eat at the restaurant. You test the recipe. You take the photos. You edit the photos. You write the post. You publish the post.

I'm exhausted just typing that. But the more times in a single day you click Publish, the more options you're serving up for your online audience. No one wants to stare at the same bowl of soup day after day after day. Variety, quite literally, is the spice of (your food blogging) life. New content is important, but it shouldn't send you into a frenzy or turn you into a blogging hermit. On the contrary, new content should never serve the sole role of space filler, as poorly crafted "fluff" posts will leave a sour taste in readers' mouths.

Consider the following questions when deciding on your posting frequency:

- **How many posts are manageable for your current schedule?** Determine a realistic number and then if you have time for more, you can always increase the number later.
- **How often is your online audience looking for new information related to your food blogging niche?** Chances are your blog isn't season- or holiday-specific, which means you can assume hungry web surfers are constantly on the lookout for new recipes, stories, tips, and techniques tied to all things food.
- **How many new ideas can you realistically generate on a consistent basis?** This ties back to defining your niche, which should be focused enough without restricting your creative endeavors.
- **How many times per day/week/month can you post and still maintain quality content?** This is the most critical question because it relates to the brand you're establishing for your blog. Posting daily with little to say isn't going to be as effective at building your audience (or your credibility) as posting twice weekly with powerful, informative, and engaging content.

Although everyone wants to be told that posting *X* times per day is going to guarantee success and put you in a fluid rhythm of traffic, the bottom line is that there is no magic number. Post as often as you can, on a consistent schedule, with the highest quality content you can create. And then remember to practice patience as you watch your following grow.

The most effective approach to keeping up with your blog's posting demands is to create an editorial calendar for your personal reference. I use Google Calendar because it allows me to easily switch around the publishing date of posts and to send myself automated reminders before a post is scheduled to be published. Any type of calendar (even nondigital) will work. An editorial calendar has countless benefits:

- It keeps you organized by displaying a futuristic view of your content.
- It reminds you to strategically plan your content around holidays, events, and most importantly, seasons.
- It allows you to schedule reminders for when posts need to be published.
- It keeps you calm, cool, and collected by eliminating last-minute scrambles because you always know what's coming up next.

In addition to an editorial calendar, the second-best strategy is to stockpile posts. *Stockpiling* consists of keeping a running list of completed posts in your blog's Dashboard. If the current week's post falls through, you automatically have another one to fall back on.

I also stockpile unfinished posts as a running collection of my inspirations, thoughts, and plans for future content. And I never limit how many drafts I create. (I currently have 40!) Some will eventually get fully fleshed out and posted, whereas others will soak in an eternal marinade, never to grace my home page. Either way, stockpiling is an effective way to prioritize your ideas and keep them all in one place.

Keep in mind that most blogging platforms allow you to schedule posts to publish automatically on a specified day and time. This feature lets you keep your content fresh without manually publishing new content at that time.

Deciding what days to post

Although only you can decide how often to post, science can help you decide *when* to post. Tools like Google Analytics, as shown in Figure 6-14, AWStats, and other statistics programs (discussed in Chapter 2) break down your blog's traffic by day, and sometimes even by hour. After you've been blogging for a few months, you can reference the statistics to see when your traffic is highest.

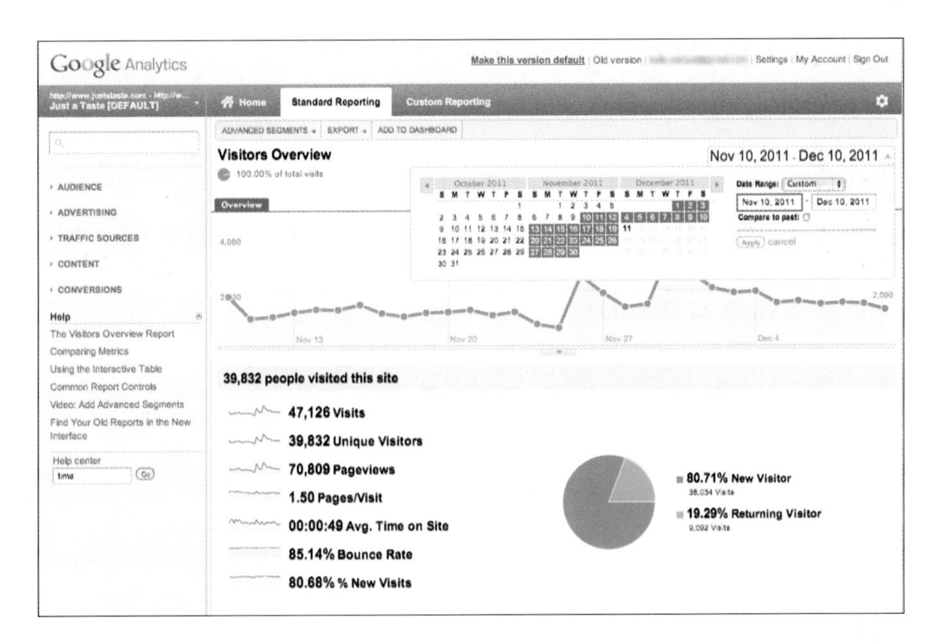

Figure 6-14: Google Analytics allows you to select your desired timeframe for analyzing traffic statistics.

Because you likely don't have the luxury of such statistics this early in your blogging career, the best approach is to begin by understanding who your audience is and when viewers are most likely to access your content. For example, if you post recipes, will readers more likely look for them on weekends or on weekdays? Will they be on the hunt in the early morning hours (prior to afternoon grocery trips) or late at night?

You can only estimate the answers to these questions at this point, so no harm is done just picking a day and trusting your gut. I would, however, discourage you from posting on Saturdays or Sunday mornings. Online blog aficionados, and web users in general, are more likely to be trolling your content during work hours and during the middle of the week.

Regardless of what day or days you decide to post on, pay attention to holidays, food events, and seasons. Timeliness is essential, and not just on the day of the holiday but during the days preceding. For example, posting a pumpkin pie recipe on Thanksgiving Day isn't very useful for your audience; after all, they'll likely already have done their grocery shopping. Instead, post the recipe a week or two in advance to give them enough time to incorporate the new recipe into their holiday spread.

Part III

The Soup to Nuts of Design

In this part . . .

Although the content you publish is undoubtedly an important aspect of your food blog, the bottom line is that the superficial stuff matters. From where to position the search bar to the color of your font, Part III invites you into the fabulous world of layout and design and helps you to craft a confusion-free roadmap for your readers.

Blog beautification just wouldn't be complete without a few final trimmings. Discover the endless options for widgets and find out the fast and easy ways of creating your very own sidebar garnish.

7

The Lay of the Land

In This Chapter

- Making a great first impression with your blog
- Utilizing a template to its fullest
- Picking a color palette for your blog
- Designing your header
- Avoiding common errors in design

Imagine spending hours baking the most decadent German chocolate cake. The salty crunch of toasted pecans, the chewy bite of flecked coconut — it's as close to flavor perfection as it gets. Now imagine that cake looks like a pile of fertilizer. Lost your appetite?

The same goes for food blogs. You can be the world's greatest wordsmith, but if your content is visually unappealing, or dare I even say appalling, you've lost your audience. Bottom line: The superficial stuff matters.

From deciding on a color palette to fretting over font styles, this chapter helps you master your food blog's first impression with tips and tricks for creating an eye-catching logo, going beyond generic templates, and avoiding common errors in style and design.

Extreme Makeover: Food Blog Edition

A critical caveat to designing your food blog is to first understand the restraints or freedoms you have based on what blog software you are running. If you are using WordPress.com, your design decisions are more limited because you are restrained to the 125 or so templates currently available. You can create a custom design, but it comes with a $30 annual price tag.

You might have trouble thinking you're "limited" to just 125 template choices, but when you compare that to what seems to be endless customization options that WordPress.org and the latest version Blogger offers, choosing from 125 templates can seem downright manageable.

WordPress.com is the hosted, free platform whereas *WordPress.org* is self-hosted and requires paying to register and host your domain. For more about blog platforms, see Chapter 3.

And if you're not the type who likes to let templates or themes control your design destiny, you can splurge by hiring a designer to build your dream blog. (Hint: Big dreams don't happen for free.) But regardless of what software route you take, the principles and considerations that I discuss in this chapter apply universally to the strategy behind any food blog's effective design.

So whether you've just set up your blog or you're looking to do a little nipping and tucking on a current layout, the key to designing an attractive blog is to think about your site as a whole.

Your food blog is a reflection of you as a writer, a cook, a recipe developer, a photographer, and any other role you star in. Now you just have to package your high-quality content in an equally as high-quality design.

Consider the following questions before deciding on the look and feel of your blog:

- What is your blogging niche and purpose?
- What is the tone of your writing?
- What types of patterns, images, and textures inspire you?
- What prominence will photos have over text?
- Which food blogs do you admire most for their aesthetics?

Keeping the answers to these questions in mind as you design your blog will help focus your goals and streamline the creative process. Maintain a running list of the food blogs you come across in your research. And then ask yourself what it is about those blogs' color schemes or tones that you find so attractive or unattractive. Are you lured in by an appealing color palette? Are they using a patterned background? Is the font too hard to distinguish?

With tens of thousands of food blogs in existence, there is very little time to woo your prospective reader. So take that pile of German chocolate cake, give it a smooth, frosted edge, and decorate it, toasted pecan by toasted pecan, so that anyone — dessert fiend or not — can't help but do a double-take at your design.

Making the best first impression

In real life, you have ten seconds or less to make a first impression. Enter the digital world, where the average Google search returns 972,000,000 results in 0.19 seconds for the phrase *food blog*. The first click to your blog has to be appealing, memorable, inspiring, and most of all, enticing enough to leave people lingering. Talk about a tall order!

Take a moment to glance at the three following blog home pages from Matt Bites (see Figure 7-1; `www.mattbites.com`), The Sophisticated Gourmet (see Figure 7-2; `www.sophisticatedgourmet.com`), and Food Blogging For Dummies (see Figure 7-3; `www.foodbloggingfordummies.com`).

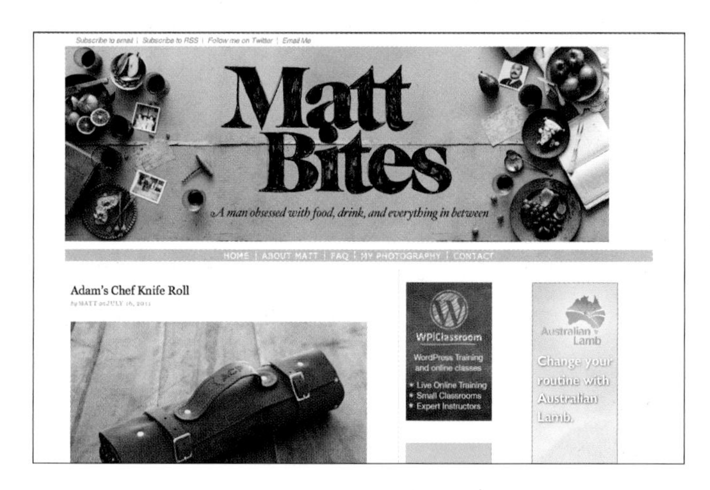

Figure 7-1: The home page of the Matt Bites blog.

Does one of these designs in particular immediately grab your attention? My guess is you're stuck staring at the eyesore that is Figure 7-3. Marshmallow pops, clashing mustard-colored headers, a random Google map, deviled pickled eggs, and a plush purple background. What's not to love?

I created the site to showcase how — despite the presence of a big, beautiful photo — a total lack of focus in design and layout creates one heck of an ugly frame for your content. Not even food porn can save a poorly designed blog. And if it's between a first glance at Matt's site, Kamran's site, and my site, chances are I'm not going to be seeing a spike in traffic anytime soon.

Figure 7-2: The home page of The Sophisticated Gourmet blog.

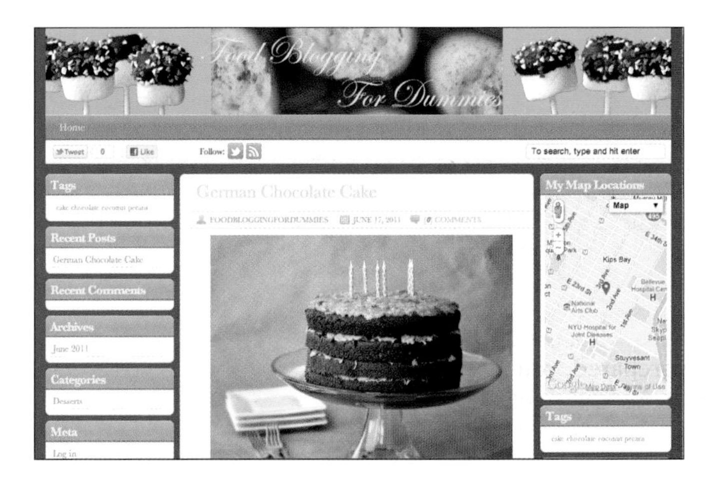

Figure 7-3: The home page of the Food Blogging For Dummies blog.

And as long as I'm on the topic of don'ts, here are a few key pointers for avoiding becoming a one-click wonder at first glance:

- Don't overwhelm your reader with a jarring color scheme.
- Don't use automated graphics, animation, or auto-play music.
- Don't let advertisements be the predominant imagery.
- Don't disguise the fact that your blog is a food blog.

Although Figure 7-3 is an obvious example of what *not* to do in terms of design and layout, the feel of your food blog is ultimately a personal decision based on your own inspirations and preferences. I've been through many a bad design on my food blog Just a Taste (`www.justataste.com`), and the way I knew they weren't right (aside from the total lack of focus, the confusing color palette, the cheap-looking logo, the absence of any navigation links, the strange mix of fonts, the . . . should I continue?) was that the second I'd type my URL and my home page would appear, I'd spot the flaws. My content didn't stand a chance engulfed in an ugly wrapper.

After countless template tweaks and endless relaunches, I finally settled on the design I have today. And now when I view my site, my attention is drawn immediately to the center content area, the clean layout, and the simple, yet memorable, header. Your blog is an extension of you. It's your voice, your color palette, your photos, your design. The non-sugar-coated version: Be you, but be the most attractive version of you.

Blogging templates for beginners

With a clear vision of what *not* to do, time to focus on how you're going to implement the right design at the most basic level. All variations of blogging software come with a pre-loaded template or theme. Although for the most part, the terms template and theme are interchangeable, WordPress specifies a *theme* as a set of files that create a graphical interface with an overall design for a blog. Those actual files are the *template files.* The nontechnical version is that *themes* give your WordPress blog its look and feel, whereas *templates* are the building blocks of the site.

Nomenclature aside, simply think of a template as a frozen dinner: It's already prepared, you just have to defrost it. Microwaving, or in your case *installing,* literally takes clicking a button. You also have further options to tailor a specific template's layout, background, font size, and style. All you have to do is salt, pepper, and customize until your template tastes right.

If you are using WordPress.com or WordPress.org, you can begin familiarizing yourself with available templates by clicking the Appearance tab from your Dashboard, as shown in Figure 7-4. From here, you can make any of the following design decisions:

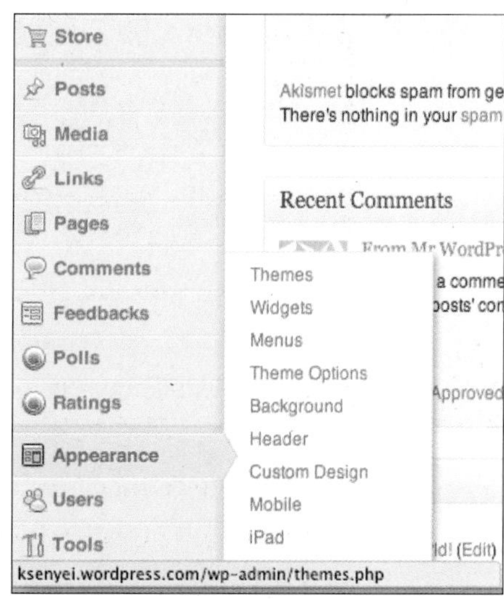

Figure 7-4: Customize a WordPress blog's look and feel via the Appearance tab on the Dashboard.

- Picking a theme
- Adding widgets (see Chapter 9)
- Uploading a custom header
- Tweaking specific theme options
- Deciding whether to buy a premium theme
- Creating a custom design

Alternately, if you use Blogger, log in to your Dashboard, choose Template from the More Options drop-down list, and then click the Customize button, as shown in Figure 7-5. From here, you can customize a range of elements, including

Figure 7-5: Blogger provides options for customizing the background, layout, and column widths of your blog.

- Picking a template
- Selecting a background image or color
- Adjusting the width of your blog display and sidebars
- Choosing from a variety of body and footer layouts
- Determining your font size, style, and color

With WordPress.org and Blogger, you can upload any free or paid template, and even further customize the code to fit your needs and wants. You can also fully customize your design on WordPress.com, although it requires purchasing an annual upgrade for $30. And if the word *code* doesn't exist in your online vocabulary just yet, have no fear. Current templates and themes have become so advanced that basic, code-free customization is easy and won't cost you a penny.

Utilizing a custom template

If you are interested in a more distinctive design, and are willing to foot the bill to either host your site using WordPress.org or to buy a template, your design options are endless. Countless free and purchasable custom templates are available online. You can either search directly for your preferences, or you can visit any range of sites that showcase libraries of themes in every color, layout, style, and feel. Most blogging platforms provide easy one-click installation for free or purchased templates, but if you're looking to go 100-percent custom, additional technical smarts may be required.

Here are three sites that provide an extensive collection of free and purchasable templates:

- **WordPress.org Free Themes Directory:** Search through the most up-to-date gallery of free WordPress templates sorted by popularity and recency. (`http://wordpress.org/extend/themes`)
- **StudioPress:** Purchase original and creative WordPress themes that are search engine-optimized. (`www.studiopress.com`)
- **BTemplates:** Sort through a library of free Blogger templates categorized by color, column layout, style, and width. This library includes access to a selection of templates inspired by popular WordPress themes. (`http://btemplates.com`)

The process of installing a custom design can vary based on your blogging software and the source of your downloaded theme. WordPress.org houses a wide range of themes that you can install by logging in to your Dashboard, and then following these steps:

1. **Click the Appearance tab.**

   The Manage Themes page appears.

2. **Click the Install Themes tab at the top of the page.**

   A page appears with options for uploading themes or searching for themes based on specific features, as shown in Figure 7-6.

3. **After you upload or select your desired theme, click the Install button.**

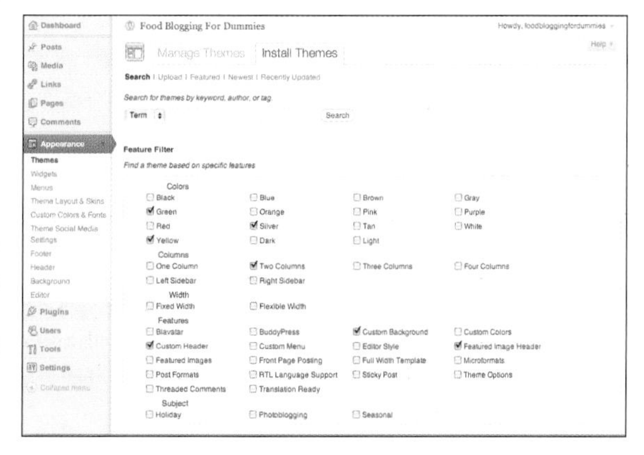

Figure 7-6: Search for themes by specifying your desired colors, column layout, width, and additional features.

To activate, preview, or delete your newly installed theme, click the Manage Themes tab at the top of the page and locate the theme from the Available Themes list at the bottom of the page.

Uploading and installing a theme from an external source requires several additional steps, including using a *File Transfer Protocol (FTP) client,* which is a tool that allows you to transmit data over the Internet. Specific installation instructions can generally be found on the site where you download the theme.

Blogger also allows installing templates from external sites. Although it's not as quick and easy as using the WordPress Administration panel, it is relatively straightforward. To upload and install a template from an external site using the Blogger software:

1. **Click the Download button on the template you choose.**

   The template downloads as a *Zip file* (a compressed package of your template files).

2. **Double-click the file to unzip it and then drag the folder that appears onto your computer's desktop.**

3. **Log in to your Blogger Dashboard and choose Template from the More Options drop-down list.**

   The Template page appears.

4. **Click the Backup/Restore button in the top-right corner.**

   The Backup/Restore pop-up window appears.

5. **Create a backup of your current template by clicking the Download Full Template button.**

   Your current template is downloaded, and then can be saved to your computer for safe-keeping.

6. **Click the Choose File button on the Backup/Restore pop-up window.**

   A pop-up window appears, which allows you to locate the template folder you dragged onto your desktop.

7. **Click Template Folder, click the template file with the `.xml` extension, as shown in Figure 7-7, and then click the Open button.**

   The template file name appears in the Backup/Restore pop-up window.

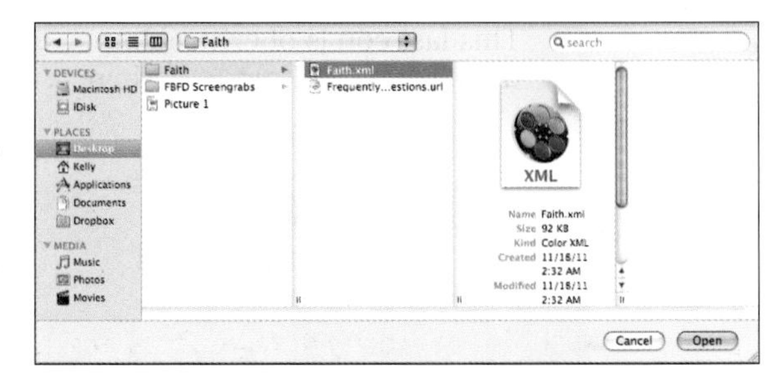

Figure 7-7: Click the template file with the .xml extension.

8. **Click the orange Upload button in the Backup/Restore pop-up window.**

   The template is uploaded and appears on your blog.

Taking advantage of the wide range of templates available allows you to further define the identity of your food blog. Such a luxury unfortunately doesn't come for free though. There are varying pros and cons to using templates and stretching your design (and your dollar) beyond the basic customizations that come with your software.

The *pros* of utilizing templates and themes include

- Getting the benefits of a personalized look without coding it yourself
- Custom-tailoring a style that's entirely in line with your specific wants and needs

On the flip side, several *cons* are associated with custom templates:

- Some custom templates cost money to download.
- You risk having a digital twin despite shelling out money for a paid template because companies can sell the same design to multiple bloggers.
- Installation can be a hassle depending on your comfort level with FTP, Zip files, and more. Uploading and activating a custom template can be as simple as a single click, but if you really have a taste for the fancier stuff, you have to know how to slice and dice your way through HTML code like a hot knife through butter. Be prepared to download, unzip, upload, activate, tweak, and troubleshoot your way to a totally custom design.

This last con is of critical importance. Dabbling in FTP and tweaking theme code without a total understanding of the steps you're taking can lead to disaster. You might not think it's possible to delete your entire site with a few stray clicks on FTP, that is, until you actually do it. Trust me; it can get ugly. Using FTP to transfer important files also opens you up to possible security risks because your transmissions can be intercepted by unwelcome eavesdroppers at any time.

If you're not ready to take off the template training wheels just yet but still crave a custom look, you can always opt to hire a designer. To avoid selecting a designer at random, find a few of your favorite food blogs and scroll all the way to the bottom of their home pages. At or near the bottom of the page, as shown in Figure 7-8, you almost always can spot whether the blogger used a designer, opted for a custom template, or kept it simple with a pre-loaded design. Using this method leads you to a designer or a specific template that you're guaranteed to mesh well with.

If (or when) you decide to hire a designer, always get multiple price quotes. I know fellow bloggers who have received quotes ranging from $500 to $5,000 for the same project. If you aren't sure what a realistic price is, reach out to design-savvy friends or fellow bloggers for some pricing perspective. And never pay a single dollar without a signed contract in place!

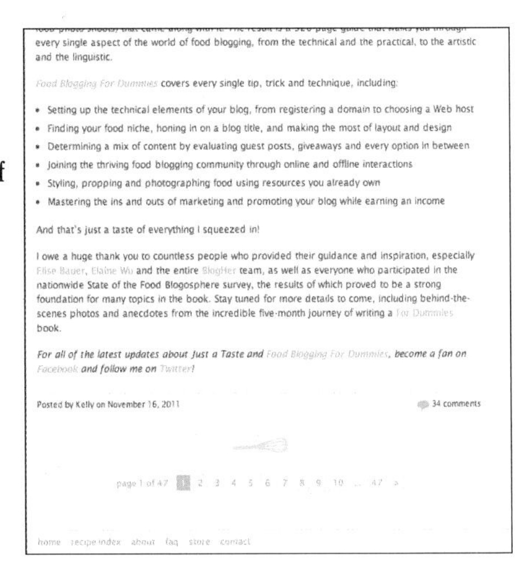

Figure 7-8: Scroll to the footer section to discover whether the designer of the blog is specified.

Regardless whether you go the DIY route or hire a designer, always test what your blog looks like on multiple screen sizes (including smartphones). Text and visuals may morph with screen size, and you want to be certain that audiences across all platforms have the same viewing experience. Also check your design on a Mac and a PC, as well as on a variety of browsers, such as Firefox, Safari, Chrome, and Internet Explorer.

Beautifying Your Blog

With a basic understanding of how templates work, you can then dive in to the specifics of your design. Being aware of a few key resources allows you to easily pinpoint your preferences for the look and feel of your blog.

Although guidelines about fonts and suggestions for header and logo treatments can steer you in the right direction, ultimately you are the judge of what is appealing or unappealing to the eye. Not everyone will agree on which nitpicky accents give a site true style and charm, but understanding the visual commonalities between the big-time blogs does prove that there is a definite strategy behind effective food blog design.

It's always a good idea to kick-start any creative process with a good old-fashioned brainstorm logged on paper. Writing your wants, needs, goals, and even any anticipated barriers, is the best way to ensure you're realizing your ultimate vision without wasting any time.

Selecting a color palette

Consider the background color of your blog as the canvas for your entire site. Now imagine all the large, colorful photos, witty headlines, and striking prose that are going to grace each page. Your goal is to keep your reader's focus on the content, and not on the canvas.

Many of the super successful food blogs, including Bakerella (`www.bakerella.com`), White On Rice Couple (`http://whiteonricecouple.com`), and Orangette (`http://orangette.blogspot.com`), utilize a basic white background for good reason.

The color white is associated with simplicity and cleanliness, and provides a sense of open space. White also just so happens to be an equal balance of all the colors in the spectrum, leaving no room for it to compete with other colors around it. Your photos, header image, and text are free to pop off the page and grab your reader's attention.

This is not to say that every food blog has to be straight vanilla. Dark backgrounds have their positive points, too. They can create a mood, define a space, or draw extra attention to a specific area of your blog.

Take for example the popular food blog Steamy Kitchen (`www.steamykitchen.com`) created by Jaden Hair. The blog, as shown in Figure 7-9, uses a neutral color palette of white, off-white, and tan, which allows the distinct red logo and photos to be the main focal points on every page.

Figure 7-9: Steamy Kitchen uses neutral background tones with color emphasis on the logo.

Other blogs, such as Chez Pim (`http://chezpim.com`) created by Pim Techamuanvivit, highlight the benefits of using darker color palettes. Her blog, as shown in Figure 7-10, demonstrates the effect that warmer hues have on photos when they're viewed in a darker context.

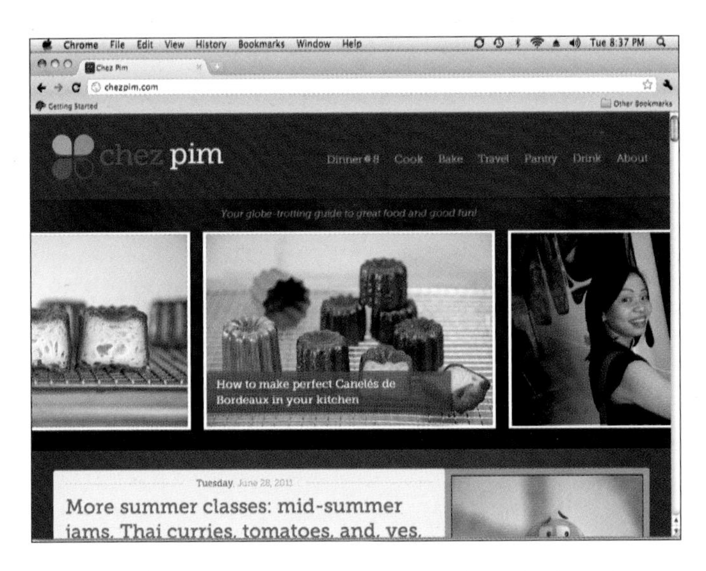

Figure 7-10: Chez Pim demonstrates the tonal effect of using a darker color palette.

The striking color palette differences in these two blogs alone is evidence that food blog design is based entirely on personal preference. Dark does not mean good, and light does not necessarily mean better. But what is best is what you feel most accurately conveys your own tone. Colors evoke emotions, so bottle up your wit, charm, tenacity, and general spice. And then assign it a custom color palette.

You can default to white or go dark, but whatever you do, steer clear of patterns as backgrounds. Patterns make your blog appear crowded, are too bold for a first impression, and distract your reader from the reason he came to your site in the first place — the content.

With a background color in place, you can begin thinking about accent colors. Consider the niche in which you are writing. Are you a bold and boisterous baker? Are you a straight-laced food scientist with molecular gastronomy on the mind? Streamline your overarching focus and then brainstorm on a color palette that complements it. For some, the color palette may be as simple as choosing your favorite color. For others, the palette may come down to the nitty-gritty elements of design.

You don't have to pull a color palette out of mid-air. If inspiration strikes, run with it! Otherwise, check out these useful sites for mixing and matching the perfect color combinations for your blog:

- **Kuler:** Adobe's color palette generator lets you find inspiration with an extensive library of predesigned palettes. You can also generate a palette based on any image that you upload. (`http://kuler.adobe.com`)
- **Color Scheme Designer:** For the more active type, find the freedom to drag and drop your cursor over a large color wheel, creating endless complementary pairings. (`www.colorschemedesigner.com`)
- **Color Hunter:** Upload an image to retrieve the color palette of your specific shot. A simple search of any food, object, or location also yields an assortment of color palettes matched to your query. (`www.colorhunter.com`)

Determining font size, style, and contrast

Something as simple as the size of your blog's text can captivate a reader or lose her with a single click. No one wants to be forced to squint. And no one wants to feel like you're SHOUTING AT THEM. To put it bluntly, when it comes to fonts, size does matter.

Begin at the top of your blog and work your way down. Your header, which I discuss in detail in the section "Designing your header" later in this chapter, needs to have an identifying font. That font should be bold, make a statement, and be as unique to your blog as possible. If you have a tagline, opt for a second style of font to highlight an interesting contrast between the name of your site and your catchphrase.

One of the best displays of the effective usage of complementary header and tagline fonts is on the food blog Love and Olive Oil (`www.loveandoliveoil.com`) written by Lindsay Landis and shown in Figure 7-11. The Gotham font is easy to read; the header text is balanced in proportion to the tagline; and the use of an actual olive oil font for the ampersand makes it memorable and in line with the blog as a brand.

Figure 7-11: Love and Olive Oil uses unique and bold fonts.

Working your way down the page from the header, your next font stop is likely at the title of your most recent post. This is where color coordination comes into play. Figure 7-12 displays the title font, Museo Sands, on Love and Olive Oil, which is the same color but a different style from the header font.

You can opt to default to black, but for a pop of color and to draw attention to your post titles, select the predominant color in your header as also the color of your title font.

Figure 7-12: The title font on Love and Olive Oil utilizes a complementary font to the blog's header text.

Below your title font is the most used font on your blog — your body text font. You can use the same font as your title font but in a slightly smaller size, or you can choose a complementary style. Figure 7-13 depicts the body text font on Love and Olive Oil, which depicts a block-style known as Lucida Sans that is easy on the eyes and in balance with the feel of the title text.

Even Taylor, who is usually so mint-averse, admitted that these were pretty darn fantastic. Or at least the few we managed to sample before bringing them to our neighbor's super bowl party, where each and every one of my brownie points were promptly gobbled up.

Figure 7-13: The body text font complements the lime green title font and is easy on the eyes.

Common fonts that work well for online design and are also *web-safe* — they appear the same on all browsers — include Arial, Georgia, Tahoma, Trebuchet MS, and Verdana.

You can experiment with various fonts, or if you've found a font on another site that you like, you can use a handful of resources to determine what it is. One such online resource, WhatTheFont (`www.whatthefont.com`), allows you to upload a screen grab of a font. WhatTheFont then generates possible matches, cluing you in to the specific font or family of fonts. Similarly, Identifont (`www.identifont.com`), regarded as the largest directory of typefaces on the Internet, assists you in finding a font based on appearance, name, or similarity.

Although some fonts may be included in your basic software setup, you can always purchase fonts online. But unless you're looking to do some serious text customization, I suggest sticking with the vast selection of available free fonts, knowing that you can upgrade at any time.

Whatever you do, steer clear of cursive or any sort of script-style font in a small size. It looks fancy, but it's difficult to digest, especially as screen sizes shrink onto mobile devices.

Another important element related to font display is the contrast between your text and your background color. If you have a white background, aim for a hue in the black or gray range. Black type on a white surface is the easiest for eyes to read. And if you have a colored background, even something as neutral as tan or light gray, choose a font color that provides enough contrast from the page. With each of these design decisions, the most important thing is to just stay consistent and to avoid a mash-up of four or five different fonts all on the same page.

Designing your header

Your *header,* or the graphic and text identifier at the top of every page, is the most quintessential reflection of you and your food blog as a brand. A header can be as simple as your name in a stylized font (known as a *word mark*), or it can contain a logo. Figure 7-14 depicts three headers, which demonstrate the wide range of colors, styles, fonts, and feels that can compose a well-balanced design from popular food blogs.

Figure 7-14: Customized food blog headers can contain a mix of images and stylized fonts.

Although Cannelle Et Vanille (`http://cannelle-vanille.blogspot.com`), Joy the Baker (`www.joythebaker.com`), and delicious:days (`http://deliciousdays.com`) use wide headers to brand their blogs, others rely on simple, stylized text to create a unique, identifying logo. Figure 7-15 depicts text-only blog logos from the popular food blogs David Lebovitz (`www.davidlebovitz.com`), Chocolate & Zucchini (`http://chocolateandzucchini.com`), and Smitten Kitchen (`http://smittenkitchen.com`).

Regardless whether you choose to go with a wide header or a basic text logo, consider the following universal points when it comes to style and size:

- **Graphics:** Graphical elements work best for logos because they tend to be clean and crisp when seen or printed in color and in black and white. For example, the sieve in the delicious:days header is identifiable without being intricate, which makes it easy to depict in digital and print.
- **Proportion:** Don't design too large of a header so that it takes up more than one-third of your home page. Your header should anchor the page, without weighing it down, and it should always be hyperlinked to your home page.

- **Size:** Use a bold font in an appropriate size so that your readers don't struggle to read the text. Italicized fonts should be used only if they're large enough to easily read, such as the word *zucchini* in the Chocolate & Zucchini header.
- **Photos:** Avoid an identity crisis by steering clear of iStock images and photos you find through Google image search. Your best bet is to stick to your own photos, which you know for certain are both original and free of any copyright restraints.

Figure 7-15: Text-only logos are made unique with identifying font styles and colors.

Most important of all, your header or logo is a snapshot of your entire brand. It is the identifying graphic or text that makes your site unique. Take your time to develop a cohesive design and don't forget to envision it and test it as part of your overall blog appearance.

Embracing negative space

One of the biggest mistakes beginner food bloggers can make is trying to fill your entire page with photos, widgets, tag clouds, mile-long blogrolls, product placements, and more. Been there, done that.

When I first launched my blog I was of the belief that "more is more." But as I began to study the sites I returned to time and time again (including Pinch My Salt, Running with Tweezers, and seven spoons), I realized that they all had one major style element in common: *Negative space,* which is the empty space found between objects, such as images, advertisements, and sidebar links.

Don't be afraid to let your page breathe. Yes, widgets are fantastic, practical, and give your blog custom flair. But be aware of the fact that your page is already going to be filled with your colorful header, eye-catching photos, and meaningful text, so a little negative space can actually be relieving to the eye. Negative space also gives your photos some breathing room, allowing them to be framed within a context that makes them stand out.

And like a trusty pair of sweatpants at an all-you-can-eat buffet, empty space actually gives you room to grow as you take on sponsor logos, ad placements, content badges, and that last king crab leg.

Steering clear of common errors in design

As you assess the overall design and feel of your blog, you'll begin to get a sense of what works and what needs tweaking. But that's the beauty of digital. You can have a generic header one second, and a fully custom design a click later.

Almost everyone has made many a design decision only to look back a few weeks, months, or even years later to ponder, "What was I thinking?" I will never forget my first theme on Just a Taste. Imagine a citrus grove exploding onto a screen and then add 19 font styles in 4 shades of yellow and a dozen or so randomly placed lemons. It wasn't pretty.

Whether you self-host or leave the technical stuff up to the pros, you can always update your blog's appearance. But although you have the luxury of being in the early phases of your style setup, consider the following overarching guidelines before pushing your design live:

- **Don't clutter the page.** Just because you can add 39 widgets doesn't mean you should.
- **Give your readers' eyes a break.** Check your font style and size on multiple platforms and devices.
- **Don't use a Flash component on your site.** Flash can slow down and disrupt the design flow of your blog.
- **Stay true to you.** Find inspiration from sites you admire while making sure you own your personal style, tone, and vision as a food blogger extraordinaire.
- **Always refer back to your blog's first impression.** Ease in your reader with a well-styled site, and he'll be back for a second serving.

8

Your Blog's Roadmap

In This Chapter

- Understanding the importance of blog navigation
- Taking advantage of your blog's prime real estate
- Establishing comment settings and guidelines

Establishing a dialogue with your readers is critical to your blog's success, but offering guidelines before inviting them to chat over your online kitchen table is also important. So, if you want to lose readers, just leave them asking any of these questions:

- Where is the search bar?
- Who is this person?
- Why can't I leave a comment?

If you want to gain readers, spend time crafting a confusion-free roadmap that allows and encourages your audience to explore your rich library of content as they interact with you as a fellow food enthusiast. The easier it is for your readers to navigate your blog, the better chance they have of finding content they truly connect with and are most likely to interact with. Put simply, your blog's navigation can ultimately mean the difference between repeat visitors and one-click wonders. And when it comes to navigation, there is no such thing as being too obvious.

From capitalizing on prime real estate to crafting a successful About page, in this chapter, you discover the strategy behind effective and meaningful blog navigation that guides readers, invites them to have a voice, and keeps them coming back for more.

Understanding Navigation Essentials

Ineffective navigation on a food blog is the equivalent of a recipe for world famous lasagna bolognese that lists 37 ingredients but is missing the method of preparation. Instead of biting into a slice of Italian comfort food at its finest, you're left staring down a pile of raw ground beef, a few sheets of dry pasta, and a basil plant. Frustration doesn't taste good, and the last thing you want to do is leave your readers stranded and starving — or worse yet, looking elsewhere for sustenance.

Before developing the specific elements of your site's roadmap, consider the following overall goals of successful blog navigation:

- To guide a reader seamlessly through your site without ever leading them to a dead-end page
- To assist a reader in finding the information he's looking for
- To provide a direct and easy overview to the content categories and primary subpages on your site
- To relay your blog's personality by strategically grouping together specific types of content into distinctive categories
- To inform a reader of where she currently is on your site and how she can get to where she's going next

Ultimately, effective blog navigation shouldn't even be noticed. The reader should be able to move from page to page without even thinking twice about where to post a comment or how to return to the home page. The latter of which leads me to a list of three of the most important internal navigation elements on your blog:

- Home
- About
- Contact

Each element of this trifecta exists as a predominant link within your navigation bar, or the sub-region of your blog that contains hyperlinks to important pages. A navigation bar is generally located at the top of your page, known as the *header*, with additional internal navigation links to categories and subpages placed in the sides of the page, known as the *left* and *right rails* or *sidebars,* as shown in Figure 8-1. You may think a stylistic decision as to whether you select a template with left or right rail sub-navigation is simple, but think again!

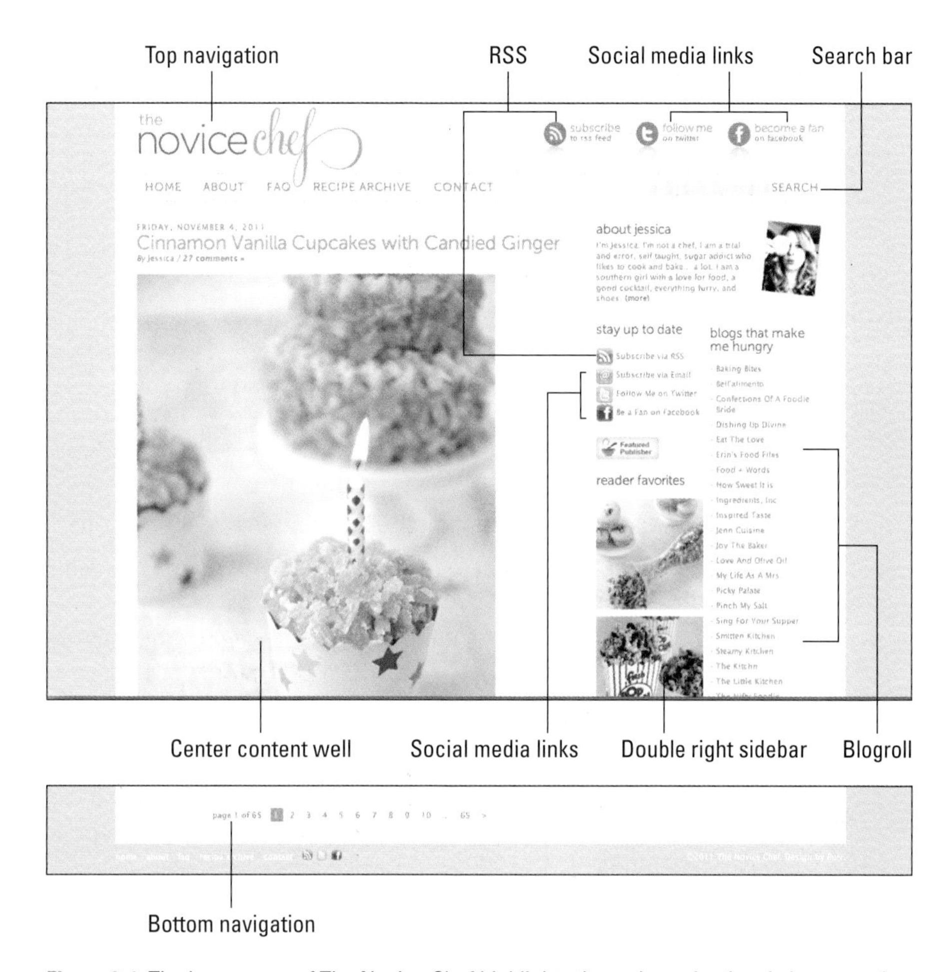

Figure 8-1: The home page of The Novice Chef highlights the main navigational elements of a standard blog layout.

A 2006 research study reported by Usability.gov, the government's source for user-centered design, showed that left rail navigation provides a performance advantage over right rail navigation. This is likely because English-speaking users read top to bottom and left to right, and thus the layout of the site parallels learned visual habits. Similar studies have shown that users tend to ignore the right side because a majority of advertising generally appears in the right sidebar. That's not to say that right is wrong and left is right, but it's important to keep in mind that even the smallest navigational decision can impact a reader's experience on your blog.

Aside from the navigation bar's main placement in the header, an abbreviated version of it with links to your About and Contact pages can also appear on the bottom, or the *footer,* of your blog. Regardless of which layout you choose, the most important thing is to be consistent with the location of your navigation bar; it needs to be in the same place on every page to ensure reader-friendly access and use.

Establishing your home page

The link to your home page should be the most visible link in your navigation and can exist as a text link, as depicted in the header navigation bar on the blog Simple Bites, as shown in Figure 8-2. In this example, the word *Home,* located in the navigation bar, intuitively directs readers back to the home page. In addition to the text link, the blog's logo is also hyperlinked so that clicking it will bring a user back to the home page.

The Home link should always be visible.

SIMPLE BITES
WHOLE FOOD FOR THE FAMILY TABLE
Home About Recipes Topics Simple Living
Butternut Squash Gratin: A New Family Favorite Side Dish
by AIMEE on OCTOBER 13, 2010
in DINNER
SEARCH: Lijit Search
TWITTER 6,560 RSS + EMAIL 11
RECENT SERIES:
eat well spend less
HOME for the HOLIDAYS Nov 28–Dec 2

Figure 8-2: The home page link on Simple Bites is a text link in the top navigation bar and a hyperlinked logo.

The home page link can also appear only as a hyperlinked logo, as depicted on the Sprouted Kitchen blog, as shown in Figure 8-3. There is no home text link on Sprouted Kitchen; instead, readers click the logo in the header to return to the blog's main page.

Figure 8-3: The Sprouted Kitchen home page can be reached via clicking the blog's logo.

Hyperlinking your logo to your home page comes with the added benefit of reinforcing your brand to a reader because he associates your logo more with your blog if he continuously clicks it to return to the home page. All other links should be conveyed via direct, obvious text so that a reader never has to rely on standalone images to navigate your content. A right rail image of an overflowing bowl of spaghetti linked to the Pasta category may be visually appealing, but without the word Pasta included on the image, you force your readers to guess where they'll land with their next click.

The subpages on your blog function like a breadcrumb trail that guides a reader from page to page while leaving a clearly defined route back to your home page. Consider the appearance of your links with regards to your overall site design. The same rules for font style, size, and color, which I discuss in Chapter 7, apply to the navigational links on your blog as well. Think clean, crisp, and easy on the eyes.

Crafting your About page

The million-dollar question: Who are you?

A short and seemingly simple question, which often doesn't have a simple answer! But luckily, you can create a page on your blog to at least give your audience a glimpse into who you are and what your food blog is about. An About page can include any variety of information, but before getting into the details, remember that it needs to at least address the following:

- Who you are
- What your food blog is about
- When you started your food blog
- Why you started your food blog

Approach the answers to these topics from the reader's viewpoint. Ask yourself: If you were to arrive at a food blog, what information would you want to know about the author and her site? Maintaining this perspective will help you jot down the essentials. Even if you aren't aware of who your audience is just yet, you can at least bet on the fact that they have some interest, big or small, in food. Aside from your culinary passion, focus this section on the qualities and achievements that define you as an individual, in the kitchen or beyond.

You and your blog's specific focus are what make it unique. I discuss finding your blogging niche in Chapter 2, and your About page is the place for your eight-second elevator pitch. Be short, be sweet, and be direct. Your personality is best conveyed through the tone of your writing. If you're a witty baker, butter them up with your humor and charm. If you're a grilling guru, let your meat geek flag fly. No matter what your specialty, it is best and easiest to just let you be *you.* A false front is easier to pick out than a stray eggshell in an omelet. And no one wants their meal to be ruined by a bite of superficiality. Many blog readers often head straight for the About page the first time they visit your blog in order to get a taste of the person creating the content, which means the page should be a candid, comprehensive, and entertaining read for intrigued visitors.

In addressing who you are, many blog authors provide their full name, whereas others use only their first name. And a rare few choose not to share even the slightest glimpse of their real world identity. But I encourage you to provide at least a taste of who you are. Not only does it help in owning your online identity (and eventually your expertise in a subject field), but it also addresses the popular blogging topic of transparency.

Being transparent with your readers regarding your identity, and even your food blogging motives and goals, is an important step in earning their trust. There's a certain comfort that comes with knowing that there actually is a real, live person who is cooking, writing, photographing, and creating the content that appears on the blog. Making your identity known can also help boost career aspirations if your goal is to become an expert in the field you're blogging in. Don't be shy about flaunting your abilities, but just make sure to do it in a tasteful, non-cocky way.

Regardless of how much information you choose to share about yourself, remember that the tone in which you convey the information says just as much as the actual words themselves. A brief introductory paragraph about who you are and why you've started your food blog is the best place to start.

The About page on my blog Just a Taste, as shown in Figure 8-4, features a short and sweet introduction at the top of the page, which describes the site and explains my approach to food.

Although the written text is both concise and direct, the layout of the page also grabs a reader's attention with an important stylistic element: a photo of the author.

Figure 8-4: The introductory paragraphs on Just a Taste's About page.

Readers will have a hard time missing the centrally located image, which not only gives them a better sense of who I am, but also personalizes the tone and feel of my blog. You can match a face to the writing and food photography on the site, which will hopefully prompt an even stronger connection between reader and author.

Aside from the essential elements of identifying yourself and your inspirations, the About page can also optionally include details about your related areas of expertise, your current city, or your hobbies outside the realm of food blogging. Although all these details personalize the page, keep in mind that short and sweet attracts readers, whereas long and sour leaves them drifting. I provide a more detailed bio below the image so that interested readers can get the full details but not everyone is forced to face the additional text at first glance.

Most importantly, never let your About page get outdated! Consider it a living and breathing résumé viewable by the entire online public, which includes your mom, fellow food lovers, casual browsers, interested advertisers, and maybe even potential employers. You never know who may grace your About page, and you don't want to come across as indifferent or careless when it comes to the details (and that includes proper spelling and grammar). Update your About page with any major new developments so that it constantly reflects your latest interests and current career status.

Creating a Contact page

Inviting your readers to contact you is a great way to build community and give them a place to engage in a dialogue with you outside the public comments realm. That's not to say you need to post your cellphone number and home address. Remember your Contact page is viewable by the entire online public, so share only the same amount of contact information you'd feel comfortable handing out to a stranger on the street. Here are the two simple ways to implement a method of contact via your blog:

- Set up an e-mail address separate from your personal e-mail account.
- Add a contact form that requires readers to include their name and e-mail address when contacting you.

A contact form can be added to any post or page on a WordPress.com blog via the Contact Form icon in the top portion of the Text editor. Clicking the icon causes a pop-up window to appear (see Figure 8-5), which you can customize. A contact form also exists as a plug-in on WordPress.org blogs, and I discuss installing and activating a variety of plug-ins in Chapter 9. Specialized code is required to install a contact form on a Blogger blog because a basic contact form button or gadget does not yet exist.

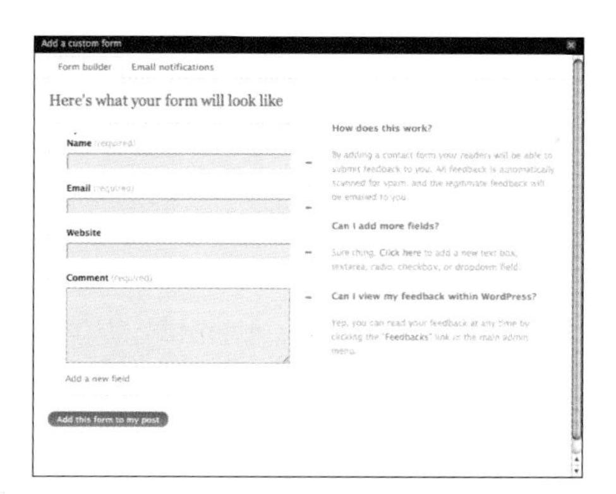

Figure 8-5: A WordPress.com contact form can be added to any post or page.

Regardless of what route you go, providing your readers with a format in which they can contact you is a critical aspect of building relationships with your audience. A Contact page also secures a direct line of communication between you and the endless opportunities that may result from your food blog.

Claiming Your Blog's Prime Real Estate

From header to footer, center content well to right rail, every inch of your blog can be a valuable destination for content, or a just as valuable canvas for some welcome empty space. You already know about the importance of centrally locating your Home, About, and Contact links, but additional navigational and organizational elements are most effective when you consider their strategic placement on your home page.

Much like a newspaper, your blog's real estate can be broken down into two basic areas: above the fold and below the fold. The area *above the fold* refers to the part of your page that can be seen without using the scroll bar, whereas the area *below the fold* represents everything beyond that demarcation.

Mapping out your blog above the fold

The above the fold area of your blog should be home to the most important navigational and organizational elements, including:

- **Navigation bar:** Aside from the home, About, and Contact pages, your navigation bar may include additional links that you consider the most important or relevant. I talk more about this in a moment.
- **Social media links:** You can't ignore social media, nor would you want to — through social media platforms, you can easily spread the word about your blog and attract more readers. Find out more in the later section, "Getting social or getting lost (literally)."
- **RSS feed:** A Really Simple Syndication (RSS) feed is a critical component for your above-the-fold blog real estate and provides another opportunity for your readers to access and enjoy your content.
- **Advertisements:** Certainly not a required element, but ads are often required to be viewable in a prime location.

  Even if you don't plan to run ads when you launch your blog, be aware that if and when you do make a run for the money, your predominant ad will likely get a front row seat in the top portion of your site.
- **Search bar:** A search bar is the fastest way for readers to find specific content on your blog, which means your search bar should be in an easily visible location either in your header or high atop your sidebar.

Navigation bar

The navigation bar should contain the important and necessary links: Home, About, and Contact. But there are others you can include, such as

- **Frequently Asked Questions (FAQs):** On this page, you provide responses to often sought-after information related to your food blog. The FAQs page can include details about what photo equipment you use, whether you accept promotional products, and answers to any other questions that are an extension of the work you display on your site.
- **Affiliate Programs:** Affiliate marketing programs allow you to earn an income by featuring links to a company's products on your blog. Amazon, Barnes and Noble, Target, and Buy.com are a handful of brands with affiliate programs, with Amazon Associates being the largest of the group. Creating an Amazon Store allows you to features your own personal product page run through the program, and it happens to be a great way to kick-start the ad revenue-making process on your blog. I discuss logistics and details of the program in Chapter 14, and although you might not be concerned with making money just yet, it is a good idea to at least consider the link's placement as you lay out your general navigation.

Basic Techniques

The Ultimate Chocolate Chip Cookie
Puff Pastry – Video
Quick Puff Pastry
Quick Puff Pastry – 2 (Step-by-Step photos)
Pie Dough
Pie Science
Making Chocolate At Home
Perfect Hard Boiled Eggs
Rendering Lard
Making Danish
Home Coffee Roasting
How to Shuck and Oyster

Bread

Baguettes
Chocolate Chip Banana Bread
Cranberry Pecan Rolls
Hamburger Buns

Breakfast and Brunch

Balsamic Strawberries
Roasted Strawberry Danish

Figure 8-6: Recipes listed by category on the Not Without Salt index page.

- **Recipe Index:** If recipes are a focus of your blog, you can create an index to house all the recipe links on one page. The best, though most manual, way of building an index page is to create a new page and add the recipe text links as you post them.

TIP

An index page is most useful when it's organized by category or ingredient. Keeping your index page updated as you post will prevent you from having to add countless links at one time.

The recipe index page on the Not Without Salt blog, as shown in Figure 8-6, displays a link to every recipe and includes categories such as Breakfast and Brunch, Cookies, and Vegetables.

An easier alternative to creating each recipe link individually is to feature a page with links to specific categories or tags. To do this, search for your desired category in your search bar, and then use the URL of the page the search provides as the link for your category. For example, if I want to create a Chocolate category, I search for *chocolate* on my blog and then create a link with the URL the search provides, which is `www.justataste.com/?s=chocolate`.

- **Press Announcements and Awards:** After you're up and running, you want a page where you can organize and log your press mentions, tout awards, and maybe even stroke your ego. You deserve a little shameless self-promotion for your hard work being recognized!

RSS feed

An *RSS feed* allows you to easily distribute and syndicate your content with readers who subscribe to your feed. Your blog updates appear in a subscriber's chosen newsreader, or via e-mail, giving her fast access to your latest posts and content updates.

Although an RSS feed can appear as a simple text link, it is most commonly represented by the universal icon shown here. Including this icon on your home page, preferably in close proximity to your social media links, provides readers with an identifiable symbol for how they can subscribe to your feed.

A majority of the more current WordPress themes and Blogger templates automatically include an RSS link as part of the design. And if you already have an RSS feed and want to take your subscription savviness a step further, utilize a web feed management tool, such as FeedBurner or FeedBlitz, to get a better sense of the scope and activity of your subscribers.

FeedBurner allows you to track and analyze the traffic to your feed, providing statistics about post popularity and the number of subscribers. Implementing FeedBurner is simple, and step-by-step instructions can be found at `www.feedburner.com`, although a Google account is required to use it. Similarly, FeedBlitz manages all aspects of your feed and is also an easy option for readers to get your content delivered fresh to their inbox as an e-mail, rather than as an item in their feed reader. (See Chapter 13 for more on RSS readers.)

For more in-depth information about your RSS feed, check out *Blogging For Dummies* by Susannah Gardner and Shane Birley, which provides extensive coverage of the uses and benefits of reaching out with RSS.

Organizing the essential navigational elements

Have no fear if you're thinking this laundry list of requirements for a small part of your site is going to leave you feeling like you're squeezing in a second piece of pumpkin pie after Thanksgiving dinner. Rest assured, it can be done! (Both the blog layout and the second round of pie.)

The above the fold section of the Homesick Texan blog, as shown in Figure 8-7, is a prime example of how to include a wide variety of navigational and organizational elements in the top portion of your blog — all without compromising the look and feel of your site.

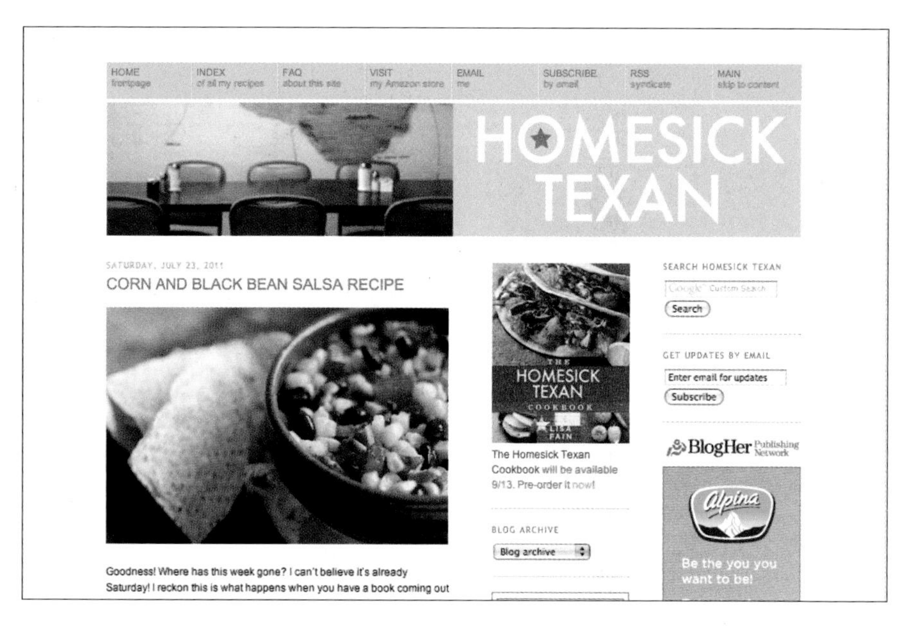

Figure 8-7: The well-designed above the fold area of the Homesick Texan blog.

Lisa Fain, the founder of Homesick Texan, utilizes a header navigation bar to house her most important links, which include her home page, FAQ/About page, recipe index page, contact page, and more. She also gives prominent placement to her search bar, RSS feed, advertisements, and header.

And there you have it! Living proof that you can fit every important element imaginable in your above the fold space without making the page feel cluttered or text heavy. The key is to make every link, and every inch, of your precious prime real estate count.

Mapping out your blog below the fold

After you pack all the information possible above the fold to guide your readers, focus on the important secondary navigational elements on your blog. These can provide direction internally or route readers to extensions of your blog externally — in the social media space and beyond. The *below the fold* section of your blog is made up of your categories, informational links, tag cloud, center content well, and footer.

Categories and subcategories

Categories and subcategories that allow readers to easily browse through your blog's content are highly effective secondary navigational aids. I discuss the details of categories and subcategories, including how to create them, in Chapter 5, but here I want to note that your list of categories can be located either above the fold or below the fold on your blog, as the placement depends entirely on your specific design and layout. Unless your blog's top navigation bar includes a drop-down feature, your categories will likely fall below the fold to give priority to social media links and your search bar.

Informational links

In addition to content categories, your rails can be home to a host of informational links that drive navigation internally and direct readers to extensions of your site. Common additions include a link to your archives, recent posts (up to five), recent comments (up to five), and resource pages.

Another common sidebar addition is a *blogroll,* which is a list of links to other blogs and sites. The links serve as recommendations for your readers and can include other food blogs, food magazine sites, and commonly used resource pages for topics like measurement conversions and cooking temperatures. (See Chapter 9 for more on blogrolls.)

I discuss implementing each of these *plug-ins* (tools that extend the functionality or appearance of your blog) in Chapter 9, but for now, keep in mind that they are some of the most popular, and most useful, enhancements to display in your sidebar.

Tag clouds

One common element often viewed below the fold is a *tag cloud,* or a grouping of the words or phrases that appear sized according to how often they're used on your blog. Although a tag cloud visually represents the popular topics on your site, it often serves as an eyesore from a design perspective. A large grouping of words, often random words at that, doesn't exactly aid in creating a smooth roadmap around your blog.

The center content well

With so many available plug-ins to choose from, it's important to not over-indulge and take the focus away from the most important display area: the *center content well,* which is the main portion of your blog where your latest posts are displayed. From a design perspective, your sidebar should be roughly one-third the width of your content well. This places less emphasis on the bells and whistles and draws the reader's eye toward the main content, which is likely the reason he came to your blog in the first place.

The footer

The last bit of navigation below the fold can be found all the way at the bottom of your blog in the footer. Don't waste this space! The *footer,* which is the section of text and links appearing on the very bottom of each page, is a prime location for a limited version of your navigation bar and can include links to your Contact, About, and Index pages. This is also a smart spot to display any copyright information related to the content on your blog.

An example

The below the fold area of Jenny Flake's Picky Palate blog, as shown in Figure 8-8, demonstrates the look and feel of a balanced blog with regard to the center content well and right rail. Jenny displays her categories and subcategories, a link to her real-time social media, as well as archives and additional blog badges, all without drawing attention away from her blog's main content. All the elements are featured in a *double right rail,* which consists of two narrower columns, rather than one wide one.

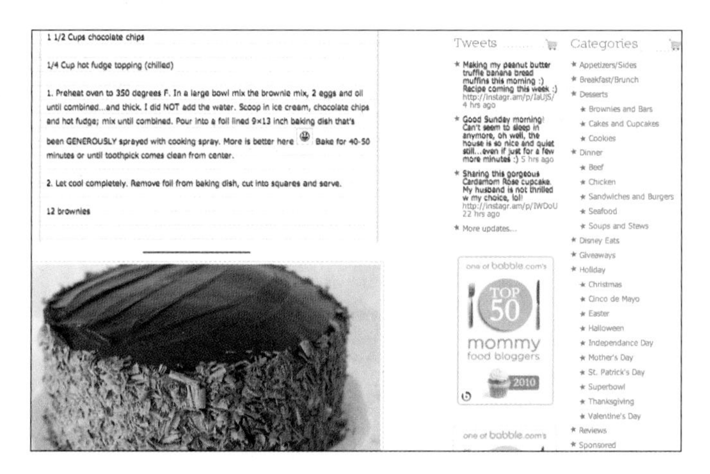

Figure 8-8: The Picky Palate blog utilizes sidebar elements while keeping content the focus.

Jenny also reinforces the placement and importance of her blog's links by distinguishing them in a reddish-orange color that's in an easy-to-read typeface. Her categories are broad enough to encompass a wide range of topics, whereas her subcategories are detailed enough to cover specific ingredients and holidays. A reader can easily scan the right rail, find a topic, and access the content with a single click. And at no point does the reader arrive at a dead end because the header and sidebar navigational elements appear in the same location on every page.

Getting social or getting lost (literally)

Face it: You can't tune out of the world of social media. People tweet, facebook, foursquare, foodspot, and stumbleupon to connect with one another more than ever before. And that interaction, in turn, drives the way people publish, view, and connect with content, and the people who are create it.

Social media links guide your readers to navigate through the online extensions of your blog, including your blog's Facebook page and Twitter feed. And although Chapter 3 introduces you to the power, reach, and purpose of social media, it's time to make your presence known via the visual cues on your blog. The most important design elements related to social media are the universal icons for Facebook and Twitter, as shown in the margin.

The Facebook and Twitter icons aren't just symbols that hyperlink to their respective sites. When displayed on your blog, they signify your extended presence to your readers. Yes, you have a Facebook and Twitter account for your blog. Yes, you are tuned in to what is being sautéed, sliced, and served up across the web. And yes, you are totally soaking up the social media scene.

When locating the landing spot for your social media links, look high toward your header in terms of placement. Although the shining blue shields are obvious indicators of what they link to, you can also take a little design liberty and opt for a different color or complementary design that best suits the tone of your blog. Garrett McCord, author of the food blog Vanilla Garlic, displays the Fab Four (RSS, Facebook, Twitter, and Contact) icons in a fun color palette, as shown in Figure 8-9.

Figure 8-9: The Vanilla Garlic blog uses complementary colors to highlight the four primary icons.

Garrett redesigned the classic Facebook and Twitter icons, but they're still intuitive to readers looking to connect with Garrett outside his blog. You can even take the customization a step further by opting for an original look to your links, as depicted on the My Baking Addiction blog (`www.mybakingaddiction.com`) in Figure 8-10. The stylized icons appear in the header portion of the blog and are incorporated seamlessly into the overall look and feel of the site. Although the icons claim an important area of real estate, they aren't flashy or distracting to the reader. The blog also features double navigation elements at both the top of the page and directly below the header. Including additional navigation links high atop the page provides more guidance for your readers to quickly and easily access specific content.

Social media links that are blended into a blog's look and feel.

www.mybakingaddiction.com

Figure 8-10: Stylized social media icons appear in the header of the My Baking Addiction blog.

Although Facebook and Twitter undeniably maintain the biggest presence in the social media circuit, you can extend your content, and thus your brand, through countless other platforms outside of your blog.

Less obvious, but still among the giants, is the photo-sharing site Flickr. As of May 2011, more than 80 million unique visitors worldwide frequented the site, uploading and sharing nearly 4.5 million photos a day. Everyone knows the power of some solid food porn, which makes Flickr the place to be for food photo swapping and sharing. I discuss adding the Flickr widget to your blog in Chapter 9, and although including it in your sidebar is a great way to advertise your albums, the link itself can exist simply in text form in your navigation bar or rail.

If you're content with dabbling in any of the big trio (Facebook, Twitter, and RSS), you can let your social media skills rest at that. But for those looking to add even more options for interacting with your audience and staying tuned in to the wide world of food, consider any of the following networking and aggregation sites:

- **LinkedIn:** LinkedIn is the professional version of Facebook. And with 100 million members and counting, it's not a bad place to have a presence. Create a profile to display your work experience and also to connect with other users in your area of expertise and beyond. Bottom line: If you're serious about turning your food blog into a business, show off your skills with a safe-for-work profile (unflattering photos not included). (`www.linkedin.com`)
- **Technorati:** Technorati is an online media company that not only publishes content tied to every aspect of the Internet, but it also indexes more than one million blogs listed in its expansive blog directory. The Food Blogs category within the directory features more than 15,000 blogs, which the site ranks according to Technorati Authority (a calculated measurement of a blog's standing in the blogosphere). (`http://technorati.com`)
- **StumbleUpon:** StumbleUpon is a web search engine directory that finds and recommends content specific to a user's tastes and preferences. The site is a great way to access content from other like-minded users, and it also drives traffic to your food blog because more users access and stumble upon your posts. (`www.stumbleupon.com`)
- **Reddit:** Reddit is a social news site that displays user-generated links. The links are voted on by readers to move up or down the page according to popularity. Similar to StumbleUpon, a link from your blog that gains traction on Reddit translates to a serious spike in traffic. (`www.reddit.com`)
- **Pinterest:** Pinterest allows users to catalog and organize content they find on the web. In doing so, readers create pin boards based on their inspirations and connect with users who share their common interests. If your blog content is pinned (and re-pinned), it results in increased traffic. (`http://pinterest.com`)

Each of these platforms, in addition to countless others, serve as valuable ways for your content to be accessed and enjoyed by a wide-ranging audience. They put your blog in front of eyes that may not otherwise grace your page, and in doing so, act as a useful guide leading readers to your content, and in turn, to you.

Keeping up with all the extensions of social media can consume just as much time as blogging itself. There are specific applications that exist for the sole purpose of consolidating all your live feeds in one location. One such program, HootSuite, displays a Dashboard with tabs for each of your social media accounts. Clicking from your Twitter tab to your Facebook tab and beyond gives you easy, instant access to all your accounts and displays real-time activity.

Social media is a critical component to any blog and provides valuable benefits, including helping you network with readers while allowing you to navigate through a mass of information. Engaging in a dialogue with the broader online food community can be a positive aspect of the blogging experience. But before you add another setting to your digital table, make sure everyone is aware of the online etiquette required to join the discussion. All it takes is one negative comment to spoil an entire meal.

Inviting Readers to Have a Voice

Comments are a vital part of the blogging experience because they transform a blog from a single, static voice into an engaging, collective space for readers to weigh in and share their opinions. This exchange defines and builds your blog's community and provides you with direct insights to your audience's inspirations and preferences. And to be honest, you're also getting a solid stroke for your ego. Who doesn't want to hear what an amazingly talented photographer you are? Or how you've inspired someone to go vegan? Or, how no one else thought of making a chocolate-covered ham?

Comments give a blog a highly interactive edge. Your voice may guide the topics of discussion, but ultimately, your readers' feedback molds your blog into more than a one-sided story. Although you hope that every person on the planet who passes by your page has a positive response, the reality is that not everyone is going to share your love of deep-fried salad or embrace the taste of your avocado brownies. But learning to take the good with the bad strengthens your blog's community and gives you the chance to lay down the rules before a harmless post turns into a digital food fight.

Adjusting your comment settings

By adjusting the comment settings on your blog, you can control how much or how little information a reader must include when posting a comment.

To adjust the comment settings on a WordPress blog:

1. **Log in to your Dashboard and then click the Settings link in the left rail.**

   A drop-down list of links appears below the Settings link, and the General Settings page appears.

2. **Click the Discussion link.**

   The Discussion Settings page appears and includes a long list of available customizations for comment moderation and posting requirements.

3. **(Optional) Control the level of anonymity required to post a comment on your blog by selecting or deselecting either of the following check boxes in the Other Comment Settings heading:**

   - *Comment Author Must Fill Out Name and Email*
   - *Users Must be Registered and Logged In to Comment*

4. **(Optional) Select or deselect the following check boxes under the Before a Comment Appears heading to determine whether you have to approve each comment:**

   - *An Administrator Must Always Approve the Comment*
   - *Comment Author Must Have a Previously Approved Comment*

   Additional settings related to notifications, blacklists, and avatars can be found on your WordPress Discussion Settings page.

5. **Click the Save Changes button at the bottom of the page.**

To adjust the comment settings on a Blogger blog:

1. **Log in to your Dashboard, and click the drop-down arrow icon to the left of the View Blog button.**

   A drop-down list appears.

2. **Choose Settings from the drop-down list.**

   The Basic Settings page appears.

3. **Click the Posts and Comments link from the list of links appearing below the Settings link in the left sidebar.**

   The Posts and Comments page appears. From here, you can customize your comment settings with a variety of options related to the comment form placement, moderation, and level of anonymity.

4. **Select the Show check box to enable comments on your blog and then select from the following options regarding who can comment:**
   - *Anyone:* Includes anonymous users
   - *Registered Users:* Includes OpenID (an online program that allows web users to create a single sign-in account and password for multiple websites)
   - *Users with Google Accounts*
   - *Only Members of This Blog*
5. **Click the Save Settings button in the top-right corner.**

All platforms provide the option to moderate comments prior to their publication on your blog. I prefer a moderation setting that allows only users with a previously approved comment to comment freely on my blog. I know and trust my routine commenters, and this setting lets me vet a new commenter before giving him free run of my comments field. Similarly, moderating your comments is one way to block specific users from posting comments, and some platforms even require your users to register an account on your blog before they're allowed to even submit a comment.

Regardless of what custom blend of settings you implement on your blog, it is beneficial to not allow anonymous comments. Unfortunately the phrase, "If you don't have anything nice to say, don't say anything at all," isn't followed by the entire online world. So if someone gets nasty, you can at least prevent her from hiding behind a shield of anonymity. Put bluntly: Anonymous comments are for cowards. And there is no guarantee that requiring readers to use their name, or *a* name, when posting a comment will prevent vitriol and negativity. But this will at least hopefully encourage them to think twice before commenting. And this is where the realm of comment etiquette begins to take shape.

Establishing comment guidelines

Elise Bauer, author of the food blog Simply Recipes, outlines comment etiquette best in her Comment Policy (`www.simplyrecipes.com/commentpolicy.php`), which asks readers to think of her site as her family's home and to not say anything you wouldn't say as an invited guest in someone's home. Elise encourages constructive, thoughtful feedback on her posts but does not allow (as in, will not approve) mean, obnoxious, or rude comments of any form. After all, the latter goes against the entire purpose of comments to create a positive dialogue, build a community, and allow you to form a relationship with your readers. So if someone is looking to trade blows over your apple cobbler, he's come to the wrong place. Avoid any possible confrontations by posting a Comment Policy on your blog in which you lay out the rules of acceptable and unacceptable behavior in your online home.

When leaving comments on other food blogs, I live by my Boss & Grandmother Rule. Would I feel uncomfortable if my boss and grandmother read the comment? If the answer is yes, chances are I need to hit the brakes and rethink my approach. Constructive feedback, specifically about recipe methods of preparation, actually helps the author and fellow readers.

Establishing a comment policy as part of your FAQs page, or as a page of its own, is a great way to lay down the rules and be totally transparent regarding what you will and will not tolerate on your blog. Here are a few tips for fostering a positive environment — both in your online home, as well as on others' blogs:

- **Respond to comments left by your readers.** This is critical because responding lets them know that you read and appreciate the feedback they provide.
- **Leave comments on other blogs.** If you see something that inspires you on another blog, share it with the author. Everyone loves to know that their work is enjoyed!
- **Keep self-promotion to a minimum in comment fields.** Yes, it's fine to include a link to your blog. But there is a tacky way and a tasteful way to toot your own horn. Letting the author know you published a similar recipe as theirs for fried broccoli is tasteful. Commenting on their Fried Broccoli recipe post with a link to your award-winning, and far better, fried broccoli recipe is downright tacky.
- **"Disgusting" is a relative term.** Taste buds are as unique as people, so just because you don't enjoy chicken livers wrapped in bacon does not mean the author's recipe tastes disgusting or is flawed. Take this into consideration when commenting on the flavor of a dish.
- **Defend your work without defaming your name.** Take a professional approach to responding to negative comments. Although a haiku of four-letter words might be tempting, remember that the Internet makes everything permanent.

Hopefully negative comments will be few and far between. And there's also no rule that says you have to approve every comment left on your blog. Ultimately, the overlying hope and goal is that readers who are given the opportunity to share their insights and opinions will respect your online home, are positive contributors, and most importantly, comment with a conscious.

9

Getting Your Garnish On

In This Chapter

- Understanding the benefits of widgets
- Implementing basic and customized widgets
- Displaying badges and buttons
- Creating hyperlinked sidebar images from scratch
- Building a better blogroll

Your navigation bar is in place. Your header image is beaming. Your audience is engaging with page after page of your content without a dead end in sight. With this sturdy foundation laid, it's time to bring on the digital accessories and let the decorating begin.

From displaying related posts to installing your real-time Twitter feed, explore the endless possibilities for enhancing and customizing your blog through widgets, gadgets, plug-ins, badges, buttons, and more. You'll discover how to take advantage of some of the web's best pre-made widgets, while also finding out how to create your very own hyperlinked sidebar images from scratch.

Master the techniques and strategies for adding a touch of flair without overdoing it, and build a blogroll worthy of jump-starting your culinary community. Grab your go-to garnishes and enter the fabulous world of food blog bling.

Exploring the Wide World of Widgets

Widgets. Even the word alone sounds useful. And after you dabble in them, you realize that "useful" doesn't even begin to cover the multitude of enhancements widgets you can add to your blog.

Widgets are tiny packets of pre-programmed software that are designed to enhance your blog's functionality, appearance, or usability. Looking to add a measurement converter to your blog's sidebar? There's a widget for that. Interested in displaying your real-time Twitter feed? There's a widget for that. Wishing every recipe could be accompanied by an FDA-style nutrition label? Believe it or not, there's a widget for that, too.

Best of all, you don't have to be a connoisseur of code to utilize widgets. If you know how to cut and paste, or even just how to drag and drop, consider yourself a wizard of widgets. They're literally that simple.

Thousands of widgets are available to add flare of every form. Beyond the superficial, widgets also provide countless benefits for your blog, including

- **Making your blog more interactive:** Up the interactive element of your blog by incorporating widgets that feature polls and quizzes, as well as the option to be in direct communication with your readers via a contact form widget.
- **Providing additional entertainment value:** Increase the amount of content your readers are exposed to by utilizing widgets that display additional content in your sidebar, including features such as the most popular posts, slide shows, videos, and more.
- **Making it easier and faster to access your content:** A wide variety of widgets exist to enhance how your readers access your content. Search bar and categories widgets improve internal navigation, while search engine optimization-specific widgets, such as the All In One SEO Pack and Google XML Sitemaps, increase the likelihood of readers finding your blog through external searches.
- **Providing an avenue for marketing and advertising:** Specific widgets, such as AddThis and ShareThis, make it possible for readers to share your content across the web by easily adding your post links to sites such as Pinterest, StumbleUpon, and Reddit. Your audience then becomes the biggest marketers and advertisers of your blog.
- **Enhancing your blog's appearance:** Better your blog's design with endless custom widgets that allow you to feature hyperlinked photos in your sidebar, add a custom logo to your header, and feature a blogroll of your favorite links.
- **Extending your content to social media platforms and beyond:** Widgets for sites such as Facebook, Twitter, and Flickr allow you to promote your brand's presence across the social media sphere by providing direct links to your fan page and feeds in the header or sidebar of your blog.

Widgets may also be referred to as plug-ins, badges, portlets, gadgets, and a slew of other names. But to keep things simple, I refer to them strictly as widgets.

Implementing widgets

So you know the wide array of available widgets and their many functions, but how can you put these bells and whistles into motion?

To implement the available pre-loaded widgets on a WordPress.com or WordPress.org blog:

1. **Log in to your WordPress.com Dashboard and then click the Appearance link in the left rail.**

   The Manage Themes page appears.

2. **Click the Widgets link.**

   The Widgets page appears with your library of pre-loaded widgets, as shown in Figure 9-1.

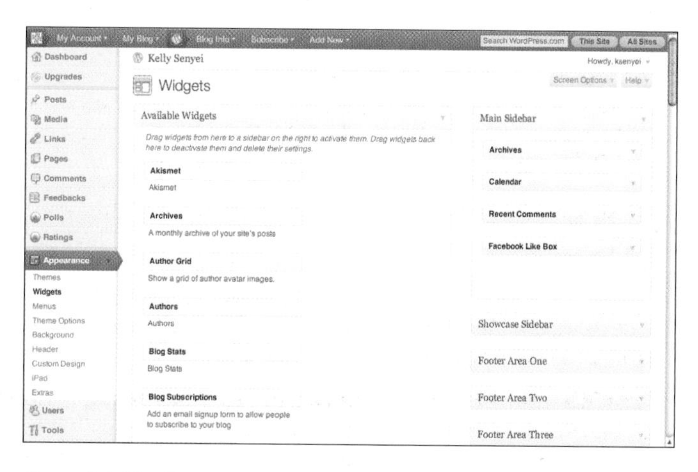

Figure 9-1: The library of pre-loaded widgets on a WordPress.com blog.

3. **Drag and drop a widget from the Available Widgets list into the Main Sidebar field located on the right side of the page to activate it.**

   Add as many widgets as you want into your sidebar field and rearrange their setup by dragging them into your desired order.

   A checkered box appears designating a place for you to drop your widget.

4. **Edit any customizations, such as the title of the widget, per your preferences, and then click the Save button.**

   Your widget is activated.

5. **Check your blog to confirm that the widget appears correctly on your page's sidebar.**

If the widget does not appear correctly on your page, refresh the page to ensure it's been saved. If the widget still doesn't appear, revisit the Main Sidebar, confirm the widget's placement, and then click Save again. Depending on your blog's setup, you may also be able to drag and drop widgets into a second sidebar or even into the footer of your blog, two fields that are featured on a variety of blog templates.

Figure 9-1 depicts four widgets implemented on my blog's sidebar, along with countless other available widgets that have not yet been activated.

And to kick your enhancements up a notch, tap into the vast network of plug-ins available strictly on WordPress.org blogs by following these steps:

1. **Log in to your WordPress.org Dashboard and then click the Plugins link in the left rail.**

   The Plugins page appears.

2. **Click Add New at the top of the page; and then either enter the name of the desired plug-in and click Search, or choose from the popular options.**

   You redirect to the specific plug-in listing.

3. **Click the Install Now link.**

   A page appears, depicting the status of your installation, as shown in Figure 9-2.

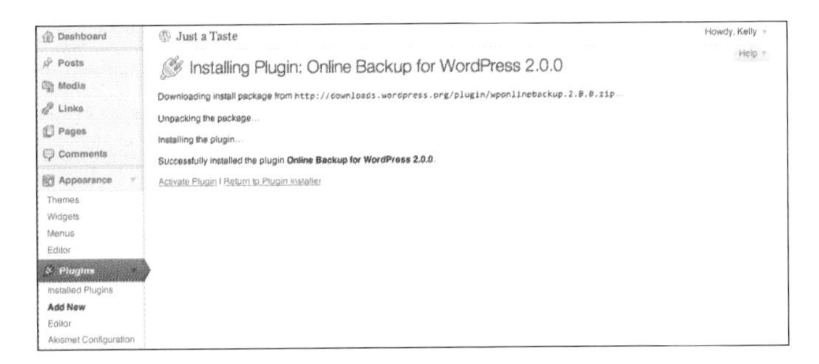

Figure 9-2: A status update appears after installing a plug-in on a WordPress.org blog.

4. **After the installation is complete, click the Activate Plugin link.**

   The plug-in is now active, and the Plugins page appears.

5. **Click Installed Plugins (below the Plugins link) in the left rail to confirm your successful installation and activation.**

   The Online Backup for WordPress plug-in is now active on the blog, which will automatically generate a backup of all blog files and store them in a desired location, such as a secure online server or e-mail inbox.

Adding gadgets to a Blogger blog follows a similar drag-and-drop process:

1. **Log in to your Blogger Dashboard and then click the More Options tab.**

   A drop-down list appears.

2. **Choose Layout from the drop-down list.**

   The Layout page appears.

3. **Click the Add a Gadget link in the area where you wish to implement your gadget.**

   The Add a Gadget pop-up window appears, as shown in Figure 9-3.

4. **Search for or select your desired gadget from the options provided and then click the blue + icon.**

   Gadgets can be rearranged at any time via dragging and dropping them into your desired locations, which include the sidebar, header, and footer portions of your page. To move a gadget, click it and drag it to your desired location, and then click the Save Arrangement button.

5. **Specify your desired customizations and then click the Save button.**

   Customizations are specific to each widget and can include designating a title, providing a number of comments to appear in a Recent Comments widget, selecting the size of a widget, and more.

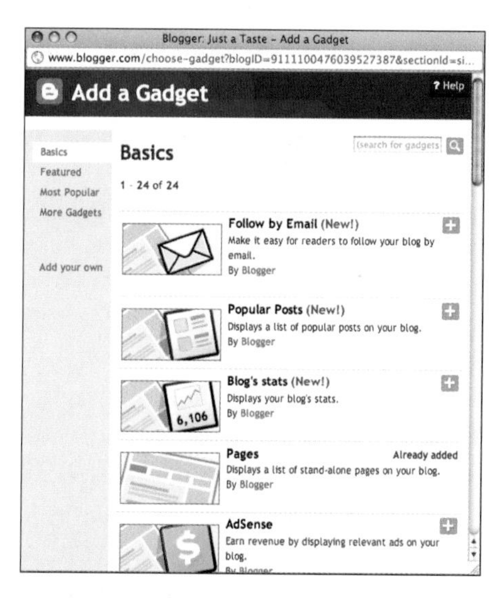

Figure 9-3: A pop-up window provides a selection of gadgets on a Blogger blog.

6. **Verify that the installed gadget appears on your Page Elements page and on your blog.**

   If the gadget does not appear, refresh your page and then check again. If it's still missing, return to the Layout page and verify you've followed the exact steps detailed here.

Following these setup guidelines proves how simple it is to implement pre-loaded widgets and to mix and match your way to the perfect blend of functionality and interactivity.

But if the pre-loaded options just aren't doing it for you, chances are you'll want to dig a bit deeper into the smorgasbord of widgets with customized creations from across the web. As you'll discover, customized widgets also stay true to the theme of simplicity, so keep on reading even if you're code-averse.

Going beyond basic widgets

Pre-loaded widgets on a blog are like vanilla icing on a cake. They're one flavor fits all when it comes to their uses on food blogs of every style and substance. But sometimes generic just isn't enough. Sometimes you don't want to be *just plain vanilla.* And this is where the flavoring extracts, food coloring, sprinkles, sugar flowers, and fondant in the form of customized widgets come into play.

Countless libraries of customizable widgets are online, including two of the largest resources, Widgipedia and Widgetbox. Both of these resources function by allowing you to copy the code for a specific widget and paste it into your blog's sidebar. This is the equivalent of the setup process you follow to implement a pre-loaded widget, but there are just a few additional steps.

To embed a widget's code into a WordPress.com or WordPress.org blog, follow these steps:

1. **Choose Dashboard⇨Appearance⇨Widgets.**

   The Widgets page appears with a list of available widgets.

2. **Drag and drop the pre-loaded Text widget into the Sidebar field located on the right side of the page.**

   You're prompted with the option to name your widget in the title bar, which appears on your blog exactly as you type it. Some widgets already have titles, so leave the title bar blank to avoid double-titling.

3. **Create your widget on the external site by following the specific setup guidelines for your desired widget.**

   The site provides the specific HTML code for your custom widget in the last step of the setup process.

4. **Copy the provided code from the external site, paste it in the Text field below the Title field, as shown in Figure 9-4, and click the Save button.**

   Your custom widget appears in your sidebar.

5. **Verify its placement by refreshing your blog's home page.**

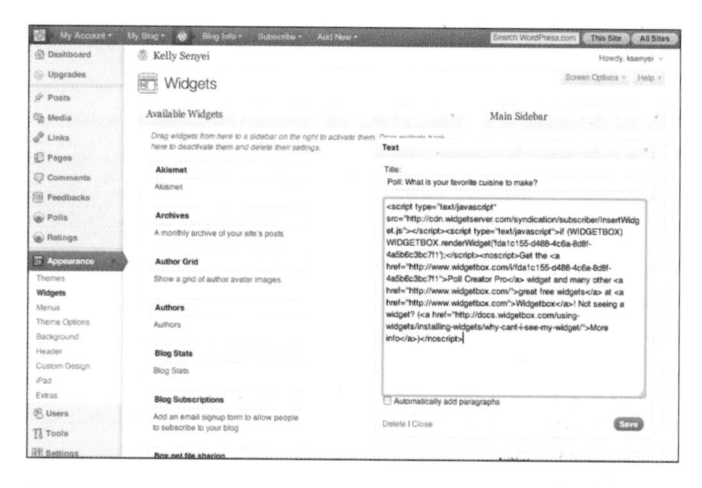

Figure 9-4: The Text widget on a WordPress blog stores the code for your custom widgets.

To implement a custom widget on a Blogger blog, follow these steps:

1. **On the Dashboard, click the drop-down icon button and then choose Layout from the drop-down list.**

   The Layout page appears.

2. **Click any of the Add a Gadget links appearing on the Layout page.**

   The Add a Gadget pop-up window appears.

3. **Scroll down to the Text widget and click the blue + icon.**

   The Configure Text page appears.

4. **(Optional) Enter a title for your widget.**

5. **Copy the custom code from the external site, paste it into the Content field, and click Save.**

   The custom widget is saved to your blog, and the Layout page appears.

6. **Click the Save Arrangement button in the top navigation, and then click the Preview button to confirm the widget's placement on your blog.**

   Your custom widget appears on your Page Elements page and on your blog.

Now that you know the process, take advantage of the wide array of widgets available online. The best place to start is with a spiced up version of your social media essentials. Although your blog likely comes with pre-loaded widgets for Facebook, Twitter, and Flickr, you can also access the widgets' codes and customize them further via the sites' resource pages:

- **Facebook:** Go beyond the blue icon with a customized widget detailing your number of fans via a two-column, horizontal, or vertical widget layout. (`www.facebook.com/badges/page.php`)
- **Twitter:** Keep your readers up to date with your social musings by adding your real-time Twitter feed to your blog's sidebar. (`http://twitter.com/about/resources/widgets`)

  You can also find other widgets for Twitter at `www.widgetbox.com/widget/twidget` and `http://twitstamp.com`.
- **Flickr:** After you create a Flickr account, generate a badge for your blog by choosing from assorted stylistic customizations. (`www.flickr.com/badge.gne`)

The sidebar of the Bitten Word blog, as shown in Figure 9-5, features the vertical version of the Facebook badge in action, as well as links to the blog's Twitter and Facebook pages via the social media icons.

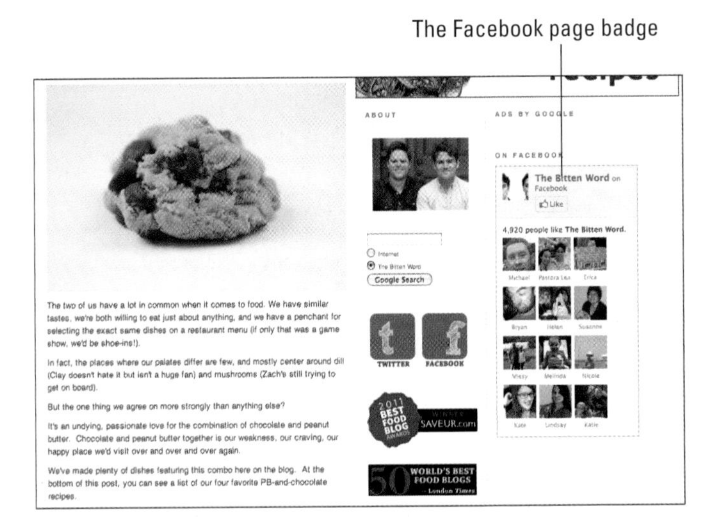

Figure 9-5: The sidebar of the Bitten Word blog displays the Facebook page badge.

In addition to upping your social media presence in your sidebar, widgets can promote your content both within your blog and on external sites. Two of the most effective and popular widgets are

- **AddThis:** AddThis allows readers to share your content by placing a collection of icons below each post (see Figure 9-6). Specific setup instructions can be found online at `www.addthis.com/help/installing-addthis`.
- **LinkWithin:** The LinkWithin widget displays related posts under each post on your blog, which in turn, increases page views by guiding readers to similar topics. Thumbnail images, as shown in Figure 9-7, also serve as visual cues to related content. This widget is not currently available for WordPress.com blogs.

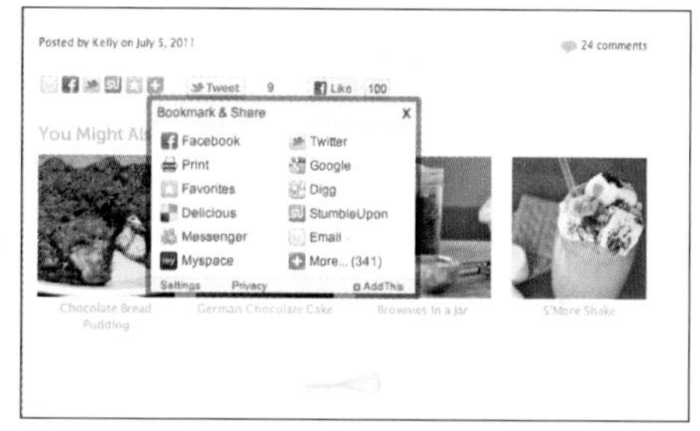

Figure 9-6: Allow your readers to share your content across the web.

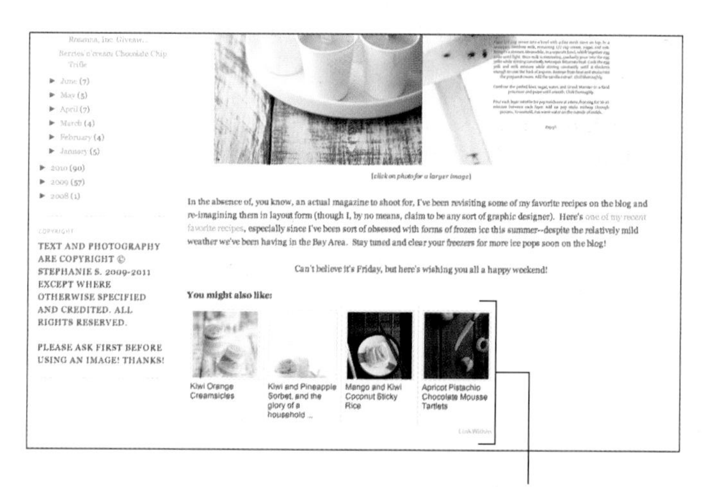

Figure 9-7: The LinkWithin widget guides readers to related content on your blog.

Displaying badges and buttons

Every blog deserves a bit of garnish, and this is where badges and buttons make their debut. *Badges* and *buttons* displayed on your blog can be any graphic or text element that serve a wide variety of functions, including

- Showing your support for a specific cause
- Announcing your involvement in an organization
- Displaying awards or accolades you've received
- Linking to extensions of your blog on external sites
- Informing readers of your upcoming events or activities

The sidebar of the Orangette blog, as shown in Figure 9-8, features a variety of badges and buttons on the right, including badges designating the blog as one of *Times Online's* 50 Best Food Blogs, a 2009 Winner of the FoodBuzz Blog Awards, and a button announcing that the blog author, Molly Wizenberg, took the handmade pledge.

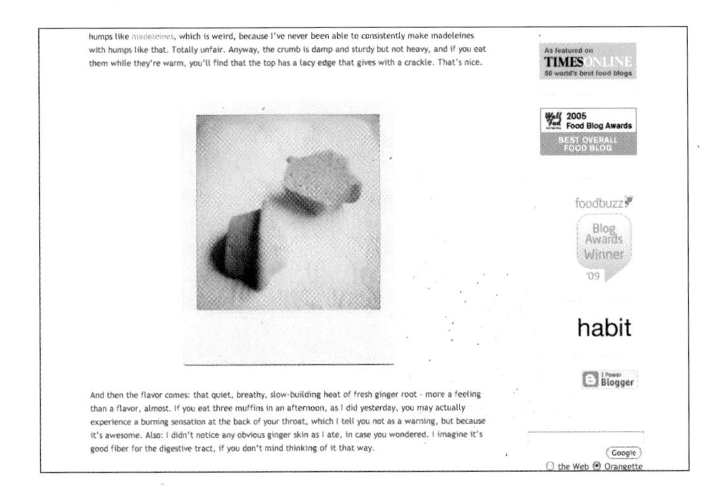

Figure 9-8: A variety of badges and buttons display on the Orangette blog.

Badges and buttons almost always link to their respective sites. Hyperlinking an image, be it a company's logo or a graphic you've created, is a simple additional step in implementing widgets. This leads me to show you the fun and fast method for designing, uploading, and implementing your very own custom badge and button creations.

Creating Your Own Blog Garnish

Basic and customized widgets are effective ways to extend your blog's functionality and style. But what if you want to take it a step further and give your sidebar an image makeover? You may think the answer lies in expensive photo-editing software, advanced knowledge of HTML code, and hours of labor. But the truth is, if you have Microsoft Word, you're in business.

Adding images to your sidebar that link to various pages or categories on your blog is an attractive way to present your content and to keep your readers clicking. For example, rather than include a text link to your page of Super Bowl snacks, up the design ante by adding an image of one of the recipes to the sidebar with a text reference to where it links. Getting this custom look is all about knowing how to utilize the tools that you likely already have in your online arsenal.

Hyperlinking a graphic

The process of adding a hyperlinked graphic to your sidebar involves selecting an image, adding text to that image designating where it leads (an optional step), and then uploading and publishing it on your blog. The entire process is essentially creating a post that you just never publish.

Adding text atop sidebar images ensures readers don't have to guess where clicking the image will lead them, which makes the images part of your blog's easy-to-follow internal navigation.

To illustrate the process of adding text to an image, I use a photo of corn with the word Vegetables to link to the Vegetable category on my blog. To add text to the image, follow these steps:

1. **Open a blank Microsoft Word document and click Insert on the top toolbar.**
2. **In the drop-down list that appears, choose Picture and then click From File from the list of options.**

   The Choose a Picture window appears.
3. **Select the image from its location on your computer and click the Insert button.**

   The image appears in your document.
4. **Double-click the image.**

   A Format Picture/Image window appears.
5. **Click the Layout tab, select Behind Text as the Wrapping Style option, and click OK.**

   The Behind Text option positions text on top of the image. Additional options for text placement include In Line with Text (text flows around the outline of the image), Square (text flows in a square shape around the image), Tight (text flows closely around the outline of the image), and In Front of Text (text flows behind the image). After you click OK, you return to the Word document.
6. **Type your text using your desired font style, size, and color, and align the text on top of the image by using the spacebar and Tab key to position it in your preferred placement.**

7. **Take a *screengrab* (an image of what's currently visible on your computer's screen) of the completed image with overlaid text.**

   To take a screengrab on a PC:

   a. *Locate the Print Screen button on your keyboard, make sure the Word document shows on your screen, and then press the Print Screen+Alt keys consecutively.*

   b. *Open the Microsoft Paint application and press Ctrl+P to paste the screengrab into the blank canvas.*

   c. *Use the Crop tool to select the portion of the screengrab you want to use and then save it to your desktop by choosing File➪Save As.*

   To take a screengrab on a Mac:

   a. *Press ⌘+Shift+4.*

      Your cursor becomes a screengrab capture tool.

   b. *Position the Capture tool in the top-left corner of the image, drag it down to the bottom-right corner, and then release.*

      The screengrab appears on your desktop.

8. **Log in to your blog's Dashboard, and then create a new post.**

   See Chapter 4 for how to create a new post.

9. **Confirm that you're in the Visual Text editor tab (the default), and then insert the image as if you were writing any other entry.**

   On WordPress blogs, the Visual tab is located next to the HTML tab in the Post editor. On Blogger blogs, the Visual tab is the same as the Compose tab, which is located next to the HTML tab in the Post editor. To switch from one to the other, simply click your desired tab.

10. **Center the image in the Text editor, as shown in Figure 9-9, by clicking the image and then clicking the Center Align button.**

    You can also center the image by selecting from the alignment options while inserting the image.

11. **Link the image URL to your desired page by selecting it and inserting it via the link icon in the Text editor.**

    This is the exact same process as hyperlinking text, except you apply the link to an image.

12. **Click the HTML tab at the top of your Text editor.**

    The HTML code version of what you're viewing in the Visual tab appears.

13. **Select the code in your HTML tab, as shown in Figure 9-10, and then copy and paste it into the Text widget in your sidebar.**

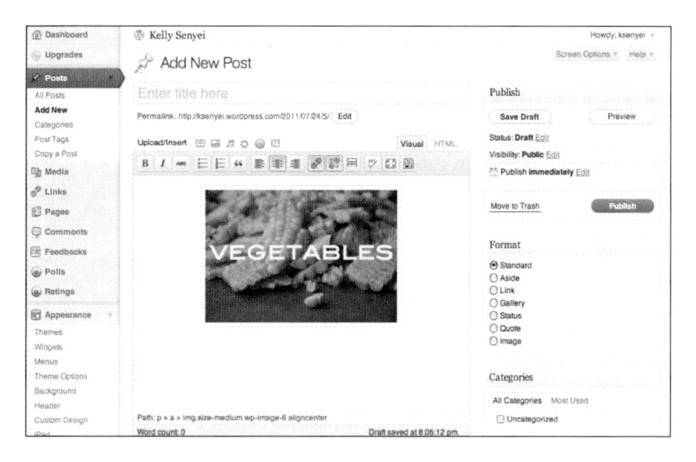

Figure 9-9: Insert the custom image into a post and link it to your desired URL.

14. **Click the Save button.**

    A custom image appears in your sidebar that links to the specified page or category on your blog.

Figure 9-10: Copy your hyperlinked image code from your HTML tab into a Text widget.

You can also tweak the code that's pasted directly into the Text widget. For example, if you implement your custom image and it's too small or too large for your sidebar, simply edit the width of the image in the Text field, as highlighted in blue in Figure 9-11. To keep your image width and height proportions to scale, change the width to your desired size and delete the number designating the height. This forces your image height to automatically scale in proportion to the designated width. Keep in mind it's always better to scale down your image size, rather than scale up. Increasing an image beyond its original size will cause it to appear blurry and distorted.

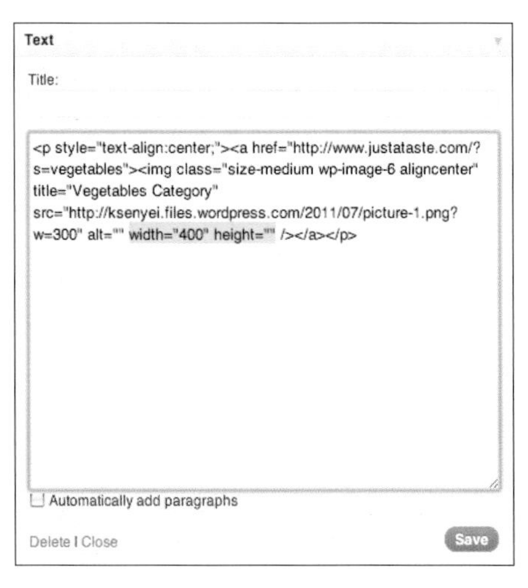

Figure 9-11: Change the width and delete the height of your image to scale the proportions.

Now that you know the basic process, you can add as many customized, hyperlinked images as you see fit. But given the vast number of available widgets and badges, it's important to not get too carried away when it comes to garnishing out your blog. Consider your sidebar as the top tier of a cake. You want your sidebar to be decorative and pronounced, but you don't want it to take away from the rest of the layers that support it. Applying the same principles of layout and design that I discuss in Chapter 7 ensures that you create a sidebar that's balanced, visually appealing, and useful for navigation.

Memorizing common HTML tags

Now that you've dabbled a bit in the HTML tab, it's not a bad idea to familiarize yourself with a handful of the most commonly used HTML tags, outlined in Table 9-1. These tags can be inserted when you're working in the HTML viewer of your Text editor, rather than the Visual tab, which already creates the custom formatting for you.

Table 9-1 Common HTML Tags

HTML Tag	*Function*
`<p></p>`	Creates a new paragraph
` `	Forces a line break on the page
`<b></b>`	Bolds text
`<i></i>`	Italicizes text
`<center></center>`	Centers content

You need to place the text you want to apply the style to inside the set of tags. For example, if you want to make only the word *chocolate* in the following sentence appear in bold type, write the sentence in the HTML tab of your Text editor as

Two of my favorite foods are <b>chocolate</b> and cheese.

That sentence would appear on your blog as

Two of my favorite foods are **chocolate** and cheese.

There really is no need to have to venture into the HTML tab, other than to get your custom code when making hyperlinked sidebar images. That's the beauty of using a blogging software that already has these functionalities built into it. But if you are feeling adventurous, or are looking to solve a headache from dysfunctional formatting, it's not a bad idea to keep the five commonly used HTML tags from Table 9-1 handy.

Building your blogroll

A *blogroll*, or a list of links to recommended sites, is a great way to foster community with fellow food bloggers. Reaching out with links to sites you frequent may prompt those sites to return the favor, which can bring a whole new audience to your blog and kick the notion that you're competitors to the curb. Community is at the core of food blogging, and there's no better way to meet new friends, find inspiration, and get access to endless experts than by embracing and promoting your fellow food enthusiasts.

If you use WordPress or Blogger, the blogroll widget is included in your library of pre-loaded widgets, and it can be implemented easily on your blog's sidebar just like any other widget. Add as many blogs as you see fit, keeping in mind that your blogroll gives your readers a sense of your interests and your recommended reading. Your blogroll doesn't have to be food-centric and can include your favorite sites dedicated to current events, education, sports, entertainment, and more. You may also opt to include links to valuable resource pages, such as

- Metric conversion tables for cooking volumes
- Fresh and dry herb comparison charts
- Guides for safe food handling and preparation
- Online store destinations for kitchenware essentials
- Dictionaries for cooking techniques and ingredients

I keep my blogroll updated to reflect my current favorite sites, which includes a selection of personal food blogs as well as larger sites, such as Serious Eats, the *New York Times* Diner's Journal, Eater, and more. My blogroll grows and wanes as my interests change, but it's generally a pretty strong indication of both my all-time favorite blogs and great resources for staying atop food news and trends. There is no perfect number for how many links to include, but remember that your blogroll becomes part of the visual layout of your blog, so it's best to avoid a 200-link list that overwhelms rather than inspires readers. You can also opt to create multiple blogrolls that feature distinctive groups of links, such as one blogroll for the blogs you're reading and a second blogroll for resources.

Part IV
Eating with Your Eyes

"Just how accurately should my blog reflect my place of business?"

In this part . . .

Photographs are one of the biggest draws to any popular food blog. No matter how eloquent and gripping your prose, the truth is that pictures show what even the most appetizing written description can't tell.

Not everyone has the resources, space, or time to splurge on a professional photography setup. In Part IV, I introduce you to the variety of high- and low-end cameras, as well as a few budget-friendly tips for creating your very own in-home studio. Before you take a single shot, make sure your model looks its best with a lesson in Food Styling 101.

10

Food Photography Basics

In This Chapter

- Understanding the fundamentals of digital photography
- Obeying the rules of composition
- Lighting a shot
- Getting the most out of natural and artificial light

Not surprisingly, one of the biggest draws to any popular food blog is the photographs — big, colorful, taste-it-through-the-screen photographs. They singlehandedly transform your blog from blah to brilliant by providing visual appeal and, if you're successful, leaving your readers drooling.

In this chapter, I introduce you to the essentials of digital food photography, which begin first and foremost with the fundamentals. Understanding the ins and outs, from lighting to composition, helps you take the best shot, regardless whether you're shooting in Auto mode or if you're aiming to wean yourself into Manual.

Before getting a grasp of the basics, you discover the importance of developing your unique photo style. From fun and playful to elegant and formal, the tone and feel of your photos will be a direct reflection of you and your blog's personality.

Developing Your Photo Style

Just as you develop your original voice as a writer, you also develop your original style as a photographer. And the more unique and identifiable that style, the better because your blog will become one-stop shopping for food photo fanatics from every corner of the web.

You may already be aware of a handful of food blogs with truly distinctive photo styles, but if not, familiarize yourself with the variety of styles by visiting food photo-sharing sites, such as foodgawker or TasteSpotting, both of which display endless photos in an easily digestible format.

As you study the photos on other food blogs and sites, ask yourself the following questions:

- Do the photos evoke a certain tone? Are they elegant and refined, or fun and playful?
- What role do props play in the photos? Are props a focal point or an afterthought?
- What role does light play in the appearance of the photos? Do the photos look light and airy, or dark and moody?

The last question is most likely to lead you to your preferred photo style because light plays the biggest role in determining the tone, and thus the appearance, of a photo. For example, take a look at the photo in Figure 10-1, which features a plate of black quinoa with shrimp by Bev Weidner of Bev Cooks.

Figure 10-1: Use brighter light to capture a sense of airiness and fun within a photo.

Bev embodies an airy, casual photo style through her use of light and props. The entire dish is illuminated by a strong cast of natural light, which enhances the variety of colors and textures of the ingredients. A vibrant blue plate provides ample contrast against the dark grains and also adds a sense of informality and playfulness.

Compare the light and airy feel of Bev's photo with the photo of rosemary shortbread bars by Stephanie Shih of Desserts for Breakfast, as shown in Figure 10-2.

Stephanie displays a warmer, moodier photo style by using *directional light* (light coming from a specific source). Strong highlights and shadows are cast across the image by a light source on the right. A dark green backdrop and maroon surface add a sense of warmth and richness.

Bev and Stephanie have developed their own original styles, using light and props to create the mood and feel of their photos. Your photos will be a direct reflection of your own preferences and inspirations, so feel free to experiment as you home in on the characteristics that define your unique visual voice.

Figure 10-2: Directional light helps convey a warmer, moodier photo style.

Starting with the Fundamentals

You're starting a food blog and you know photos are essential. But you're on a budget, your camera is a dinosaur, and your first attempts are blurry, overexposed, or both. Where do you even begin?

For starters, forget any past failures, put down your extinct equipment, and stop staring longingly at the galleries on foodgawker wondering when your photos will make the leap from the rejected pile to the accepted throne.

Every amateur photographer benefits from understanding the founding concepts of photography — regardless of your equipment, current skill level, or dependency on automatic versus manual settings. Time to crack the code for how to best capture food through your lens and to set you on the path to becoming the Annie Leibovitz of lasagna.

Seeing the bigger, clearer picture

Taking a photograph can be as simple as setting your point-and-shoot camera on Auto mode, or as involved as manually setting your aperture and shutter speed on your digital single-lens reflex (dSLR) camera. And if *shutter speed* and *aperture* leave you confused or nervous, you've come to the right place.

At the most basic level, photography is broken down into three main elements:

- Aperture
- Shutter speed
- International Organization for Standardization (ISO)

All three of these elements work in conjunction with light (either natural or artificial) to determine the exposure of the static image captured through your camera's lens.

Aperture and shutter speed

Aperture is the hole in your lens that determines the amount of light let into your camera. Think of aperture as the iris of your eye; when it's larger, more light is let in, and when it's smaller, less light is let in. Aperture works directly with *shutter speed,* which determines how slow or fast the lens shutter opens to allow light to access the sensor. Together, aperture and shutter speed determine the exposure of your image. Aperture also determines the depth of field of an image, which I discuss in full later in this chapter in the section "Wanted: Depth of field."

Aperture is designated by an *f-stop* (or *f-number*) — a number that relates to the focal length, which includes a range of low to high values. Figure 10-3 depicts a selection of f-stops in relation to the size of the aperture. Lower f-stops, such as f/1.4, f/2.8, or f/3.5, translate to a larger opening, letting in more light and a faster shutter speed. Higher f-stops, such as f/11, f/16, or f/22, are associated with a smaller opening, allowing less light and a slower shutter speed.

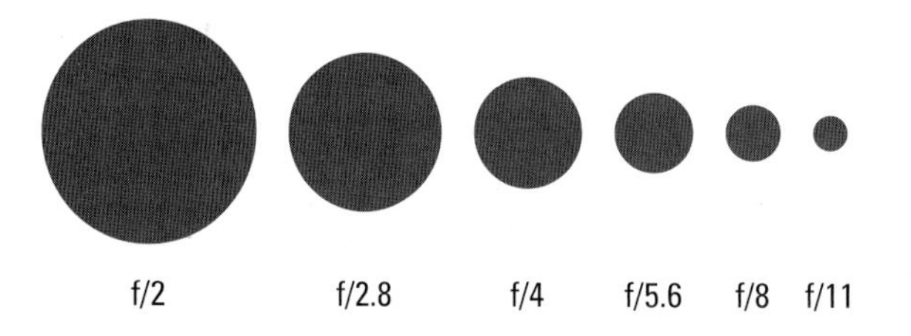

Figure 10-3: The higher the f-stop, the smaller the aperture.

ISO

ISO is a measure of how sensitive your camera's image sensor is to light. The ISO range depends on the specific camera, but it generally stretches anywhere from 50 to 3200. The lower the number, the less sensitive your camera is to light.

If you use a dSLR camera, the aperture, shutter speed, and ISO can be viewed from the display screen, as shown in Figure 10-4.

I only skim the surface of these three basic elements, but if you're interested in finding out more about digital photography, check out *Digital Photography For Dummies* by Julie Adair King.

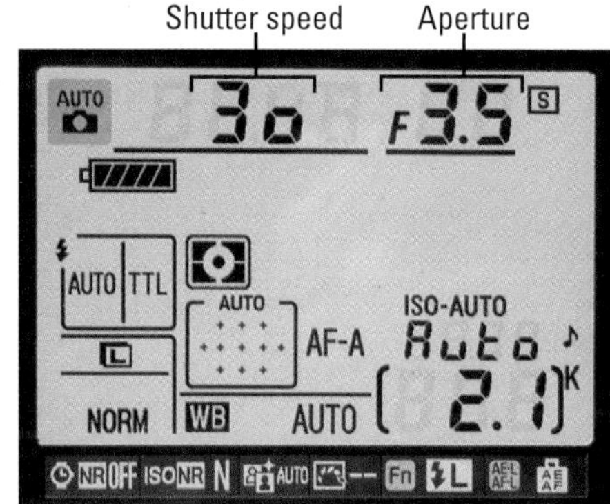

Figure 10-4: The display screen of a dSLR camera.

You can utilize these elements in two ways to create the best image. The first way is to set your camera to the Auto setting via the camera menu or set the Mode dial to the green camera icon, as shown in Figure 10-5. The second way is to use your camera's Manual mode, which I discuss in the section, "Shooting in Manual mode."

Figure 10-5: Use the Mode dial on a dSLR camera to set it to Auto.

Turning the Mode dial on your camera to Auto tells your camera to decide the best settings for aperture, shutter speed, ISO, white balance, flash, and focus. Leaving all the decision-making up to your camera means all you have to do to take a picture is press the shutter button.

Amateur photographers should start on the Auto setting, regardless whether they're hoping to switch to the Manual mode at some point because you need to understand what happens to the three main elements when your camera does the driving. If you're using a point-and-shoot camera, you'll most likely always be on the Auto setting, either because your camera doesn't offer a Manual mode or because it's easier and faster to use.

Although point-and-shoot cameras provide some options for manually adjusting the elements, the controls are often hard to locate and have limited usability. But that doesn't mean you still can't take a stellar photo! Later in this chapter, I address the basic rules for composing the ultimate shot, regardless of what camera you use.

Shooting in Manual mode

When you're comfortable taking the wheel, switch your digital SLR to manual and start setting the aperture, shutter speed, and ISO yourself. Manual mode is set by turning your Mode dial to M.

Start with the *ISO,* a control of your camera's sensitivity to light, which can be adjusted in any mode and is typically configured at 100, 200, 400, 800, 1600, and higher (depending on your camera). The lower the number, the less sensitive the sensor; the higher the number, the more sensitive the sensor. A more sensitive sensor makes it possible for you to take photos in low-light situations, such as on an overcast day or even at night.

The ISO is controlled via your specific camera's menu settings, and is increased or decreased depending on the amount of light required to create the best image. ISO also has a direct impact on the graininess (or *noise*) of your image. Take for example Figure 10-6, which depicts eggplant Parmesan sliders with an ISO of 6400 (the highest possible ISO setting on my Nikon dSLR).

Figure 10-6: A high ISO value causes your image to appear grainy.

The background appears pixilated and confetti-like, and even the sliders themselves have a certain graininess to them. To adjust for this problem, simply decrease the ISO. Figure 10-7 depicts the adjusted image, which has an ISO of 400. By decreasing the ISO, the sensor is less sensitive to light and thus prevents the image noise.

Figure 10-7: Lower your ISO settings to prevent image noise.

Next up is setting the aperture and shutter speed using your camera's exposure meter, which is viewed either on your display or by looking through your viewfinder. The meter indicates a spectrum from positive to negative, as shown in Figure 10-8, providing clues as to how to adjust your image's exposure via the dials on your specific camera model.

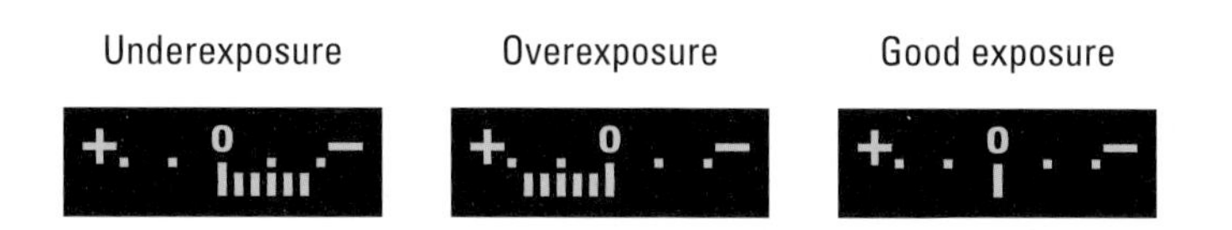

Figure 10-8: A positive to negative spectrum indicates your level of exposure.

If lines appear more toward the negative side, the image will be underexposed. If lines appear more toward the positive side of the spectrum, your image will be overexposed. The goal is to have no lines on the exposure meter, indicating a "0" value and thus good exposure.

To correct for the negative reading on your exposure meter, decrease the f-stop number and decrease the shutter speed to make it slower.

To correct for the positive reading on your exposure meter, increase the f-stop number and increase the shutter speed to make it faster.

For example, in Figure 10-9, the left image is an image I shot of sushi and sashimi with my exposure meter indicating a negative reading (an underexposed image), which was the result of shooting indoors on a cloudy day. In this photo, my settings were f/8 with a shutter speed of 100. The resulting photo is too dark because my aperture wasn't big enough to allow in enough light to illuminate the subject. To correct for the underexposure, I used my dials to decrease my shutter speed from 100 to 25 and to shift my f-stop from f/8 to f/5.6, which made my aperture bigger and produced a meter reading exactly on the "0" mark, indicating proper exposure. The resulting photo, as shown on the right in Figure 10-9, is much brighter and no longer underexposed.

Figure 10-9: Decrease the shutter speed to allow in more light, which corrects underexposure.

Shooting in Manual mode involves some guesswork, as you shift and re-shift your ISO, f-stop, and shutter speed to get the perfect exposure balance. The good news is that despite being in Manual mode, you still have the option to auto-focus in order to have one less thing to worry about.

Honing your Manual mode skills takes time, but luckily three intermediary "cheat" settings enable you to wean yourself into Manual without quitting the Auto mode cold turkey.

Putting on the "manual" training wheels

Shooting in Manual mode lets you control the specific look of your shot. However, you may not have the time (or perhaps even the interest) to adjust and re-adjust your settings until you get them just right. By the time you've figured out the f-stop, the ice cream will have melted, the kids will have missed dinner, and you'll realize it's 3:30 a.m. and you're still not entirely happy with the resulting photo.

If you can relate to any of that, take it easy on yourself by strapping on the training wheels and slowly weaning yourself from Auto to Manual. Utilizing these three semi-Manual modes on your digital SLR will split the decision-making between you and your camera:

- **Aperture-Priority mode:** Setting your camera to the A on your Mode dial means you determine the aperture (f-stop) and your camera then determines the appropriate shutter speed.
- **Shutter-Priority mode:** Indicated by the S on your Mode dial, this mode makes you responsible for setting the shutter speed while your camera takes care of the aperture to create the best shot.
- **Programmed Autoexposure mode:** In the P mode, your camera determines the aperture and shutter speed, which is essentially the equivalent of the Auto mode. However, in P mode, you can override any of the decisions your camera makes to custom blend your ideal exposure.

Regardless whether you're riding the Manual mode bike with or without training wheels, remember that departing from the world of automatic requires patience and practice as you gain your balance.

Wanted: Depth of field

You can recognize it in an instant, a sharp focal point fading gradually into the distance — known unscientifically as "that cool blurry effect." That effect is the *depth of field,* which is the range between the nearest and farthest objects in a photo that appear in focus. So how do you make it happen in your next shot? Become best buddies with your aperture.

Remember that aperture is tied to focal length (the f-stop), which in turn relates to how shallow or deep the focus is on the subject of your photo. Here are the two scenarios for creating a variety in depth of field:

- **Larger depth of field:** Decrease the aperture (which in turn increases the f-stop) to increase the depth of field and make more of your image appear in focus.
- **Shallower depth of field:** Increase the aperture (which in turn decreases the f-stop) to decrease the depth of field and make less of your image appear in focus.

Figure 10-10 depicts a photo of strawberry Fruit Roll-Ups in which there is a very shallow depth of field.

Figure 10-10: A larger aperture and smaller f-stop creates a shallower depth of field.

A larger aperture and a setting of f/5.6 provided a smaller depth of field, making less of the Fruit Roll-Up appear in focus against the rest of the image. This in turn created the often desired blurred effect, which you can now pinpoint as depth of field.

Sticking to the Basic Photography Rules

Countless elements stand between what constitutes a good food photo and what constitutes a spectacular food photo. Regardless whether you use a smartphone camera, a point-and-shoot camera, or a digital SLR camera, the same standard principles apply to every shot:

- The Rule of Thirds
- Composition
- Perspective
- Background
- Lighting

I'd be remiss to not include lighting among the standard principles of photography. But the truth is, lighting is so important that it deserves its own entire section later in this chapter, as well as its own technical how-to in Chapter 11.

All five of these principles work together to translate what you see through your lens into what you publish on your blog. Every photo serves a purpose, whether it's purely for entertainment or entirely for instruction. Adhering to these basic rules allows you to best convey the emotion, look, and feel of a real-life moment with an audience who can experience it only in digital form.

Obeying the Rule of Thirds

A balanced person is a centered person. A balanced photograph is an off-centered photograph. As ironic as it sounds, to find balance within a shot, you have to place your subject in anywhere but the middle of the frame. And this is where the granddaddy of all photography rules comes into play.

The *Rule of Thirds* is a fundamental principle of *composition* (the visual arrangement of elements); it refers to deconstructing a photograph into horizontal and vertical thirds to create a grid of nine squares with intersecting points.

Figure 10-11 depicts The Rule of Thirds grid, with red circles indicating the four key intersecting points, which are the prime placements for the subject of your photograph.

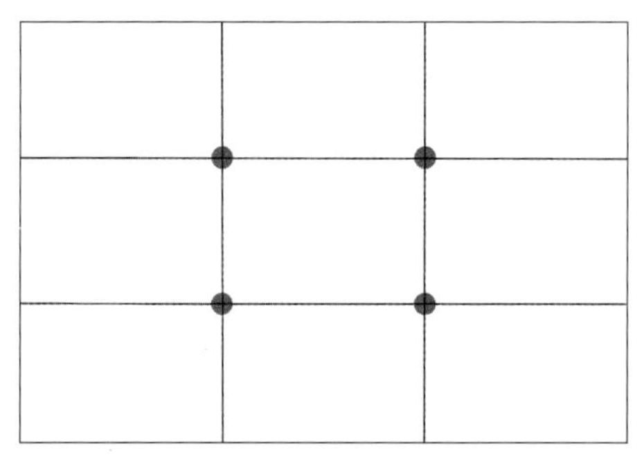

Figure 10-11: The Rule of Thirds divides an image into nine parts and designates four key intersecting points.

This grid, with its four key intersecting points, has become the standard guide for creating a balanced photo. And in fact, the concept of dividing an image into thirds dates as far back as the late 1700s when it was put into practice by painters.

Aside from its more than 200-year history, The Rule of Thirds is a critical component of a photograph's composition. Framing subjects according to the key intersecting areas actually creates a more pleasing experience for viewers' eyes as they gravitate toward the focal point. Placing a subject in the dead-center of a frame creates an image without dimensions, without tension, and thus without much interest. Consider Figure 10-12, which depicts baked apples with apricot glaze framed in the center of the shot.

Figure 10-12: A photograph with the subject in the center of the frame doesn't adhere to The Rule of Thirds.

Now consider applying The Rule of Thirds and re-framing the subject so that it rests at one of the four key intersecting points, as shown in Figure 10-13. Aligning the main focal point (the pouring of the apricot glaze) of the baked apples in the right third of the frame draws the viewer's eyes to that point, while at the same time it creates dimension and a sense of tension in the photo.

Figure 10-13: Create balance and interest in your image by placing your subject at one of the four key intersecting points.

The goal for amateur photographers is to not just point and shoot (even despite having a point-and-shoot camera). Instead, look through your viewfinder, imagine the invisible grid, and frame your shot with the critical intersecting points in mind. This strategy will take practice, and may even seem counterintuitive at first. After all, your subject is the focal point of your photograph, so why wouldn't you want it in the center of the frame? But the more you can train your eyes to obey The Rule of Thirds, the more balanced and interesting your photographs will be.

With that being said, you also don't want to become a photography robot, capturing all your photos with the exact same framing. Remember that food photography is an art, and like all forms of art, it thrives on creativity and imagination. Allow yourself to experiment on occasion to ensure your unique personality and style shines through in each shot.

Composing the perfect shot

Although The Rule of Thirds is the granddaddy of composition, countless other elements are involved in framing and creating a visually appealing shot.

Patterns and textures play a big role in photography; a fact that is especially true for food photography. For example, envision the look and feel of freshly whipped chocolate buttercream slathered atop a moist and spongy vanilla cake. Picture the swirls of frosting and how each cake crumb falls naturally into place on the plate. These tiny details, paired with the visual patterns on linens, napkins, and other props, create dimension and a sense of place. Your job is to use those textures and patterns to your image's benefit.

But patterns don't just exist on placemats and tablecloths. They are also created by grouping multiples of the same food in a shot. For example, Figure 10-14 depicts eight pickled deviled eggs on a checkerboard tray. The repetitiveness of the shapes of the eggs and the wooden squares creates a stimulating effect on the eye by drawing it to the varying focal points of the shot. When in doubt, default to multiples to create a striking pattern, but be careful the photos aren't hypnotic or draining on the eye.

Another way of creating visual appeal through composition is to utilize leading lines to their fullest. *Leading lines,* which are strong straight or curvy lines in a photo, usher your eyes through an image by pinpointing where to start and suggesting a natural flow within the frame.

Notice the leading lines apparent in Figure 10-15, which depicts a simple in-process shot of a potato being sliced on a mandoline.

Figure 10-15: Leading lines direct the focus of your eyes as they wander across an image.

The arch of the mandoline frames the top portion of the image while the strong parallel line of the wooden cutting board defines the lower space of the photo. Together the two leading lines bookend the image and direct your eyes to the subject (the potato slices). There is a sense of balance, interest, and a defined path your eyes take through the image. Leading lines help create movement while directing the focus of your gaze, and they appear either intentionally or unintentionally within an image.

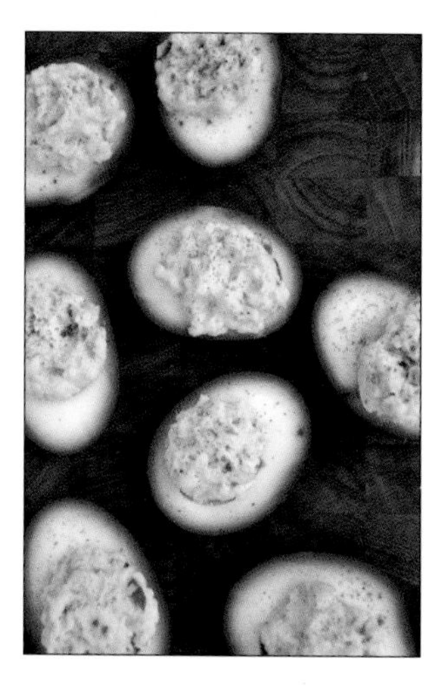

Figure 10-14: Multiples of the same foods create eye-catching patterns and textures.

Gaining perspective

Perspective is about the way you see your subject through your lens and how you move yourself and your camera to find the point of view that best suits what's standing, sitting, dripping, steaming, flaming, or melting in front of you.

So do you shoot *at* your subject, or down onto it? Do you get up close and personal with the Parmesan, or keep your distance? Although your setup depends on your personal style and preferences, it's important to keep in mind the variety of options when deciding on your camera angle:

- **Eye-level:** Known by the pros as the *hero shot,* going eye-to-eye with your subject puts you both on the same plane.
- **Three-quarters:** Slightly above eye-level but not overhead, a three-quarters shot gives you prime angling to see down into and onto your subject.
- **Overhead:** Get a bird's-eye view by positioning your camera to look down onto your subject.

Something about the textures, colors, and shapes of food make it an undeniably mesmerizing subject to photograph. Every twist of a noodle, dollop of tomato sauce, and curl of Parmesan cheese changes its appeal as you move your camera to best capture the bowl. From high above, the noodles look like tangled waterslides dipping and diving into each other's shadows. From eye-level, they appear like hills of undulating ropes, dripping with sauce and spilling onto the table below. Change your perspective, and you've changed your whole shot.

For example, on the left in Figure 10-16 is an eye-level shot of a recipe for pickled onion and carrot relish. Pay attention to what your eye is drawn to in the frame. Now consider the exact same subject, but shift your perspective to photograph the relish from the overhead angle, as shown on the right in Figure 10-16.

Figure 10-16: Change your angle to get a different perspective.

There is no right or wrong answer as to which shot is better. The perspective you choose is based entirely on your preference and style. I prefer the overhead shot for this particular setup because it gives me a better sense of the relish (the focus of the recipe) in the context of its placement atop a grilled sausage in a bun. My eyes travel along the twists and turns of the pickled onion, making stops at each carrot cube before continuing onward.

The key is to consider multiple perspectives for each shot because you never know what a shift in your camera angle may create. As you experiment with a variety of points of view, keep in mind your distance from the subject. The range of your photo dictates the focal point and falls into one of three general categories:

- **Wide shot:** This is a shot of your specific subject within a larger context, such as your whole Thanksgiving table rather than just the turkey.
- **Medium shot:** A medium shot provides some hint of the larger context while placing your subject as the main focal point in the frame. Figure 10-17 is an example of a medium shot in that you can clearly see the sausages topped with relish, but you can also distinguish their place atop a tray and next to a jar of the condiment.
- **Tight shot:** From close-up to extreme close-up, tight shots are a favorite among food photographers because they allow you to capture every crack and crevice while exposing the intricate textures and shapes of a dish or ingredient.

Figure 10-17: A medium shot provides context while keeping your subject the focal point.

With camera angles and ranges in mind, the third component to structuring your photo is to contemplate a horizontal versus a vertical setup. Which option you choose depends on your styling preferences, what your subject is, and the blog layout. Some blogging templates better showcase horizontal versus vertical images, and it takes some trial and error in posting to decide what looks best for your specific design.

Regardless whether you opt for horizontal or vertical photos, all images should be labeled according to best practices for search engine optimization (SEO). (See Chapter 13 for more on SEO and naming images.)

Paying attention to backgrounds

You may be so focused on the subject of your shot that you forget to see what exists behind it, such as that tree branch sticking out from behind the chef's head. You've now unintentionally turned his toque into a flowerpot for the nearby shrubbery.

Backgrounds play a critical role in your framing and setup, and they can impact the overall feel of your photo. I go into detail about the role of backgrounds in propping and styling in Chapter 12, but for now remember to always look beyond your subject in order to minimize distractions and maximize the focal point. Too busy of a background and you're interrupting the frame, too little contrast with a background and you're doing a disservice to the subject.

Seeing the (Natural and Artificial) Light

Lighting singlehandedly expresses the mood and tone of your entire photo, be it flashy and overexposed, or authentic and balanced. How you avoid the former and home in on the latter comes down to your custom blend of natural light (via the sun), artificial light (via light bulbs), or a mixture of the two.

The results from The State of the Food Blogosphere survey indicated food bloggers were relatively evenly split between using natural versus artificial light, and each method comes with its own set of pros and cons listed in Table 10-1.

Table 10-1 Natural versus Artificial Light

Light Source	*Pros*	*Cons*
Natural	It's free. No equipment is required.	You're limited to daylight hours. You have less control over the quality, depending on the weather.
Artificial	You can take photos at any time. You have total control.	Equipment costs money. Requires knowledge to set up and adjust.

In addition to your budget, a key factor in determining which type of lighting is best for you comes down to your personal schedule. For example, if you work during daylight hours, you either have to use artificial light to shoot at night, or use natural light and stick to the weekends. But there's no reason to let your day job get in the way of quality food photography for your blog! (I can hear employers everywhere groaning.)

Picture this: It's 8 p.m., and you're just plating your pan-fried tilapia with edamame succotash and are anxious about getting the perfect shot for your blog. Just as your plate touches your dining room table, the sun sets and you're left wondering if night vision goggles can be strapped to a camera lens.

Forget the goggles and allow me to introduce you to the daylight bulb — your go-to solution to faking natural light at night. Take a glance at Figure 10-18, which depicts a pomegranate I lit using a 100-watt daylight bulb (without any retouching) that was positioned above and to the right of the fruit.

Daylight bulbs can be purchased at most hardware stores and cost about $6. Who knew your sanity could cost less than $10? They're designed to simulate light from the sun, and although the bulbs do a decent job of putting out daylight-looking light, there really is no perfect substitute for the real deal.

If you're lucky enough to have daytime hours to take photos, your task then becomes finding the natural light in your setting — any way, any how. (Hint: On top of the toilet isn't off limits.)

I consider finding the best natural light in my apartment to be like an obstacle course. One minute I'm lying on the floor crammed up against my floor-to-ceiling window, the next minute I'm balancing on a bar stool while holding back the blinds and snapping a photo. I had one foot on my air conditioning vent and the other on a dining room chair to capture the natural light I used while photographing my s'more pie, as shown in Figure 10-19. You're always fighting the clock and the weather when shooting with natural light.

Figure 10-18: A daylight bulb provides natural-like daytime light in the dark.

The real inside scoop is seasoned food bloggers know that finding natural light is like finding gold. And they'll go to any length to locate it and use every last ounce of it until it's no longer at their disposal. I definitely drink the natural light Kool-Aid and have been known to lug my 22-pound stand mixer from my kitchen to my dining room table just so I can position it next to the window. Natural light really is that irresistible. In Chapter 11, I teach you a few tricks for how to best utilize natural light, but for now, start focusing on where to find it in your home (and also start stretching so you don't pull a muscle in the process).

Figure 10-19: Seeking out and using natural light is like finding photography gold.

11

Gathering Your Equipment and Tools

In This Chapter

- Saving and splurging on camera options
- Identifying your basic studio equipment needs
- Putting together your food-styling toolkit

A piece of duct tape here, a swath of your favorite pillowcase there, a $5 poster board wrapped in aluminum foil, and *voilá!* Welcome to your new in-home studio.

You don't need to empty your bank account to assemble the equipment for creating high-quality photos. In this chapter, I teach you the ways of photography frugality, which include taking advantage of the endless backgrounds and tools hiding in your kitchen and around your home. You'll also discover the camera that best suits your needs, and realize that it's not about how much you spend, but how you maximize what you have.

A primer in equipment wouldn't be complete without my list of the must-have tools for the ultimate food-styling kit. From ten-inch tweezers to offset spatulas, make the most of your meal with a few simple tools of the food-styling trade.

Knowing Your Camera Options

Taking a high-quality photograph is just as much about knowing how to use your equipment as it is about the equipment itself. Although not all cameras are created equal, you don't need to splurge to get a stellar shot.

The same standard principles of composition I discuss earlier in this chapter apply to every type of camera, regardless whether that camera also doubles as your cellphone or has a lens weighing nine pounds.

From $200 to $2,000, it's important to know what money can buy while remembering that money alone can't buy you class, taste, love, or most applicable to your situation, high-quality photos. (I guess *technically* you could fork over the cash to buy an Ansel Adams original, but that's beside the point.)

With three options, selecting your camera is a straightforward decision based on your budget and what equipment you own already. As The State of the Food Blogosphere results show in Figure 11-1, a majority of food bloggers polled utilize a dSLR camera, making it the most popular, and also the most expensive, option. Your list of options for digital cameras is short and sweet:

- **A camera phone:** Compact, portable, and easy to use, camera phones have become a popular option among professional and amateur photographers alike. Recent advancements in technology have made poor picture quality a thing of the past because many camera phones capture high-resolution images and allow you to adjust your focus for depth of field while also maximize on low-light situations. In addition to their portability, camera phones allow you to easily e-mail your photos or post them directly online.
- **A point-and-shoot camera:** A point-and-shoot camera is a simple and straightforward option that requires very little advanced technical knowledge or time to use. Much like camera phones, point-and-shoot cameras are compact and portable and, depending on the model, may feature additional options for adjusting the lighting or focus of an image.
- **A dSLR camera:** dSLR cameras are the most advanced cameras of the three options and require the most technical knowledge to use. Unlike their compact counterparts, dSLRs are larger and heavier, but with the added bulk comes endless customizations for lighting, focus, and framing because many provide the option to crop a photo within the camera itself. dSLRs offer Automatic and Manual settings, giving you the option for just how much control you want to have over capturing photos.

So can you really get the same quality shot with a camera phone, a point-and-shoot, and a dSLR? Only one way to find out. Take a glance at Figure 11-2, which depicts the same glass of dry spaghetti shot with an Apple iPhone 4 camera (left), a Nikon Coolpix point-and-shoot camera (middle), and a Nikon D90 dSLR (right).

Although not identical, I achieved relatively similar quality photos with each of the three cameras because I applied the same standard principles to all three shots, the most important of which is lighting. (See Chapter 12 for more on lighting setups.)

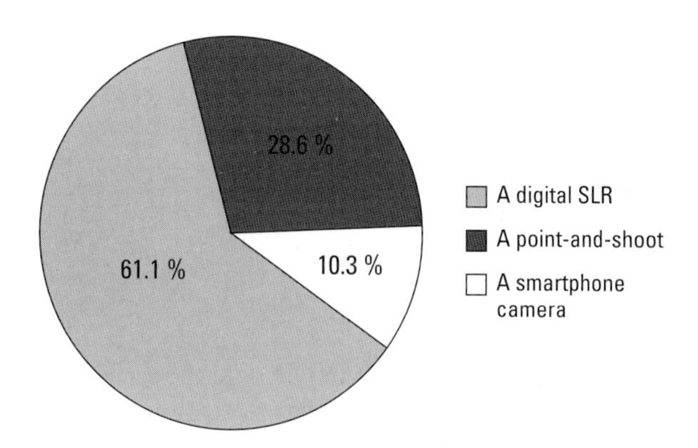

Figure 11-1: A majority of food bloggers use a dSLR camera rather than a smartphone or point-and-shoot camera.

Figure 11-2 is further proof that there's no reason to break the bank just to take food blog-worthy photos. But as long as you are checking your balance, consider the various pros, cons, and costs for each type of camera.

Camera phones

Camera phones are prized for their portability, and with current technology, the quality of the photos they produce has skyrocketed. In fact, as of September 2011, the Apple iPhone 4 bypassed four types of dSLRs as the most popular camera used in the online Flickr community. It's hard to beat portability!

Although the digital camera feature may not be a determining factor in what type of smartphone you purchase, if you are considering a smartphone with a photo function, pay attention to the *megapixels* (the measure of millions of pixels in your camera's image sensor). Although megapixels aren't the only determinant of quality photos on a camera phone, they do play a key role, and semi-serious phone photographers should aim for anywhere from 3 to 5 megapixels, and up.

The cost of a camera phone depends, not surprisingly, on the cost of your smartphone. For context, an Apple iPhone 4, which comes with a high-quality 5-megapixel camera, costs $199 (not including the price of the service plan).

Figure 11-2: A variety of low- and high-end cameras create similar levels of image quality.

Point-and-shoot cameras

Also known as compact cameras, point-and-shoot cameras are a user-friendly option for capturing a split-second image without any technical work involved. Reliant on the Auto mode, point-and-shoot cameras are prized for their simplicity and ease of use.

But with ease of use also comes lack of control because you can't manually set the aperture and shutter speed to fully determine the outcome of the image. Point-and-shoot cameras range anywhere from $110 to $500, depending on the quality and functions associated with the specific model. I recommend any of the available Nikon COOLPIX or Canon PowerShot models.

dSLR cameras

A dSLR camera is the king of the food photography throne, providing you with total image control, the ability to use multiple lenses, and the highest picture quality imaginable. The bad news? The cameras are expensive, can be rather bulky, and require advanced technical knowledge to make the most of the manual functions.

I can't recommend a single best dSLR camera because buying a camera is like buying a car, a house, or a bagel — the decision is entirely dependent on the buyer's tastes. And like every camera purchase, you get what you pay for, so start your research on the low end of pricing (around $500) before working your way up to the quadruple-digit cost options. That being said, you can't go wrong with reputable brands, such as Canon or Nikon. I have forever been a fan of Nikon's D90 model and only recently upgraded to the D7000.

Building Your Studio

I often fantasize about having a photo studio like that of White on Rice Couple's Todd Porter and Diane Cu. The powerhouse food-styling and photography duo built their dream setup, as shown in Figure 11-3, in Orange County, California, and the outcome is a stunning kitchen — prime for print and TV shoots — that's equipped with every appliance, gadget, and surface, not including the separate room dedicated entirely to props of every size, shape, and color.

I often find myself staring longingly at this photo. Eventually I snap back to reality with the reminder that Todd and Diane are professional photographers with a professional studio, who produce some seriously professional photos.

Not to disappoint you, but this section will not teach you how to create the Todd and Diane's setup for $7. Instead, I discuss when to buy and when to DIY equipment, backgrounds, editing software, and more. Time to get back in touch with the kindergarten version of yourself as you cut and paste (literally) your way to the ultimate in-home studio.

Photo credit: Todd Porter and Diane Cu, White on Rice Couple

Figure 11-3: White on Rice Couple's kitchen studio is illuminated by vast amounts of natural light.

Enhancing your light

In Chapter 10, I stress the importance of lighting and how it can singlehandedly transform your photos from blah to brilliant. So how are you going to make that big jump? With $5 and a side of elbow grease.

Making the most of your light involves utilizing *fill cards* (also known as *reflectors* or *bounce cards*), which are panels you arrange at various angles around your subject in order to balance the exposure and adjust the strength of the light.

The good news is you don't need to splurge on professional-grade fill cards when a cheap foam core board provides the same effect. But before launching into an arts and crafts session, familiarize yourself with the four most common fill card colors and their specific uses:

- **White:** Use a white fill card to bounce light onto a subject. This is known as a *positive fill* because you use the color white to diffuse the light back onto the subject to further illuminate it.
- **Black:** Use a black fill card to lessen the illumination on the subject. This is known as a *negative fill* because you use the color black to absorb light and make the subject less bright.
- **Silver:** Use a silver fill card for a stronger positive fill than with the color white. Silver gives off a punchier, metallic hue that can also cool the tones of an overly warm image.
- **Gold:** Use a gold fill card to add a warmer tone to a subject by counteracting lighting that appears too cool or gray. Gold is often used to warm a person's skin tone.

Figure 11-4 depicts standard fill cards I created from one 20-x-30-inch white foam core board I purchased at a local art supply store for $5.

Figure 11-4: A foam core board makes multiple fill cards and reflectors.

You can create fill cards, too, using an inexpensive foam core board, scissors, and tape. Cut the board into four equally sized rectangles and then tape together two of the rectangles to create your standalone tabletop fill card. The third panel can be used atop the folding reflector to bounce light onto the top of the subject, and the fourth panel can be turned into a silver or gold reflector, or kept as an extra white fill card.

Create a negative fill card by using a black poster board, craft a silver reflector by covering a poster board in aluminum foil (just make sure to crumple it up first), and make a gold reflector by rinsing off the brown sugar glaze from your holiday ham wrapper and stapling it to a poster board. (I'm providing this last suggestion in jest, though I wouldn't put it past myself!) If a spiral-sliced ham isn't in your near future, buy a roll of gold foil online or at a stationery store for around $5.

I cover how to set up and shift your homemade fill cards in Chapter 12, which is dedicated to the standard studio setup used by professional and amateur photographers alike.

If you're having trouble with natural or artificial light that's too harsh, opt for a *scrim,* which is a semi-transparent piece of fabric positioned in front of a light source to soften its intensity. You can purchase scrims at photo stores. But why buy another piece of equipment when you already own it?

Instead, head straight for the bedroom, un-tuck those white bed sheets, and put them to work! Hang the sheets in front of your window or use pillowcases or white napkins as scrims draped in front of daylight bulbs for nighttime shooting. (***Warning:*** Hot light bulb + pillowcase = potential fire hazard. Keep your scrim close enough, but never touching the bulb.)

Repurposing household items

Did you know countless backgrounds and photo surfaces are hiding in your kitchen, bedroom, and even bathroom? Take a closer look around your home — if you have a brown paper grocery bag, wrapping paper, cookie sheets, and dare I even say, prom dresses, you're in business!

Take for example the photo of my s'more shake in Figure 11-5. You might not have guessed it by looking at the photo, but the bright red background is actually the bottom portion of one of my dresses. The muted colors of the shake were begging for a pop of color to provide a contrast between the food and the background, so I specifically chose the fiery red to help convey the fun summertime vibe that inspired me to develop the recipe.

As you hunt through your closet, pay particular attention to the solid colors and patterned items to give your images a variety of looks and feels. Aprons, dish towels, and even bed sheets also make for fantastic backgrounds and can be used multiple times without looking the exact same in any two shots. All it takes is looking at your home from the perspective of a photographer, who sees any and every surface as a potential background for photos.

Food and clothes don't often mix well, so be careful to avoid spills and stains.

I often revert to my go-to background: a cookie sheet with patina. (*Patina* is just a fancy way of saying "an old and tarnished allure.") Every time I turn to my grungy cookie sheet for help, it comes to my rescue without fail. Stacking various dishes atop the matte silver sheet makes any food pop by providing a plain, shine-free surface. Bowl of murky beef stew? I turn to the cookie sheet. Neutral-colored hummus dip? I reach for the cookie sheet. Melted cheese gone awry? Super cookie sheet to the rescue.

Figure 11-5: Photo backgrounds exist everywhere in your home, including your closet.

The best part about my cookie sheet is that it photographs differently every time depending on the light, so readers aren't bored by the same look and setup in every shot. Figure 11-6 depicts that very cookie sheet in two shots, one featuring ice cream sundae toppings and another featuring a citrusy cocktail made with fruit juice.

Countless other outlets and resources provide prime photo backgrounds and surfaces for any size budget:

- **Flea markets:** Flea markets are home to a variety of options on the cheap and are best for buying weathered items, such as white-washed or distressed wood, as shown in Figure 11-7. Anything old and used tends to photograph well because it has added texture and character as a result of its age. Also keep an eye out for antique bakeware and glassware, which can be found at flea markets, as long as you're willing to hunt for them.

Figure 11-6: The same photo background takes on a different appearance in every shot depending on the lighting.

- **Home repair stores:** I often turn to home repair stores for budget-friendly surfaces. One of my favorite places to shop is at Home Depot because it sells a variety of patterned and solid vinyl flooring tiles that cost less than $1 for a 1-x-1-inch tile. I use them as surfaces for my plated dishes, or I prop them up as backgrounds. Individual wood panels sold as closet shelf inserts are another alternative. They're made in white and every grade of wood and cost around $5.
- **Stationery stores:** Stationery stores are the ultimate resource for cheap backgrounds and surfaces, especially when it comes to large sheets of decorative paper and rolls of wrapping paper. If you go the paper route, look for textured options because papers with notches or weaves provide great textural contrast for your image. Also go for matte, rather than shiny, which doesn't photograph as well.

- **Your own kitchen:** Check under your sink, above the fridge, beneath the stove — you never know where a useful background may be hiding. In addition to grungy cookie sheets, my favorite backgrounds include serving trays of every size, shape, and color as well as boards. A scratched wood cutting board is the most basic of surfaces and can make any dish appear appetizing simply by providing a natural, complementary frame for your food.

Figure 11-7: The matte finish of distressed wood panels make them prime photo surfaces.

Although surfaces and backgrounds are an important part of any photo setup, your first priority should always be the food, especially if you're the one cooking. It's much easier to style and prop a well-prepared dish than to have to make a culinary catastrophe appear edible.

Freeing up your hands

Drizzling syrup over a stack of steaming hot pancakes, squeezing a lime wedge into an ice-cold cocktail, slicing and dicing through a sweet onion with a chef's knife. Some of food photography's finest moments exist in the action shots.

But how are you going to capture your own hands in motion when you're also the photographer? The answer lies in two simple pieces of equipment: a shutter-release remote and a tripod, which I used to take the photo depicted in Figure 11-8. The reality is, not everyone has a friend, significant other, child, or talented pet nearby to lend a hand and/or paw to get the perfect shot. Desperate times call for desperate — or as I like to think of them, *extra creative* — measures.

Turn to any of the following pieces of equipment to star in your own photos:

- **Tripod:** A tripod holds your camera, which then frees you up to stir or sauté with one hand while you snap a photo with the other. Tripods also maintain the framing of your shot so repeat shots have the same setup (if desired).
- **Shutter-release cord:** Shutter-release cords are tethered to your camera at varying distances, giving you the ability to take a photo without pressing the shutter button on your actual camera. They cost around $10, depending on the quality.

- **Shutter-release remote:** Shutter-release remotes function the same as cords, however, they're wireless. They cost around $12 at the cheaper end, but more high-end options can cost up to $40.
- **Auto-timer:** If you're a patient person, skip the cords and remotes and take advantage of your camera's auto-timer function.

Figure 11-8: Star in your own photos by using a tripod and shutter-release remote.

A tripod is a photographer's best friend or biggest enemy. Many professionals swear by the three-legged camera perch, whereas others swear it off entirely. Consider the pros and cons of this basic photography tool:

- **Pros:** Advocates of tripods insist they provide stability for your photos and make it easier to get the exact same camera angle for repeat shots. Tripods also free up your hands and give you more flexibility in the process of taking a photo.
- **Cons**: Opponents of tripods argue the equipment is more of a burden than a blessing because it keeps a photographer chained to one specific camera angle. Your creativity is kept in check and your efficiency is put to the test because it's often difficult and cumbersome to constantly adjust and readjust the height and positioning of your camera.

Assembling Your Food-Styling Toolkit

I always take a quarter sheet tray stocked with my essential food-styling tools onto set with me. And by "set," I mean the space five steps outside my kitchen (you may know it by its less cool name, the "living room"). But a toolkit jam-packed with every gadget and utensil imaginable isn't necessary. Figure 11-9 depicts a few of my go-to items, including olive oil, a water spritzer, Q-tips, wooden skewers, and clear silicone earplugs (surprisingly, not used for noise!) to name a few.

The following list provides a comprehensive list of tools for your food-styling kit — including my go-to tools shown in Figure 11-9 and a few others. Every person has their unique needs and preferences, so pick and choose as you see fit. I must emphasize that these tools are for food styling and not food preparation. That's a separate (although not entirely different) list.

- **A sharp knife:** A sharp knife is the fastest way to make precise, camera-ready cuts. From slicing a cake to carving a porterhouse, always keep a sharp knife on hand to cut clean slices or to correct any less-than-perfect edges.
- **Long tweezers:** They might look like a tool from sixth grade science class, but larger-than-life tweezers are every food stylists' go-to instrument for every task from placing individual peas in a pasta dish to stacking ice cubes in a tall pitcher.

  The tweezers in Figure 11-9 are 10 inches long, but the 8- or 12-inch varieties serve the same purpose. I purchased mine on Amazon for less than $2.

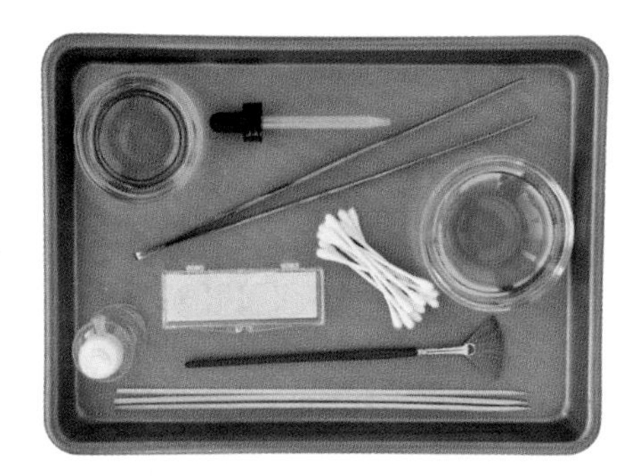

Figure 11-9: A portable quarter sheet tray ensures your essential tools are always in reach.

- **Q-tips:** Much like tweezers allow for precise placements, Q-tips allow for precise clean-ups. Keep a handful of Q-tips at your disposal to clean inside cocktail and Champagne glasses, to soak up unwanted liquids, or to swiftly clear excess crumbs.
- **A spray bottle:** Fill small spray bottles with your choice of liquids, such as Windex, water, olive oil, or glycerin. Always label your liquids to avoid confusion and remember that using Windex or glycerin will make your food inedible.
- **Various liquids:** A spritz of olive oil on meats adds a fresh-off-the-grill glow, whereas a spritz of glycerin adds sturdy beads of condensation. Water is also an all-purpose moisturizer, and a quick splash will freshen up sliced fruits and veggies. Windex just might be the answer to all your food-styling needs. From removing a sticky residue on a surface to providing a streak-free shine on a cocktail glass, there really are fewer all-purpose solutions. (A small bowl of Windex, rather than a large bottle of it, makes for easy dipping with Q-tips.)
- **Wooden skewers:** The length and fine point of wooden skewers makes them the prime tool for making intricate adjustments on any plate or in any narrow cocktail glass.

Wooden skewers also make great props. But how do you photograph a standing skewer when you're playing the roles of both food stylist and photographer? Rather than buy a block of Styrofoam, I fill a container with uncooked rice or oatmeal and use it to hold the skewers, as shown in Figure 11-10, which depicts the behind-the-scenes setup and the final shot for deep-fried tortellini on-a-stick.

- **An off-set spatula:** A small off-set spatula functions much like an artist's spatula, giving you the flexibility to swirl and shape with a natural flair. Utilize the tool for molding mashed potatoes, smearing whipped cream, and everything else in between.
- **An eyedropper:** Similar to a spray bottle, an eyedropper gives you total control over adding liquids to a dish featuring sauces or dressings.

Figure 11-10: Wooden skewers are effective as food-styling tools and props.

- **A kitchen blowtorch:** Kitchen blowtorches aren't just for adding a crackled crust to crème brûlée anymore! The next time you're having trouble getting an entire roast to keep its just-out-of-the-oven glow, hit it with the flames from a blowtorch. The fiery heat instantly causes the roast to plump, transforming it from dull to juicy in mere seconds.

  A blowtorch is also handy for heating up the blade of your knife prior to slicing through a chilled cake. A warm knife leads to precise, crumble-free slices.
- **Paper towels/spare bowls:** A *false bottom* is a fabricated, hidden place-holder that takes up space (so less food is needed to fill the plate or bowl) and prevents food from weighing itself down. A wad of paper towels and small bowls make good false bottoms.

A false bottom helps food appear more plump and lively, rather than depressed. For example, a false bottom is placed inside a salad bowl because otherwise, the lettuce would smash the lettuce beneath it.

To create a false bottom, simply ball up a wad of paper towels and encase them in plastic wrap, or place a smaller bowl upside-down inside a larger bowl, as shown in Figure 11-11.

Figure 11-11: Use a false bottom to prevent spaghetti from compressing.

- **Candle wax/silicone earplugs:** The tacky property of both candle wax and silicone earplugs make them the perfect tools for securing small props in place. Affix forks and knives on the edge of a plate, angle a spoon against a bowl, prevent objects from rolling, and more.
- **A paintbrush:** Get in touch with your inner Monet by swapping olive oil for oil paints. A few brushstrokes of the golden liquid on your seared meats and vegetables add a glistening glow, one stroke at a time.
- **Salt:** Aside from serving as a staple seasoning in your kitchen, salt is used for a variety of food-styling fixes and adornments, such as atop seared chicken or steak or simply as an often forgotten tabletop prop. Sea salt is an especially effective salt for garnishing because its larger flakes are more easily seen than regular table salt, as shown in Figure 11-12.

Figure 11-12: Large flakes of sea salt add a decorative touch atop salted caramels.

But salt isn't just for show! A glass of beer or Champagne is best captured with a foamy head. So how do you keep it frothy for more than a single shot? Add just a pinch of salt and let the carbonation work its magic. Depending on your personal taste preferences, salting a beer could make it undrinkable, and salting a glass of Champagne will *definitely* make it undrinkable. This trick is generally used only by the pros when glasses of beer and Champagne have been on set for extended periods of time and still need to retain their frothy head.

12

Styling and Photographing Food

In This Chapter

- Homing in on your personal approach to food styling
- Getting insider tricks of the food-styling trade
- Creating your timeline, from preheating to plating
- Understanding the importance and influence of props
- Constructing a studio setup in your home
- Taking photos in restaurants
- Editing your photos with free online resources

The plate of food you capture through your lens is a complete reflection of your own personal tastes, both in the form of flavor and in the form of style. How you depict every crumb, dollop, splatter, and drizzle identifies your distinctive approach. Do you keep it natural and let the lasagna do its thing? Or do you glue each grated granule of Parmesan into place to create your perfect plate?

You, as the food stylist, are left to decide whether going *au naturale* or faking your food is your route of choice. Over the years I've drawn inspiration from the countless food stylists I've observed in action. Learning the trade by studying the style of Santos Loo, master stylist for all your favorite Food Network shows, and working alongside Paul Grimes, all-star editor and stylist at *Gourmet,* taught me to hone my natural food-styling craft in the kitchen.

The techniques I share in this chapter are tried and tested tips to encourage you to find your own unique approach to plating and propping. You also learn to construct a standard in-home studio setup and discover how to transfer your photography skills from your kitchen to a restaurant table. A foray into the variety and functionality of free photo-editing programs adds the finishing touches to your culinary masterpiece.

Finding Your Style

In this section, I unveil the insider tips and tricks of the professional food-styling trade. You discover the ins and outs of two different approaches, natural and edible versus fabricated and indigestible. Although each one comes with a side of pros and cons (listed in Table 12-1), both enable you to style your food so it looks just as good as it tastes.

Table 12-1 Natural versus Artificial Food Styling

Food-Styling Approach	*Pros*	*Cons*
Natural	Food remains edible. No additional styling products are required or need to be purchased. Food remains authentic to its actual appearance.	Food may have a shorter lifespan for photographing. Food may not appear as appetizing.
Artificial	Food has a longer lifespan for photographing. Food can appear more appetizing.	Food is inedible. Additional styling products are required and will have to be purchased. Food may not remain authentic to its actual appearance.

Much like painting, sculpting, and sketching, food styling is an art form that conveys emotion, tonality, and inspiration. Whether you're a newbie to the craft or the Vincent van Gogh of gastronomy, approaching food styling from the mindset of an artist leaves the door wide open for creativity.

No matter what food styling method you choose, timing is everything. From choosing props to taking practice shots, I cover all the essential steps of your styling timeline in the later section "Timing your process." It's also important (and perhaps obvious) to point out that if you do go the artificial route, you cannot eat the faked food after you've styled it. So although I provide tips and tricks for artificially styling like the pros, the reality is that few food bloggers actually opt for the artificial route because most food bloggers eat what they cook.

Going au naturale

The natural approach to food styling is about maintaining the authenticity and edibility of a dish. It's about shining the spotlight on purity, in all its imperfect forms.

Figure 12-1 is an example of a naturally styled plate of food. You could eat every last bite of the pan-fried tilapia and edamame succotash, without fear of shoe polish poisoning or death by push pin.

Figure 12-1: The natural approach creates an edible and authentic representation of the dish.

Steering clear of glue, thumb tacks, wax, and countless other food-styling tricks preserves the real-life nature of the food. Slight blemishes (the white parts on the fish, which would be airbrushed out if that image appeared in a magazine) are embraced, rather than buffed out.

Most importantly, the natural approach provides your reader with a tangible, realistic goal if she was to make the dish in her own kitchen. For this reason, I advocate for the natural approach because the food I photograph for my blog is actually what I'm eating that day. Natural styling is about the integrity of the ingredients and not tricking your viewer's eye, no matter how crumbly the cookie or shapeless the stew.

But with purity comes a shorter shelf life because the absence of fake food means your window to capture a dish in its prime shrinks. Quality and beauty can be sacrificed as ingredients give way to the natural timeline of decay. For brownies and doughnuts, this might not be a problem. But for ice cream, cocktails, and a variety of sauces and oil-based dressings that can separate, it becomes a race against the clock.

The natural approach to food styling produces a realistic portrayal of a dish, and your job is to seize the moment when it looks its freshest to capture an image that's both authentic and appetizing.

Faking your food

From glue and glycerin to cotton balls and Karo syrup, the number of ways to fabricate food is limited only by your own imagination. Food styling the unnatural way makes use of all things edible and inedible to create an appealing presentation.

Figure 12-2: Two bowls of the same cereal highlight the differences between the natural and artificial approaches to food styling.

For example, consider the photos in Figure 12-2, which feature crunchy squares of the same oatmeal cereal. Take a closer look at the milk — or should I say, "milk" — in the photo on the left. If you were to enjoy a spoonful of the cereal shown here, you wouldn't be able to explain how sweet and satisfying it is — and not because it's gone stale, but because your mouth would be sealed shut . . . by the glue. Elmer's glue (shown in Figure 12-3) is a common substitute for milk, especially in cereal shots because the thick liquid holds its shape and still retains the illustrious shine of dairy. Edible? Not so much. Practical? Absolutely.

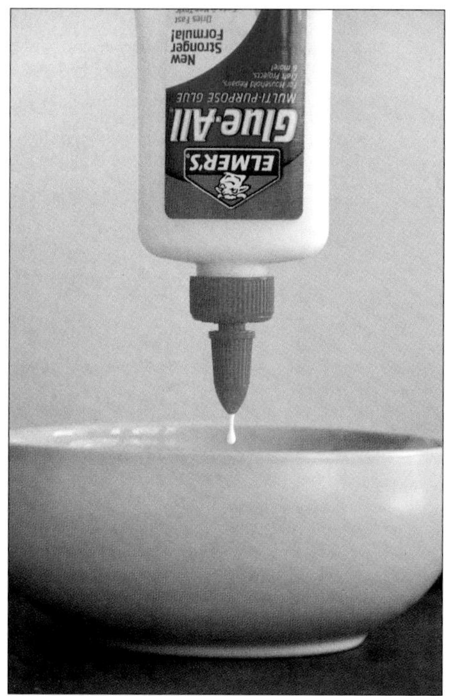

Figure 12-3: Food stylists turn to Elmer's glue as the ultimate substitute for milk.

Food stylists employ a whole bag of tricks when making food look its best for hours at a time while under hot lights on set. In addition to glue, a few of the more widely used substitutes include

- **Kitchen Bouquet:** Kitchen Bouquet is a browning and seasoning sauce that's been on grocery store shelves since 1879. It's an edible alternative for giving meat an illustrious, juicy sheen and is diluted in water to create a stand-in for coffee and iced tea.
- **Cotton balls:** Forget personal hygiene; cotton balls are your new go-to source for steam. Soak the cotton balls in water

and then microwave them until they start steaming. Stash the hot cotton balls behind a cup of coffee for a freshly brewed look to your cup of Joe.

- **Acrylic ice cubes:** Ice is one of the hardest ingredients to work with in food styling for the obvious reason that it melts. Acrylic ice cubes take the place of the real deal and look entirely authentic. The downside is they cost anywhere from $20 to $30 a bag for the higher-end options. Search for the ice cubes on Amazon.com to find the quantity and style that best suits your needs.
- **Powdered sugar:** Also on the Hard to Style List is ice's cousin: ice cream. Although mashed potatoes were originally food stylists' go-to substitute, more modern techniques involve blending store-bought frosting with powdered sugar until you achieve your desired color and texture. The pliable mixture will scoop and crumble like its real-life counterpart and won't melt in mere minutes.

Figure 12-4: Glycerin creates the illusion of condensation on foods and drinks.

- **Glycerin:** Glycerin is a colorless, odorless thick liquid that can be purchased at your local drug store for around $5. The water-soluble liquid is poured into a spray bottle and spritzed onto foods and drinks to create the illusion of condensation. The thick droplets stick to a subject and hold their shape for hours, such as the "condensation" I created on the grapes in Figure 12-4, which have the fresh appeal of being washed recently.

Each of these substitutes gives food a sustained lifespan, allowing photographers the time required to get the perfect shot. Although the swap-ins make the food inedible in real-life, they also ironically make it appear more appetizing in photographs. But there is such a thing as overdoing it. Too many tricks, and the food can start to look unappetizing. That defeats the end goal of food styling: to make your meal more attractive and enticing.

Funding your fake food habit

A bottle of Kitchen Bouquet here, a few cotton balls there, and before you know it, you're funding a fake food habit that may cost you more than the real meal itself. But the truth is that fake food-styling tricks involving glycerin, glue, and every other inedible substitute are generally used only by professional food stylists. Put more simply: Food bloggers don't fake their food because generally food bloggers eat their food.

Although the more extreme tricks, such as subbing glue for milk, are most common in the world of food advertising, it still helps to understand the sleight of hand (and added costs) as you perfect your own approach to food styling. For example, while setting up the glue shot in Figure 12-3, I actually made a false bottom from a plastic lid and tape (shown here), so I wouldn't have to buy or waste bottle after bottle of Elmer's finest on a food setup that wasn't even edible. Every small purchase adds up, so before you dive headfirst into a sea of acrylic ice cubes, keep in mind the extra budget it takes to *fake* your food.

Faking various elements of a composed dish can provide an inaccurate visual, which leads astray anyone who attempts to makes the dish. This is mostly a concern for images paired with recipes (and not advertisements), but it's always a good idea to have the integrity of the dish in mind when you're styling, regardless whether you're depicting the real deal or an inedible rendition.

Food Styling Like the Pros

Regardless whether the food in your photos is edible or otherwise, it takes an artistic eye to create a well-styled shot. But "well-styled" is a relative term because food beauty really is in the eye of the beholder.

Although everyone will be in search of different styles and tones, all stylists can benefit from a crash course in Food Styling 101:

- **Enhancing, not engulfing:** Don't over-sauce or over-garnish your food and instead let the pureness of the ingredients in the meal shine.
- **Keeping it real:** Regardless whether you're using the natural food-styling method or are turning to inedible components, pay attention to how the food would (and should) look in real life.
- **Portioning with precision:** Keep in mind the portion sizes depicted in your shot, which will also be impacted by the size of the serving dish you use.
- **Staying goal-oriented:** Always remember what the photograph you are taking will be used for. Is it for a recipe post? An advertisement? Both? This will ensure you portray an accurate tone and style for your shot.
- **Garnishing like you mean it:** Garnishes are one of my pet peeves in the culinary industry. They either artfully and relevantly enhance the appearance of a dish, or they miss the mark entirely and become useless, inedible excuses to beautify food. Garnishes can be placed atop and even around a dish, such as the chopped hardboiled egg shown as a garnish for traditional gazpacho in Figure 12-5. Regardless of where you position them, garnishes should serve a purpose by enhancing the flavor and the appearance of your dish.

Figure 12-5: Feature edible garnishes atop and around your plated dish.

Timing your process

You've just sliced your golden brown chicken breast and fanned it over a bed of couscous. The steam is seeping from each slice like smoke signals waiting to be captured by your lens. You quickly march your masterpiece to the table to take a photo, but then you can't find your camera, the tablecloth you were hoping to use is wrinkled, and your favorite silverware is missing. Ten minutes have suddenly passed, all the juices have run out of the chicken, and the last ray of optimal daylight just snuck behind a cloud.

When I first started photographing food for my blog, I scrambled in this scenario. I'd be so anxious to cook — and eat — a dish, I'd forget about setting myself up long before preheating the oven so I could have every opportunity to get the best shot imaginable. After you miss getting a great shot, it doesn't take long to learn your lesson and wise up for the next round.

The following is the timeline I follow when taking food photos; it starts with an idea and ends with a beautiful image on your home page. Begin by deciding what you'll cook. In this example, I use a recipe for banana nut pancakes to illustrate the steps in the timeline that follows:

1. **Decide on tone.**

   After you know what dish you're making, decide on the look and feel of the photograph you want to capture. Will your photo be bright and lively, or dimly lit and moody? I was eating the banana nut pancakes for breakfast, so I wanted an airy, light setup that took advantage of the morning sunlight.

2. **Choose props and set up the shot.**

   Create the shot's entire setup, which includes laying out surfaces, selecting the serving dish(es), picking out cutlery, and brainstorming the best camera angle. I knew I wanted to keep this shot very simple and fresh, so I used a blue and green-striped dish cloth as my surface, a plain white background (that would contrast well with golden-colored pancakes), and a white, circular plate with just enough of a lip to catch a river of maple syrup.

3. **Take a series of practice shots.**

   Always take a practice shot before you plate your dish so you can decide right then and there whether your props work. To get an accurate read for what your image will look like, use a suitable stand-in for the food. I stacked two yellow dishes on my white plate to resemble pancakes, as shown in Figure 12-6.

Figure 12-6: Practice photos enable you to make tweaks before shooting time-sensitive food.

4. **Get cooking.**

   Prepare your dish, keeping in mind the various components that might be better assembled tableside by your setup versus in the kitchen, such as garnishes and sauces. For the pancakes, this meant cooking seven pancakes, which is more than I'd eat in a single meal. I needed the additional pancakes for stacking purposes to create height; otherwise, it'd be a less enticing tower of three pancakes barely visible over the lip of the plate. My cooking procedure also included pre-slicing pats of butter (and stashing them in the fridge), chopping extra pecans for a garnish, and moving my syrup from the pantry to the fridge to give it a thicker consistency.

5. **Photograph any desired in-process shots.**

   While cooking your dish, photograph any essential in-process shots that would provide helpful visual cues for your reader, such as the color of a seared protein or the texture and thickness of a sauce. Similarly, photograph individual ingredients or techniques that may be better explained through photos rather than simply through words.

6. **Plate your dish.**

   Put together the components of your dish, sans any time-sensitive garnishes (such as syrup), and position it on your setup.

7. **Photograph your dish.**

   If necessary, garnish the dish, and then photograph it from every angle you see fit by moving around your light. I knew I wanted to capture the height of the pancakes stacked atop one another as well as the syrup cascading from one pancake ledge to the next, so I positioned myself at eye-level with the dish, as shown in Figure 12-7. I made the most of the early morning sun to capture the available natural light and did not use a tripod so I could quickly test various angles for the shot.

8. **Dig in!**

   With your meal immortalized in digital form, it's now time to enjoy the fruits of your labor.

Figure 12-7: Following a timeline allows you to capture your dish in its prime.

By following this exact timeline, I captured the pancakes in their prime. From a few options, I selected the image in Figure 12-7 as the lead image for my Banana Nut Pancakes recipe post. I chose this particular photo of the 15 or so images I took because the syrup was falling at just the right position and was best captured by the angle of my camera. Later images I took at a higher angle showed the syrup in a pool on the bottom of the plate (shown in Figure 12-8), which I decided was too distracting and took away from my desired focal point (the textured ridges of the pancakes).

Speeding up your process

The food styling, propping, and photographing process outlined in the previous section is a thorough approach to capturing your meal in its prime. But sometimes you don't have 20 minutes to test the lighting, take a few practice photos, and pre-assemble your garnishes while wavering between two plates or three, silver or gold, napkin or doily.

Sometimes you cook a meal and all you can do is snap a single shot before the hunger strikes and within minutes you're a member of the Clean Plate Club.

If you're racing the clock or a crowd of ravenous teenagers, stick to these strategic tips to fast-forward your process as you go from raw ingredients to a final photo in no time flat:

- **Help yourself:** The last thing you want is to be running around the house in search of a camera battery while the flank steak goes up in flames. Set your camera out next to your photo setup, along with any other equipment, such as fill cards or reflectors. All equipment should be in plain sight and easily accessible, and batteries should always be charged.

Figure 12-8: A higher camera angle features an unwanted view of a pool of syrup.

- **Read your recipe:** The fastest way to stall your progress is by forgetting to thoroughly read through your recipe before you start cooking. Mistakes in the kitchen stretch out your timeline, and even worse, could make your meal inedible. Triple-check your "teaspoons" from your "tablespoons" and, if applicable, always preheat your oven before you even pick up a knife.
- **Streamline your setup:** The more decisions you can make in advance, the more streamlined your process will be. Don't wait until you have a finished dish to decide you're better off screwing in the daylight bulb. Gauge your photography environment by picking out your photo spot, laying out any props, and selecting your plate or serving dish before you start cooking. When the food is in motion, it's difficult and cumbersome to pause for miscellaneous styling additions.
- **Don't futz:** Although speediness requires precision, it's important to not let perfection be the enemy of good. And in the world of food styling and propping, "good" translates to "authentic." No need to spend five minutes strategically placing each fork. Instead, throw a handful of forks onto the table and let them do their thing. I guarantee your photo will look more natural and appealing than an image with an engineered arc of cutlery. The same goes for backgrounds and surfaces. When in doubt, default to a cutting board. Older, textured surfaces without any sheen are your best option because they don't reflect light and won't interfere with your image's exposure.
- **Hold the phone:** Literally. When I need a quick photo, I use my camera phone. Technology has made it so that a few simple snaps with my cell captures endless, high-end photos that are quickly uploaded and shared across the web. (See Chapter 10 for a refresher on camera phone photography.)

The Power of Propping

Props of every shape, size, and color help create the mood of your photograph by establishing the scene in which your food is placed. The goal of such stylistic additions is to help tell the dish's story by playing a supporting role to the food, rather than stealing the lead.

Much like your approach to food styling, your approach to prop styling is a direct reflection of your visual preferences and design taste. Start by answering the following question: Are you a minimalist or a maximalist?

In the field of prop styling, *minimalists* prefer only the essential items exist in the shot. This can include a serving dish or utensil, or just the pure food paired only with a background, such as the marshmallow pops depicted in Figure 12-9. Open space is a welcome respite for minimalists, who lean toward clean, crisp, and simple setups. The approach may connote a modern slant, or it can relay a sense of purity and the belief that "less is more."

Figure 12-9: Emphasize the food by taking a minimalist approach to propping.

Opposite the minimalists are those *maximalist* people who embrace embellishments and champion the belief that there is no such thing as too many props — a belief I challenge! An established space is preferred to open space, and tchockes are heralded rather than feared. But like a good steak, somewhere between *rare* and *well-done* rests *medium,* a complementary blend of the best of the minimalist and maximalist worlds.

Choosing props with a purpose

Consider three key factors when selecting the props for your shot:

- **Size and scale:** Are the props in your shot to scale with the food? For example, a soup spoon paired with a cup of espresso (as shown in Figure 12-10) or a platter used as a single-serving dessert plate is not only inaccurate, but also makes the image appear unbalanced.
- **Placement:** Depth of field plays a critical role in the placement of props, and their importance determines their degree of focus. If I want to simply hint at the idea of a party atmosphere surrounding my dish, I place beer or wine bottles far in the distance of my setup. Although out

of focus, the shapes of the bottles are still seen and the entertainment element is implied. (See Chapter 10 for a refresher on depth of field.)

- **Relevancy:** Maintain the contextual role of props by ensuring their relevancy in a shot. Use props that would naturally appear in the setting, such as an ice cream scoop in a sundae image, or a sprig of cilantro in a guacamole image. Relevant props and garnishes may seem obvious, but they're often forgotten or overlooked.

Orchestrating the extras

I approach propping food photographs from the viewpoint that props serve the same role as extras on a movie set. Although they don't play a central role and often blend in with the background, they are present *enough* to establish the context for a scene.

Figure 12-10: Props, such as a spoon paired with an espresso cup, should always be in correct proportion.

Much like backgrounds and surfaces, props lurk (and are in plain sight) all over, including your bathroom, your local flea market, your kitchen, and your corner bakery. Consider the following categories of props when setting up your shots.

Plates and bowls

They might seem like the most simple and straightforward props, but plates and bowls take on an entirely new tone depending on their quantity, style, and placement. A stack of dessert plates in the background of an image establishes that multiple people are digging in to your creation, whereas a giant bowl with a few smaller bowls scattered around it suggests a casual, everyone-help-themselves setup. The style of plates and bowls also plays a role in the mood they evoke. Fine china doesn't relay the same sense of a casual get-together as a set of mismatched plates and bowls.

The stacking technique is popular among food and prop stylists because it builds the always-coveted element of height into an image. Figure 12-11 depicts the stacking technique in action for pasta arrabiata with roasted eggplant. Take note of the empty bowl in the background, which implies the portioning of the meal is still in process.

Figure 12-11: Stack bowls to add height and create a group feel.

Cutlery

The amount of cutlery featured in a shot is one of the easiest ways to understand the degree to which props convey the emotion and context of a scene. An image with a fork placed next to a bundt cake evokes an entirely different feel than an image with five or six forks. One says, "I'm having a slice of cake alone," whereas the other says, "Party time!" (I'd be up for either.)

I am a big fan of using mismatched silverware — modern-style knives, silver forks, and tarnished spoons — to evoke a casual feel. To further relay a relaxed environment, try tossing the cutlery into a pile on the table. As a general rule for all types of props: The more careful attention you pay to individually positioning each piece, the more unnatural and contrived the scene will feel.

Opposite the smorgasbord approach is the table setting arrangement, which can be either casual or refined depending on the style of your cutlery. For example, a pearl-handle steak knife adds a fancier touch whereas a wooden-handle steak knife is less formal.

Knives are an optimal, go-to prop for conveying not only the tone of an image, but also the action. Positioning a chef's knife, paring knife, or serrated knife in an image is one of my favorite ways to depict the process of a recipe. Figure 12-12 showcases freshly cooked kernels being shaved off ears of corn with a knife as a natural in-process prop for quinoa with corn and scallions.

Figure 12-12: Positioning knives in a shot conveys a sense of process and action.

Although knives play a helpful role in conveying action, there is such a thing as overdoing it when it comes to the blade's prominence and placement. For example, the sheer size and positioning of the chef's knife in Figure 12-13 is overwhelming. Your eye is immediately drawn to the shiny, distracting tip of the blade, which dwarfs the Brussels sprouts and leads you away from the food-specific focal point of the image.

Glasses and bottles

The transparency of glasses and bottles make them the prime props for reflecting light and casting soft glows in an image. They also add a variety of heights and hues, from both the color of the vessel to the color of the liquid.

Figure 12-13: Large, poorly positioned knives draw the viewers' eyes away from the food-specific focal point of your image.

The appearance of beer and wine bottles adds another stylistic element to your setup. Darker bottles evoke a richer feel and are available in a wider variety of shapes. Clear glass adds an aura of airiness. Don't forget to maintain accuracy in your images by ensuring carbonated beverages are photographed in their bubbly state.

Featuring multiple bottles in a shot implies a crowd is enjoying the meal, without specifically showing the people. For example, Figure 12-14 depicts the faintly recognizable shapes of beer bottles in the distance (a product of the depth of field in the photo). Placed in context with party-friendly sirloin sliders with smoked bacon, and it's easily understood this dish was not enjoyed as part of a seven-course, sit-down dinner party, but rather as a casual snack among friends.

Figure 12-14: Positioning bottles in your setup implies a group gathering or party.

Staggering stemmed and stem-less wine glasses around a dish also allows the warm yellow or bold burgundy reflections to work their moody magic in your photograph. The variety of colors of both wine and beer provides welcome wiggle room for experimentation, although it's hard to beat the look and feel of a tall glass of golden lager illuminated by the sun's rays.

Cooking equipment

From grills and griddles to sauté pans and stock pots, the cooking equipment found in your kitchen is realistic (and readily available) for propping your photographs. Photographing the in-process element of your food highlights its authenticity and gives it a real-life allure.

Figure 12-15: Cooking equipment provides texture and action in an image.

Found under the sad-but-true category is the fact that at times your composed dish is not as attractive as the dish's individual ingredients. Rather than struggle with the final product, capture your food in action by snapping the ingredients in their various stages of cooking. For example, Figure 12-15 shows shrimp cooking on a grill pan in my kitchen.

I wasn't entirely satisfied with the final shot for these shrimp tossed in Buffalo sauce, so I chose to highlight the bright pink color of the seafood contrasted against the dark, patterned texture of the grill pan. Cooking equipment not only adds to the authentic nature of preparing the dish, but it also provides action moments otherwise not inherent in a plated setup.

Figure 12-16: People provide context and scale and help set the tone.

Even if you aren't entirely satisfied with your final shot of the completed dish, you should still feature the dish at the top of your recipe post and remember to name it appropriately for SEO purposes. For example, the final shot of the plated shrimp would be uploaded and named Grilled Buffalo Shrimp. (See Chapter 13 for more on SEO and naming images.)

People

When relevant (and accessible), use people as props to up the action in your shots and provide perspective on the size of your food. People are also particularly helpful in setting the tone and feel of a scene via their emotions, actions, and even their ensembles. For example, Figure 12-16 shows a friend of mine at a summer party. His hand is clasped around a grilled sirloin slider, which provides perspective for the size of the food; his t-shirt and grin allude to the laidback tone of the environment in which the food is being enjoyed.

Although Chapter 11 introduces you to the possibility of starring in the shots you're taking by using a tripod and shutter-release remote, one of your hands can actually appear in a shot without any extra equipment (or amputation) required. For example, in Figure 12-17, I'm holding chocolate-dipped pretzel rods — a photo featuring my left hand and taken using my right hand.

Figure 12-17: Featuring hands in a photo provides perspective.

Forgotten touches

You may not even recognize countless items as relevant props for your image:

- Beer bottle caps
- Wine wrappers and corks
- Salt and pepper shakers
- Crumbled napkins
- Straws
- Coasters

Each of these often forgotten touches adds an element of authenticity to your image by paralleling the natural feel of a real-life setting. Figure 12-18 depicts the difference between a photo without added details and a photo with added details, including a salt dish, wine bottle, corkscrew, wine wrapper, and cork.

Figure 12-18: Forgotten touches, such as a corkscrew, bottle, or wine wrapper, add authenticity to your image.

Constructing Your Setup

If you've followed along so far, you have your background, your fill cards, and your lighting. Time to put it all together. In this section, I give you a sneak peek of a standard food photography setup.

The following layout is achieved easily in your home. Have no fear if your space is limited. If I can make this setup work in my small New York City apartment, chances are you can make it work in your home, too.

In the following setup, I assume you're shooting in prime conditions, which means using natural, rather than artificial, light. Although sunlight should be your first choice, if a light bulb is your only option, utilize this same setup.

To construct your photo setup, follow these steps:

1. **Position your basic surface, such as a table, next to a window.**
2. **Lay out your background and your fill cards.**

   Figure 12-19 demonstrates the lineup of these essential items.

   Your white fill cards are what you use to bounce the light. *Bouncing* is a photographer's way of redirecting the light to best illuminate the subject and achieve the desired mood in a photograph. In Figure 12-19, I angled the fill cards to bounce the light directly back onto the salad to fill in some of the darker areas and brighten the overall shot.
3. **Adjust the angle and position of the fill cards according to your specific lighting needs:**
   - *Less light:* To decrease the amount of light reflecting onto your subject, simply move the fill cards farther away. Increasing the distance between your subject and the fill cards gives the light a longer distance to travel after it reflects, which lessens its intensity. Also consider using a black fill card to take away some of the highlights on your subject.
   - *More light:* To increase the amount of light reflecting onto your subject, simply move the fill cards closer. Decreasing the distance between your fill cards and your subject gives the light a shorter distance to travel when it bounces back toward the subject, which in turn increases its intensity. Also consider using a silver reflector for an extra pop of bright light.
4. **Assess your image from every camera angle imaginable.**

   Don't be afraid to move yourself around the light source to test the various options. Photographing your subject with your light at the 3 o'clock position, as shown in Figure 12-19, provides a much different effect than photographing it with the light at the 12 o'clock position, as shown in Figure 12-20. Backlighting your subject by positioning the light directly behind your subject at 12 o'clock casts a deeper shadow at the front of the image.

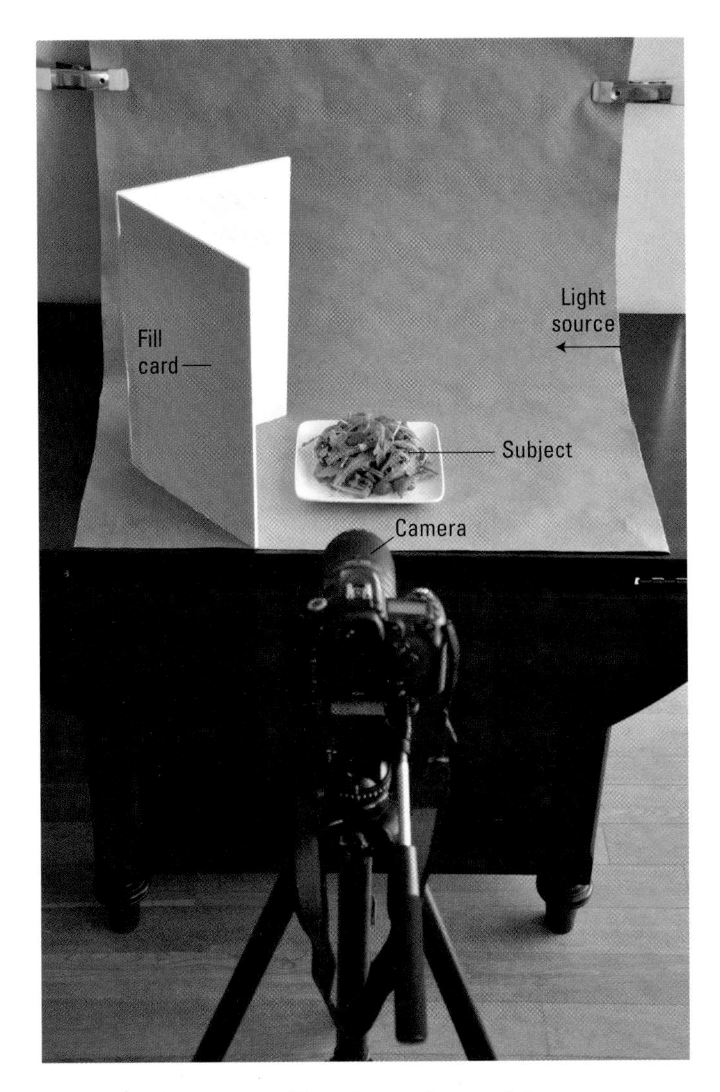

Figure 12-19: Position your fill cards opposite your light source.

5. **Capture the image.**

   Capture the image from every angle imaginable by taking multiple shots at higher and lower angles. Remember to also capture both horizontal and vertical variations of your food and to experiment with your framing and focus.

Getting just the right amount of light involves taking countless photos as you use trial and error to create your desired mood via your light source. You can also use bouncing techniques for restaurant photography, where your white napkin takes the place of your white fill cards, a technique I cover in the next section, "Photographing Food in Restaurants."

Remember to experiment with your setup to make the most of a variety of backgrounds and surfaces. If you're shooting at eye-level with your subject, such as in a hero shot, pay attention to the length of your surface. Figure 12-21 depicts one of my favorite surfaces, plain brown paper, which runs up and behind the plate of figs on what the pros call an *infinity board* setup (named for the endless appearance it takes on when photographed).

Figure 12-20: Shifting so that your light comes from the 12 o'clock position creates strong shadows in front of the subject.

Because I shot at eye-level with the figs, I had to run my surface up behind the plate; otherwise, you'd catch a glimpse of the corner of my dining room table and wall. To do this, I use a simple technique involving foam core board and spring clamps, which you can find at your local hardware store for less than $2. Figure 12-22 depicts the spring clamps in action and gives you a behind-the-scenes view of how I set up the fig shot.

Figure 12-21: When you're at eye-level with your subject, take note of the length of your surface to ensure it's long enough for the shot.

The brown paper gradually curves up behind the figs, taking the place of the painted wall behind them to provide a clean, infinite background for my photo. Switch in any type of paper or fabric to achieve the same effect, and avoid splurging on the $35 professional's version with this simple DIY setup.

Figure 12-22: Spring clamps are essential tools for your in-home studio and have a variety of uses.

Photographing Food in Restaurants

Restaurateurs, waiters, chefs, and hosts will all have their own take on tableside photography. Some restaurants have gone so far as to ban photographs from inside their establishments, either because they annoy other customers or because they fear the photos don't do their food justice. But still others embrace the idea of some (hopefully positive) free publicity blasted into the blogosphere.

If or when you decide to join the food paparazzi, keep in mind the unofficial code for restaurant photography etiquette:

- **Never use a flash.** It's incredibly disruptive, not to mention it's inevitably going to wash out your food by overexposing it, so the results won't be worth the effort.
- **Be discrete.** There's no need to remodel the dining room to get the perfect shot. Don't move tables, chairs, and fish tanks for the sake of your photo.

- **Remember your dining mates.** As much as that life-changing slice of lemon cake makes you want to immortalize it via a TwitPic, keep in mind other people are around you who actually came to the restaurant for the sole purpose of eating. (Crazy, right?)
- **Ask permission.** If you doubt whether the chef will mind a quick photo or two, ask your waiter for the go-ahead before letting loose with your lens.
- **Keep it to a minimum.** It's a meal, not a spread in *Vogue.* Avoid becoming a snap-happy Sally by limiting your number of clicks.

Although I cover the ideal in-home studio setup in Chapter 11, taking photos in a restaurant is an entirely different experience than shooting in your own home. If you decide to dabble in restaurant photography, pay attention to these important considerations:

- **Composition:** Composition of restaurant photos relates to framing and food styling. The good news is that because you're at a restaurant, the food is already styled for you. Try not to disrupt the authenticity of how a dish is presented and instead focus on best capturing the plate.

  Figure 12-23 depicts a photo I took at Per Se in New York City. I didn't so much as rearrange a single grain of salt on the plate. Then again, it'd be impossible to improve the look of anything created by master chef Thomas Keller and his team, so my job was a total, tasty breeze.

Figure 12-23: Avoid re-styling the composition of a restaurant dish in order to preserve its authenticity.

- **Lighting:** If at all possible, try to sit by the window to take advantage of any available natural light. Figure 12-24 depicts a photo I took inside Hill Country Chicken in New York City. I purposefully situated myself next to a large glass window to utilize the ample natural light to illuminate the fried chicken and fries.

  Of course window seating won't matter if you're past daylight hours. But regardless of the time, never use a flash because it disturbs other diners and overexposes your food. Instead, take advantage of the tools you're given to enhance your shot, including your white napkin. White napkins serve the same purpose as white poster boards for bouncing light onto your food. Napkins — they're not just for wiping your mouth anymore!

Figure 12-24: Positioning yourself by the window lets you take full advantage of any available natural light.

- **Perspective:** You can either sit or stand when taking photos in restaurants (your fellow dining patrons likely won't appreciate you sprawled across the floor or perched atop the bar). Make the most of your shot while minimizing disturbance by capturing your plate from the point of view of where you're sitting.
- **Props:** At the risk of crossing the annoying threshold, utilize the available tabletop props to maximize your photo. An upside-down water glass serves as a makeshift tripod to steady your shot, while the natural table setting (including candles, flowers, salt and pepper shakers, or wine glasses) provides context for your photo by placing it within a restaurant scene.
- **Notes:** When taking restaurant photos for the purpose of publishing them on your blog, don't forget to write down the name of the dish, the components, and of course, the taste (that is, assuming you're reviewing the restaurant's food and not their choice of china). You'd be surprised how easy it is to forget this step!

Using Free Programs to Edit Your Photos

Think of editing your photos like applying a final layer of frosting to a cake. The most essential part is already established (and hopefully drool-worthy), and now you just have to pretty it up with a few final swirls and sprinkles.

The goal of food photography is not to spend 5 minutes capturing your photo and 45 minutes editing it. Correcting for exposure, temperature, framing, and focus are all valuable uses for photo-editing software, but your first priority should be to get the best possible shot in the moment in which you are taking the picture. But for those times when the ice cream is melting quickly and the syrup is pooling faster than you can handle, editing software is your friend.

Typical editing tasks

You just finished photographing (and then eating) your favorite homemade pizza complete with Mom's marinara, spicy Italian sausage, and mounds of crunchy green peppers. With a full stomach, you settle down to upload your photos and start writing your post. One by one the photos appear on your computer screen and suddenly your mind launches into a game of 20 Questions. *Is that a stray mushroom in the shot? Is the cheese really that yellow? Did I forget to turn off the florescent kitchen light? Why is the pizza so centered in the frame?*

Photographing food requires an attention to detail, but lucky for you, photo-editing software can bare some of that burden. Although it's never a good idea to rely entirely on editing to create the best image, a handful of typical editing tasks enable you to take your photo from blah to brilliant, including the ability to adjust these things:

- **Brightness:** Increases or decreases lightness
- **Contrast:** Alters the difference between the lightest and darkest areas
- **Cropping:** Adjusts the focal point to improve framing
- **Exposure:** Brightens or darkens highlights
- **Rotation:** Moves or flips alignment
- **Saturation:** Increases or decreases the strength or purity of colors
- **Size:** Scales up or down

Each of these adjustments can enhance the appearance of your photos, but your best bet is to avoid making such tweaks by remembering the following details while in the process of capturing your image:

- **Focus on framing:** As obvious as it may sound, always remain conscious of exactly what you see through your lens. Look up and down, left and right to ensure you see every element within your framed shot.
- **Give yourself options:** Take both horizontal and vertical versions of your image, regardless whether you think you'll use both options. I can't even count how many times I've stared down a slew of vertical images only wishing I'd taken a single horizontal shot.
- **Preview your shots:** After you take your first photo, immediately review it on your camera. Previewing your shots in your camera gives you the option early on to make any necessary tweaks, such as removing stray crumbs or re-positioning a garnish. It's always better to fix a flub in the moment than to rely on post-production.

Assessing free editor options

Save your dollars for dinner by opting for any of the wide variety of free photo-editing programs, such as Pixlr (`www.pixlr.com`), Photoscape (`www.photoscape.org`), or Picasa (`www.picasa.google.com`). Although a majority of the free programs offer the same basic editing functions, the most popular and comprehensive editor is the GNU Image Manipulation Program (GIMP), which is downloadable software.

Regardless of what program you choose, be careful not to overdo it with the photo-editing. It's easy to get carried away with the editing process, so be mindful of the common errors in overexposing and over-saturating an image, both of which detract from the authenticity of your original photo.

Splurging versus saving on software

Adobe Photoshop and Adobe Lightroom are two of the premiere photo-editing software options with a level of quality and functionality that are hard to beat. But they also come with a hefty price tag in the hundreds of dollars range. So if you're looking to save and still do some more than basic touch-ups, consider either of the following mid-level software programs:

- **PaintShop Photo Pro:** PaintShop Photo Pro is a powerful photo-editing software with a user-friendly interface and extensive editing tools for all your cropping, framing, and formatting needs. The program costs around $100 and includes a comprehensive Learning Center to answer questions at any point along the photo-editing process.
- **Photoshop Elements:** Photoshop Elements is a simple, straightforward photo-editing software perfect for first-time photo editors. The program costs around $80 and includes a wide range of special effects options, such as the ability to merge two photos into one or airbrush specific sections of an image.

Available on multiple platforms, GIMP is easy to install and run and can be downloaded via `www.gimp.org`. With just a few simple clicks, you'll be maximizing the quality of your photos without splurging on a professional-grade program. Figure 12-25 depicts the GIMP interface along with a pre-edited version of my photo of garlic knots. The colors in this image are washed out (not saturated enough); the image has too cold of a tone; and the image isn't bright enough.

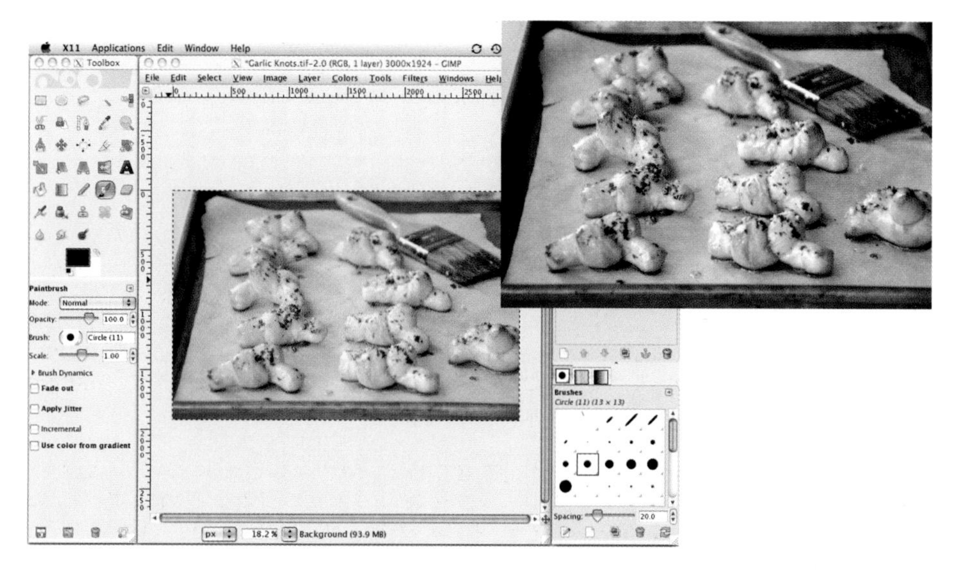

Figure 12-25: The GNU Image Manipulation Program provides advanced photo-editing functionality for free.

I spent two minutes tweaking a few elements of the photo, including balancing the color scheme by lessening the blue hues and enhancing the saturation of the colors. I also increased the contrast so that the garlic knots appeared more pronounced against the white parchment paper. Figure 12-25 depicts the resulting photo, post-editing. GIMP provides comprehensive tutorials for the most basic editing needs all the way through its most advanced editing functions.

Part V
Marketing & Monetization

"Oh, we're doing just great. Philip and I are selling decorative jelly jars on my blog. I run the Web site and Philip sort of controls the inventory."

In this part . . .

After your blog is up and running, focus on getting your content in front of as many readers as possible while entertaining the thought of how you're going to make a profit from all your hard work.

In Part V, you discover the strategic tips for using search engine optimization (SEO) to get the most out of every post as you up your rank and extend your brand across the blogosphere. Discover the pros and cons of ad networks, find out how to effectively interact with sponsors, and master the many ways of bringing home the bacon.

13

(Super) Marketing

In This Chapter

- Promoting your content on other blogs and sites
- Organizing your content
- Understanding the impact of search engine optimization
- Interacting outside the pages of your own blog
- Tracking your day-to-day traffic

"If you build it, they will come."

Sure, *they* will come. But in the case of beginner food bloggers, the "they" is generally your immediate and extended family. Other than readers related to you by blood or marriage, who else is going to spend time on your blog?

The answer depends entirely on you because you are the biggest champion of your blog. Although a future *Oprah* moment may be in your cards, you can't rely on anyone but yourself to spread the word about your brand. Rather than "set it and forget it," if you really want people to consume all the content you're creating, you need to "set it and spread it" — everywhere.

In this chapter, I share the strategic ways of widening your blog's visibility online. Discover the tools for effectively and efficiently getting the most out of search engine optimization (SEO), tracking your progress, and becoming an integral part of the greater food blogging community.

Envisioning Your Blog as a Brand

After your blog is up and running, your main job is creating stellar content for your specific niche, regardless whether you joined the blogosphere in search of a casual hobby or to establish a serious business. As the steady stream of posts gracing your home page grows, so too will the eyes that read and interact with your content.

But relying on your immediate circle of readers and organic traffic from search engine results isn't enough to propel you into Major League Blogging. To make the jump from the minors, you need to positively and proactively get your content in front of as many eyeballs as possible.

Before you market and publicize your content, if you really want to hit it big with traffic or revenue, you have to view your blog, and more importantly yourself, as your brand. You aren't just promoting your blog as a landing spot for the best grilling recipes or the most exclusive restaurant reviews. You are promoting yourself as *the* valuable and credible resource within your niche. I discuss the technical elements of building your blog into a brand through the consistency and frequency of your content in Chapter 6, but now it's time to look at the big picture and to envision your prime seat at the food blogging table.

For example, I visit David Lebovitz's self-titled blog (`www.davidlebovitz.com`), as shown in Figure 13-1, because I know that I can trust David as an expert recipe developer and cookbook author who publishes recipes that he has created, tested, and perfected. I find added reassurance in the thriving comments section, which includes constructive feedback from my fellow, passionate foodies who have also cooked and tasted his recipes while testing his technique tips.

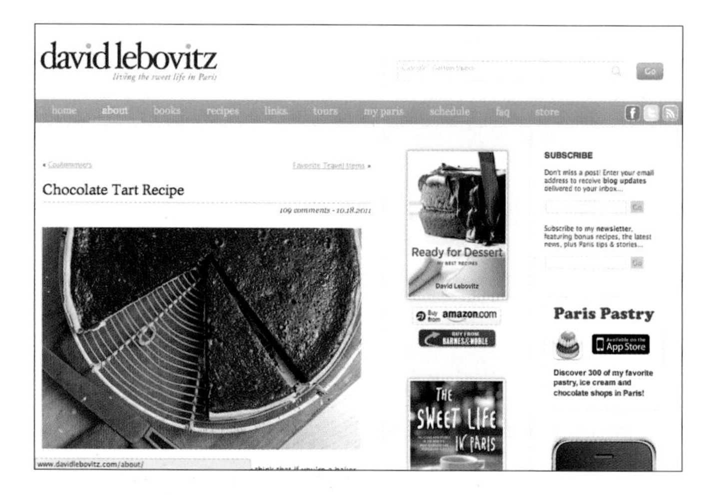

Figure 13-1: David Lebovitz has established himself as a food blogger you can trust.

Becoming Your Own Publicist

After cook, food stylist, writer, editor, and photographer, you have one more role to add to your growing list of duties: publicist. Broadly speaking, a *publicist* is responsible for creating and managing the attention generated by and around a client, as well as serving as the communication bridge between that client and the public (hence the industry name *public relations*).

Publicity is generated in the form of reviews, mentions, event appearances, interviews, TV segments, and any other form of media tied to fostering a client's positive image. In the case of your food blog, you are the publicist *and* the client, so I hope you like working with yourself!

Some press attention may result organically from the inventive content you're creating, such as your Peanut Butter Whoopie Pies recipe post being named as Best of the Web by *SAVEUR* or a link from Epicurious to your ingenious tips for preparing artichokes. Other mentions may result from you actively pushing your content into the best places to be seen, such as by submitting your food photos to foodgawker or TasteSpotting. (I discuss both in the later section, "Promoting your visual content.")

Regardless of what way you attract press, keep track of the attention and acclaim you and your food blog receive. In Chapter 8, I cover the essential elements of blog navigation, which includes featuring a separate page dedicated to press mentions and awards. The page doesn't have to be elaborate and can simply display a chronological list of any important acknowledgments, such as the Press page on Savory Sweet Life, as shown in Figure 13-2.

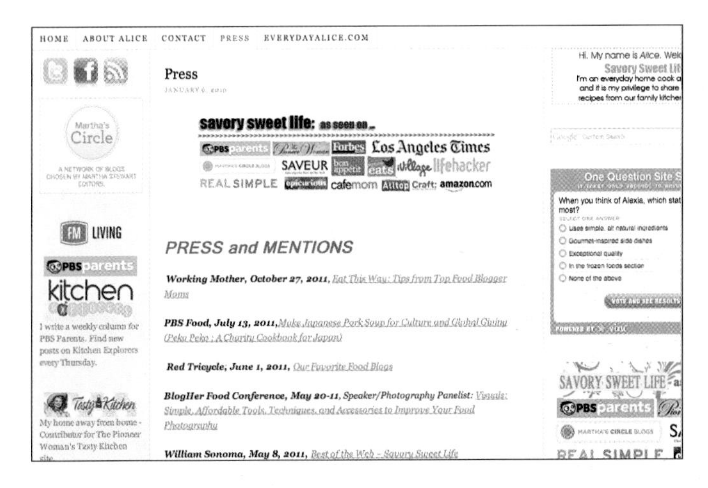

Figure 13-2: Alice Currah of Savory Sweet Life keeps a running list of notable press mentions.

Other than reading the list of incoming links from your statistics tracker (which I discuss later in this chapter), the easiest way to stay tuned to your brand's mentions across the web is to create a Google alert for the name of your blog and for your own name. To create an alert, go to `www.google.com/alerts`, enter as many variations of your name and your blog's name as desired, and then select how often you want to receive alerts.

In addition to maintaining a Press page, displaying badges for food blog awards or nominations you receive alerts readers to your press-worthy achievements. Badges are generally displayed in your sidebar (see Chapter 9 for more on uploading badges). A few of the more widely recognized distinctions include badges for the *SAVEUR* Sites We Love, the *SAVEUR* Food Blog Awards, and the James Beard Award for Excellence (see Figure 13-3).

Figure 13-3: Highlight your achievements in your blog's sidebar.

Acknowledgments range in scale from a fellow blogger featuring your recipe for quinoa with corn and scallions, to the *New York Times* Diner's Journal linking to your review of the now shuttered elBulli. Regardless of their weight, maintaining a running log of your press mentions and awards has several important purposes:

- It demonstrates a degree of authority and achievement, regardless whether you have 5 acknowledgments or 500.
- It helps you easily and effectively keep track of the praise you garner.
- It provides a place for anyone and everyone to quickly gauge your position as a recognized leader or expert in your niche.

Although critical acclaim may not be your only meter for success, it never hurts to receive positive feedback for your work. Who doesn't love a little recognition for a job well done? As your blog grows, so too will the likelihood of it being recognized. Press — and specifically positive press — affects three key elements of your blog:

- **Credibility:** Acknowledgements from industry professionals, big and small, help establish your blog as a credible landing spot and valuable resource.

- **Traffic:** Press mentions increase your blog's traffic by surfacing your content in front of a new audience that may not have otherwise come across your site.
- **Revenue:** If you run ads on your site, as your traffic increases, so does your ad revenue. (See Chapter 14 for more on ads.)

Sharing Your Content

The online audience is always in search of the next entertaining read, captivating photograph, or informative video. Don't let such a starving group go hungry.

High-quality, creative content naturally promotes itself. But even a perfectly seared filet mignon can benefit from a few extra touches in the form of a peppercorn crust or red wine reduction to increase its appeal. Sharing your content — be it text, photos, or videos — across a variety of highly trafficked sites exposes your brand to a whole new audience. Similarly, making your content easily accessible to your readers gives them one more reason to return for another helping.

In this section, I discuss two things: how RSS feeders help you — and your readers — distribute your blog posts; and ways to promote your visual content. These techniques are effective ways to increase your reach with the end goal of boosting your traffic and visibility online. The follow-up strategy is to then make it simple enough for your readers to share and spread your content. (See Chapter 9 for more on implementing content-sharing widgets.)

Feeding your readers' cravings

One of the best ways to keep your readers in tune with your blog updates is to use a Really Simple Syndication (RSS) feed (originally known as the RDF Site Summary). An *RSS feed* functions like a magazine subscription model by allowing readers who sign up to automatically receive updates when you publish new content.

In addition to giving your audience members a taste of your latest content updates, RSS feeds are an efficient tool with a variety of benefits, including

- **Accessibility:** An RSS feed makes content more easily accessible and quickly digestible by your audience. And with so many food blogs in existence, the faster and easier it is for readers to see your content, the better.

- **Reach:** The easier readers can engage with your content, the larger audience it will attract. An RSS feed drives more traffic (and repeat traffic) to your blog and also extends its reach across the web.
- **Communication:** An RSS feed streamlines communication between you and your audience by providing them with the opportunity to opt in to automatic updates.

Rather than your readers visiting every one of their favorite blogs to see whether new content has been uploaded, RSS feeds do the work for them by pulling in updates from all the blogs they subscribe to. They can then access the content via an RSS reader or e-mail.

Receiving feeds through an RSS reader

An *RSS reader* (or *feed reader*) is the software that houses all the various feeds your readers subscribe to. Think of an RSS reader as the mailbox outside your home. Every time a new publication is released, it's delivered to the reader, which aggregates all the fresh content into one easily accessible place. You can choose from thousands of readers. A few of the most popular are Google Reader, shown in Figure 13-4, which displays your feeds in an easily digestible format; Bloglines (`www.bloglines.com`); and NewsGator (`www.newsgator.com`).

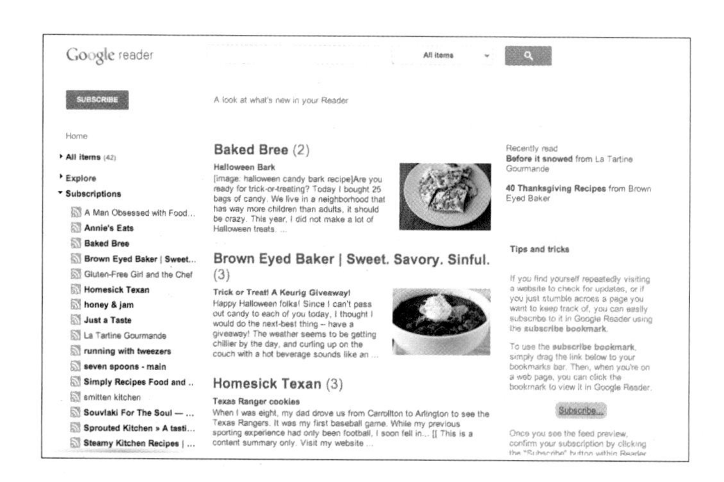

Figure 13-4: Google Reader aggregates feeds you subscribe to.

To subscribe to each of the feeds listed in Google Reader, I clicked the RSS icon on the various blogs I read and selected Google Reader as the destination for my content delivery. Every time a blog I subscribe to publishes a new post, I see the update in my reader, scan the content, and click the headlines that interest me the most.

Receiving feeds through e-mail

If you'd rather not juggle a separate portal in the form of an RSS reader, you can receive updates as e-mails. Fresh content is delivered straight to your inbox at a frequency determined by the feed creator. You can get a new e-mail serving once a week, once a month, or every time a new post is published.

An RSS feed contains either an entire post or a short summary of a post, with the option to include photos. Although you decide how much information you include, I opt for the summary version so your audience is driven to your blog for the full meal.

Figure 13-5 depicts a sample e-mail that subscribers to my feed receive every time I publish a new post. In addition to a linked headline and intro text, the e-mail also includes share functionalities, such as Digg This! or Stumble It!, for my blog readers to easily redistribute the content.

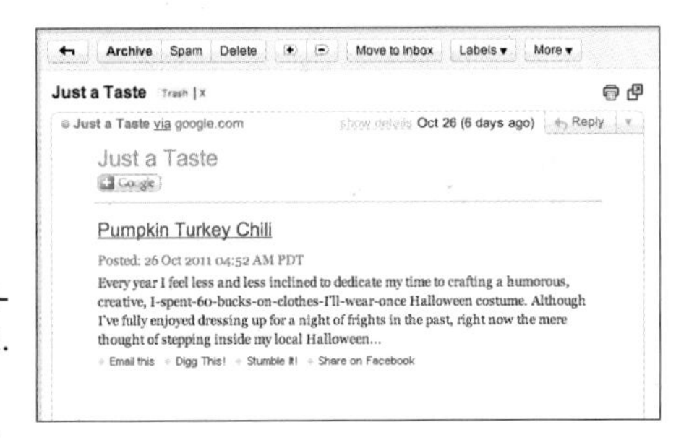

Figure 13-5: E-mail updates alert blog readers to new content.

When a reader "diggs" your content, she is submitting it to the sharing site, Digg (`www.digg.com`), which displays a list of the most popular content being shared across the web. Your content moves up or down in popularity based on how many people "digg" (read: like) it. Similarly, when a reader "stumbles" your content, she is sharing it on StumbleUpon (`www.stumbleupon.com`), a platform that finds and recommends content to its users based on previous content they've read. For example, after I log in to my StumbleUpon account, I browse through a wide variety of sites with the option to "like" or "dislike" the similar sites StumbleUpon suggests. StumbleUpon is then able to tailor my browsing experience to my specific tastes while introducing me to a wide variety of new content.

Setting up your own RSS feed

A majority of blog platforms feature themes and templates that come with RSS feed functionality (indicated by the square orange RSS icon) as part of the design. But the best way to control exactly what appears in your feed, and keep track of how many people subscribe to it, is to utilize a *web feed management provider* (a publishing tool that handles the distribution of your content). A few of the more popular web feed management providers include FeedBlitz, RapidFeeds, and FeedBurner.

FeedBurner (`www.feedburner.com`), which is owned by and run via Google, manages all aspects of RSS, including the appearance, statistics, promotion, and monetization of your feed. Begin by registering for a free account and then burning and configuring your feed. FeedBurner provides detailed step-by-step instructions on its site for configuring your feed so that it appears on your blog.

After your feed has been configured, click your RSS feed icon to be directed to your FeedBurner page, where you're given the choice to select a reader or opt-in via e-mail (see Figure 13-6). FeedBurner tracks your number of subscribers as well as your click-through rate, bundling all the statistics into an easy-to-read report.

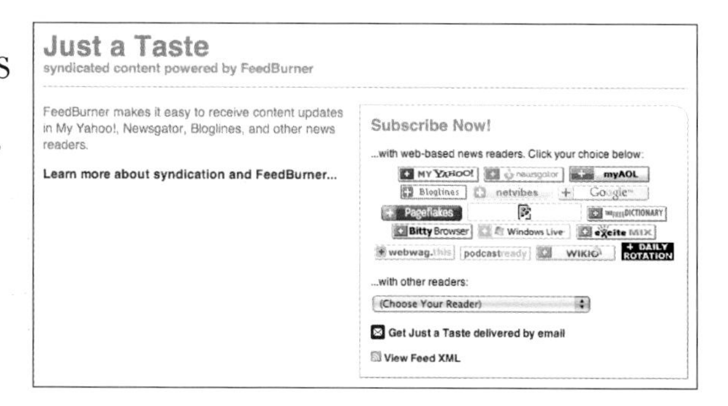

Figure 13-6: The FeedBurner page provides endless options for subscribing to your favorite blogs.

Promoting your visual content

Food photography is one of the best and fastest ways to get your content in front of a larger audience. After publishing a photo on your own blog, submit it to a variety of food photo-aggregator sites for a chance to be published in their online galleries. The most popular sites display endless photos (with links back to the original posts), and keep quality high by moderating submissions and featuring only the *crème de la crème* of food porn.

The real key is the link back to your original post, which ushers an entirely new audience from the photo gallery sites to your blog. As readers click through to a featured post on your blog, they're more likely to stick around and explore additional content that interests them. Although countless food photo-gallery sites are available, I discuss briefly three of the most popular in this section.

TasteSpotting

TasteSpotting (`www.tastespotting.com`) was created in 2007 by Sarah Gim and Jennifer Bartoli as a visual potluck of user-submitted food photos tied to recipes, culinary techniques, products, and more.

Register an account on the site and then submit your choice photo along with a link to the blog post where the image originally appeared. After you submit the photo, it's moderated by the TasteSpotting team and either accepted and displayed in the constantly updating gallery, as shown in Figure 13-7, or rejected and not shown on the site. If one of your photos is rejected, you can still submit additional photos for consideration.

Figure 13-7: TasteSpotting features a constantly updated home page of food photos from across the web.

foodgawker

foodgawker (`www.foodgawker.com`) was created in 2008 by Chuck Lai and serves as an online gallery of user-submitted food photos relating to every aspect of the culinary scene.

An account and a link to the original post where the photo was published are required to submit photos. Include a short, catchy description of your image and *tag* it (label it with applicable keywords) before submitting it for approval, as shown in Figure 13-8. If accepted, the photo appears in the foodgawker gallery.

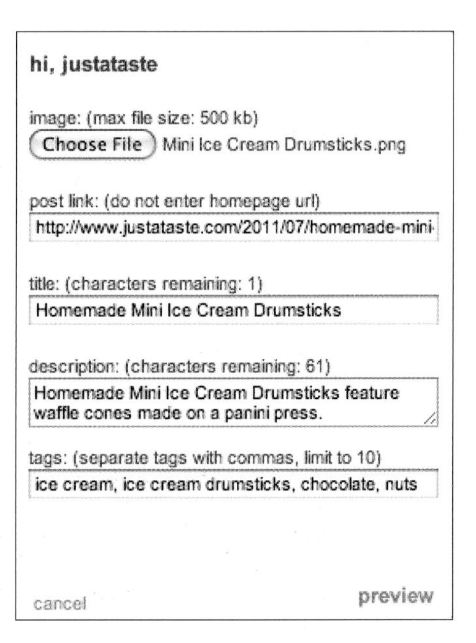

Figure 13-8: Submitting a photo to foodgawker.

If your photo is rejected, you receive feedback with specific comments regarding why it didn't make the cut. Comments like "low lighting and/or underexposed" or "composition - too tight" serve as valuable and constructive criticism for your food photography skills and help guide you in future submissions.

Although I find the feedback feature to be incredibly constructive, it can also be confusing. I can attest that the same photo can be accepted on TasteSpotting and rejected on foodgawker, or vice versa. Keep this insight in mind when weighing the importance of acceptances and rejections on photo gallery sites across the web.

Food Porn Daily

A third popular site for syndicating your food photos is Food Porn Daily (`www.foodporndaily.com`), created by Amanda Simpson. Rather than submit your photos to a gallery of smaller images, Food Porn Daily features one user-submitted photo every day and links to the original blog post.

Much like TasteSpotting and foodgawker, a feature on Food Porn Daily drives traffic to your site and increases your visibility to new readers.

The Ins and Outs of SEO

Search Engine Optimization.

Those words alone are enough to strike panic and confusion in the hearts of even the most seasoned of bloggers. Search engine optimization (SEO) is like the deep-dish pizza of all pizzas — it's big, overwhelming, full of hearty ingredients, often times daunting to digest, and yet also tasty.

In this section, I barely skim the surface of this expansive subject, but I provide enough information to put you at ease. If you're interested in diving in further, check out *Search Engine Optimization All-In-One For Dummies* by Bruce Clay and Susan Esparza, who will have you chowing down on SEO pizza faster than Joey Chestnut at a hot dog-eating competition.

At the most basic level, *SEO* is the process of making your blog as visible as possible to search engines such as Google, Yahoo!, and Bing. The more visible your blog to search engines, the higher it appears in search engines' results, and therefore, the more likely an online user is to find it.

The basic concept of SEO is a straightforward one, but it's the science behind how it works that might leave you stumped. I skip over the seven-course meal answer, which involves words like "crawlers," "indexing," and "algorithm," and instead giving you the appetizer-size explanation: Search engines scan web pages to collect information. They then store that information in their databases so they can reproduce it when an Internet user searches for a specific word or phrase. A variety of factors influence how and why the search results appear in the order they do, and those factors change as the search engines change their algorithms.

Here are the two main approaches to SEO:

- **Organic:** Also known as the natural or free approach, organic SEO does not involve any sort of payment and instead relies on techniques tied to keywords, relevancy, links, frequency of posts, and other factors to naturally rank sites in search engine results. You're required to be the SEO expert when it comes to this DIY approach, however, you have tools, such as Google Recipe View and Google Insights, at your disposal to help guide you.
- **Paid:** Paid SEO tactics involve buying your way to higher search engine rankings via such tactics as *pay-per-click campaigns* (paid advertisements that appear in search listings) and purchased links. You take the DIY element out of the process by paying an SEO company to run an expert SEO campaign for your blog, which requires more of your dollars but less of your time.

Before you begin dabbling in rankings and results, remember that quality content comes first, and SEO is simply a way of polishing your already attractive posts to make them even more attractive to search engines. In this section, I guide you through strictly organic SEO practices.

Clueing in to keywords

Keywords, or the basic words and phrases associated with a topic, are one of the easiest and fastest ways to optimize the content on your blog. They also prompt you to write from the perspective of what Internet users are searching for, and thus, angle your content to the widest audience possible.

Search engines rely on *keyword density,* or the number of keywords on a given page, to determine how relevant a page is to a given topic. For example, if I write a post about the classic Thanksgiving dinner, I'd include these keywords in my post:

- Thanksgiving
- Turkey
- Stuffing
- Mashed potatoes
- Cranberry sauce
- Pumpkin pie

For SEO purposes, I'd work these words and phrases naturally into the text of my post so as the search engines index the page, they catalog the references to the keywords and then know to list my post as a search result for the phrase *Thanksgiving dinner.*

Keywords are an effective way to optimize your blog, but there is such a thing as overdoing it. When a blogger publishes a post in which she first focused on keywords and then focused on the actual content and tone of her writing, it's painfully obvious. Search engines can actually recognize posts intentionally jam-packed with keywords (known as *keyword stuffing*) and will penalize the page by ranking it lower in results. Your new keyword mantra: Use them, don't abuse them.

Keywords also play a critical role in how you title your blog posts, meaning you should use the most commonly searched terms when titling your posts. Here semantics mean the difference between what 10 million people search for and what 10 people search for. For example, imagine writing a Chocolate Cake with Vanilla *Frosting* recipe post. Or is it Chocolate Cake with Vanilla *Icing?* Frosting or icing — which one is more likely to be searched for? No need to call on the cake gods for an answer. Instead, head over to Google Insights for Search (`www.google.com/insights/search`) for one-stop shopping to find out who, what, when, where, and how many times Internet users have searched for a given word or phrase.

Figure 13-9 shows the Google Insights for Search results comparing *vanilla frosting* with *vanilla icing* for the timeframe from 2004 to the present in the United States. As the results indicate, the phrase *vanilla frosting* was searched for roughly one-and-a-half times as often as *vanilla icing,* so I know more Internet users are likely to find my recipe if I title it "Chocolate Cake with Vanilla Frosting." Of course, my recipe would have to actually be a recipe for frosting and not icing. (The two terms are interchangeable to me although professional bakers might disagree.) Keywords in titles are critical, but clarity and accuracy should always win out over trying to trick the search engines into ranking your blog first in their results.

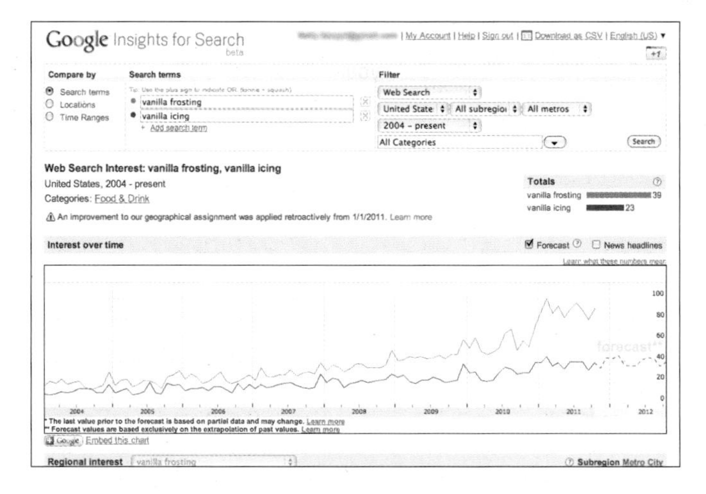

Figure 13-9: Results from Google Insights for Search gauges which words and phrases are most commonly searched for.

Understanding Google Recipe View

In early 2011, Google rolled out its new recipe search feature, *Google Recipe View,* a useful online search tool that allows you to narrow your search to include only recipes and to even further focus your search by designating specific ingredients, cooking times, and calories. For example, the figure depicts the search results for *fish tacos,* which I further specified by selecting Tilapia and Lime from the ingredient list on the left sidebar.

Refine your search

Google Recipe View also has an impact on search results and on SEO as a whole. Your recipes appear only in Recipe View's search results if they're marked in a particular code formatting known as *Google Rich Snippets,* which alerts Google to catalog your recipe page as an actual recipe. If you're using WordPress.org, you're in luck because the Recipe plug-in formats everything after you install it on your blog. Otherwise, you have to manually mark up the code with Rich Snippets in each recipe post, which can be a long and trying process if you aren't familiar with the basics of HTML.

For more information on manually formatting your recipes with Google Rich Snippets, visit the Google Webmaster Tools Help page:

```
www.google.com/support/
     webmasters/bin/answer.
     py?answer=173379
```

Such insights into search results are further proof to avoid titling your posts with obscure, albeit witty, names. A delicate balance has to take place between SEO and creativity. For example, although "Heaven in Seven Layers" is a clever title for your new favorite lasagna recipe, the lack of the word *lasagna* in the title isn't going to win you any friends in the SEO department. On the flip side, "Seven Layers of Lasagna Heaven" is going to attract a lot more people than a generic title such as "Cheese Lasagna."

Pay particular attention to keywords that not only distinguish the ingredients in your recipe, but also the technique. For example, "easy" is a popular recipe search term, so rather than get cutesy and title your post, "Speedy Spring Roll Sauce" (trust me, I too am tempted by alliteration), instead title your post, "Easy Spring Roll Sauce."

"Cocktail" is another keyword that can make or break the rank of your recipe. Many cocktails don't contain the word "cocktail" in their name, such as the Manhattan, the Mai Tai, or my personal favorite, the French 75. But for SEO purposes, you should always include the word "cocktail" in the titles of your beverage posts, such as "The French 75 Cocktail."

The keyword titling strategy also applies to images, which are indexed similar to the text that appears on each page (meaning they're catalogued into image search results). Never publish an image with an obscure name, which happens all too often if you don't sensibly name your images prior to uploading them. Published images with names, such as *DSC_0543,* do nothing for SEO. Instead, title your image with a keyword-friendly name, such as *chocolate-covered strawberries,* and then reap the search result rewards.

Giving and getting link love

Hyperlinks, often referred to simply as *links,* are words and phrases on a web page that, when clicked, lead readers directly to another web page — a page that is either on the same site or on a different site altogether. Links are a critical SEO component because search engines track how many websites link back to your blog (which is an indicator of your blog's popularity). The three main types of links differ based on direction and destination:

- **Internal:** Internal links point to and from one page to another page within your blog, such as from your spaghetti post to your homemade meatballs post.
- **Outbound:** Outbound links point from your blog to another site, such as from your spaghetti post to a pasta vendor's site.
- **Inbound:** Inbound links point from another site to your blog, such as from Eataly's blogroll to your blog.

Inbound links to your blog tell the search engines how popular your blog is across the web. The more popular your blog is, the more visible it is, and thus, the higher it ranks in search engine results. Inbound links are especially effective in boosting your blog up the results page when those links come from credible, highly trafficked sites (which are very highly ranked).

Creating original, quality content is your best shot at getting some inbound link love from the bigger sites. You can also attract other sites' attention as a result of your outbound links, which you can use to connect to larger sites and display as a sign of community support in your blogroll. (See Chapter 9 for more on blogrolls.)

The key to using links effectively on your blog is knowing what words and phrases are best to link. Always hyperlink the *anchor text,* or the keywords in a sentence that most accurately describe the page they're linking to. Links are often displayed in a different color or style (underlined, bolded, or italicized) than the rest of the text on the page so they stand out. For example, the underlined words in the following sentence link to a post containing a recipe for homemade ricotta.

> Last weekend I shared my homemade ricotta recipe, which I served on toasted crostini topped with a drizzle of honey.

The words *homemade ricotta recipe* are the anchor text within the sentence because they clearly describe what content will be found on the linked page. Links should always center on anchor text and be as descriptive as possible. Phrases that are too generic don't display in search engine results because they don't specify the content appearing on the pages they link to. Never link any of the following phrases:

- Here
- Click here
- Get it now
- Find out more
- Download

On rare occasions, the preceding phrases are the most helpful to readers, such as directing them straight to the download page for an application. In such instances, however, including additional words — for example, "Download the free app" — in the link also helps.

When adding links on your own blog, your blogging software lets you decide whether to have the link open either in the same window (or tab) or in a new one, as shown on WordPress.org in Figure 13-10. Both options involve a simple, single-click process.

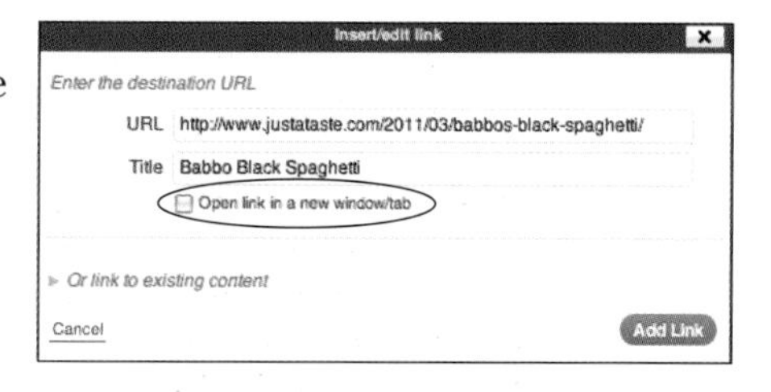

Figure 13-10: Choose whether you want a link to open in the same or new window.

You decide how the links on your blog open because some people think one way is better than the other. I prefer my internal links open in the same window and my outbound links open in a new window so readers aren't directed entirely away from my blog via an outbound link.

Regardless of how you use links on your blog, avoid engaging in a *link exchange*, which is swapping links with another blogger or site (a sort of reciprocal "you scratch my back, and I'll scratch yours" approach). Link exchanges are bad practice because they can prompt you to link to a site not necessarily in line with your niche, preferences, or genuine interests. Linking to another site for the sole goal of getting a link back in return devalues the content on your blog and misleads readers who trust you. Refer your readers to other sites because you actually find worthwhile content there.

Interacting Online and Offline

Technology is a wonderful tool because it allows you to be in touch with nearly every corner of the globe, all from the comfort of your couch. Although effective as a digital bridge, technology has also stifled the degree of face-to-face interactions people engage in on a daily basis.

From communicating via online comments to attending conferences, becoming an integral part of the food blogging community requires staking your brand's claim in the digital and real-life realms.

Building community

The best way to build a community around your blog is to foster a dialogue with your readers — and between your readers — in the comments section. Start the conversation by posing a question for your readers at the end of a post. Invite them to share their favorite recipe, best restaurant recommendation, or any other open-ended topic to kick-start the conversation.

Whether the comments section thrives on your blog, actively establish your voice on other food blogs. If you see something you like, why not leave a comment for the author? Chances are he'll return the favor with a comment on your blog, too.

And after he does, respond to the comments and questions posed on your blog by him, and by any other bloggers. You may get to a point where there are too many comments to respond to them all (talk about a good problem to have!), in which case, do your best to have as prominent of a presence as possible.

The next step toward community-building is an obvious one: Establish your voice in the social media spheres. After you launch into social media for marketing purposes, Twitter and Facebook are the places to be. As the results from The State of the Food Blogosphere survey indicate in Figure 13-11, a majority of food bloggers rely specifically on Twitter for spreading the word about their blogs. But social media isn't just for marketing. The online social media scene is the prime place for meeting fellow food-lovers and cultivating relationships online. (See Chapter 8 for more on the power of social media.)

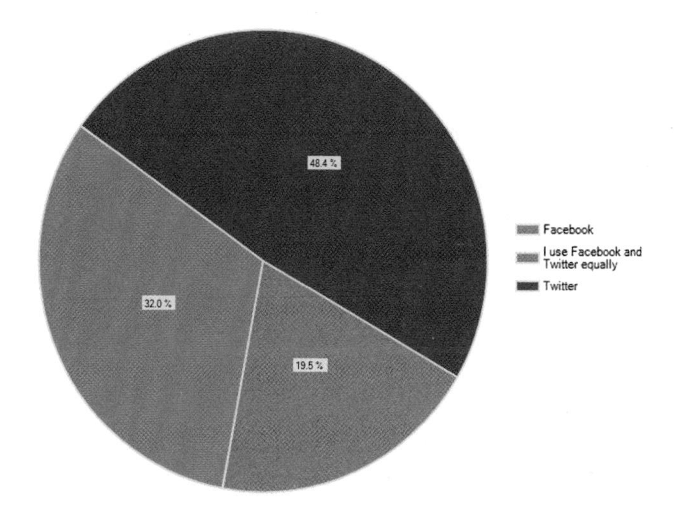

Figure 13-11: Food bloggers prefer Twitter as a marketing tool.

Meeting and greeting bloggers offline

Although you can easily get sucked into the online world, it's absolutely critical to step out from behind your screen, put down your smartphone, and engage in face-to-face interactions with your fellow food bloggers. If not for the marketing advantage, then for the pure purpose of experiencing a real-life exchange with your culinary cohorts.

Why the need to interact the old-fashioned way? Because doing so helps reiterate that a real human being is responsible for all the amazing content that appears on your blog. There are countless opportunities for building your brand outside the digital sphere and increasing your visibility offline:

- **Conferences:** Food and food blogging conferences are some of the best ways to engage in face-to-face interactions with other impassioned foodies. From the annual International Association of Culinary Professionals (IACP) conference to the frequent Food Blog Forum events, stay up-to-date with the culinary conference circuit for the chance to put a face to those Twitter avatars.
- **Eat-ups:** Get in touch with your fellow local food bloggers and arrange an *eat-up,* where you meet at a local restaurant or host a potluck, and swap stories and inspirations for your blogs.
- **Events:** From seasonal food festivals to annual food media events, tune in to the event-sphere to snag tickets to popular culinary events nationwide.

Each of these in-person interactions is a chance to connect with your fellow food bloggers (or potential readers) and spread the word about your blog. Don't forget to bring business cards for networking, which can be homemade or created by the variety of affordable, and even free, online printing companies, such as MOO (www.moo.com) and Vistaprint (www.vistaprint.com). Although the main aim in attending conferences should be to see your online friends and nurture new relationships, you are your most valuable marketing asset, so put yourself to work!

Tracking Your Progress

There are endless ways to measure success on your food blog. From the number of comments to the number of Facebook fan page members, how you measure your success is as individualized as your blog.

The visitor and pageview statistics are either a big boost to your self-confidence or a crushing blow to your self-esteem. Poor statistics can leave you feeling defeated, but only if you fail to understand them in the context of time. No blog is a multi-million pageview success overnight. You need time to build an audience, and more importantly, a *consistent* audience. Breaking down the basics of food blogging statistics allows you to set more realistic goals when making and breaking your traffic records.

Implementing a statistics tracker

Before you can digest your blog's statistics, implement any of the variety of statistics trackers for cataloging your traffic. I discuss three of the more popular statistics trackers (Google Analytics, Site Meter, and AWStats) in Chapter 2. Installation of the major trackers involves following a specific step-by-step process according to your tracker of choice.

Installing Google Analytics requires registering a Google Mail account and logging in at www.google.com/analytics. After you log in, decide whether you want to complete the installation by manually adding the tracking code to your blog, or if you're a WordPress.org user, by relying on a plug-in for easy installation.

The Google Analytics for WordPress plug-in is one of the most popular installation tools (because it's user-friendly) for quickly setting up tracking on your blog. It's also my personal tracker of choice thanks to a perfect mix of simplicity and reliability. After retrieving your tracking code from Analytics, install and activate the plug-in, and then follow these steps:

1. **Log in to your blog's Dashboard.**

2. **Click the Settings tab and then click the Google Analytics link.**

   A new page with a Web Property ID text field appears.

3. **Enter the Web Property ID in the text field (see Figure 13-12).**

   The *Web Property ID* is the account ID you receive after registering your blog's URL with Google Analytics.

4. **Click the Save Changes button.**

   Google Analytics has been successfully installed on your blog and will begin collecting statistics.

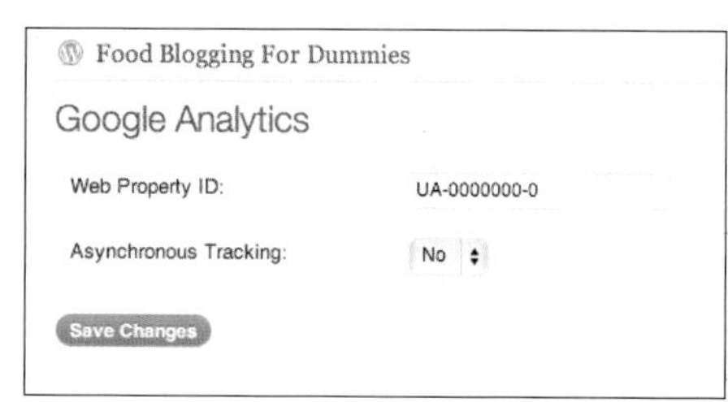

Figure 13-12: Installing a statistics tracker.

To install Site Meter, register an account at `www.sitemeter.com`, and then log in and click the HTML Code link in the list of menu options, which directs you to a setup page. Site Meter provides detailed step-by-step instructions for installing the tracking code on more than 45 types of blogging platforms, including WordPress.com, WordPress.org, Blogger, and more.

Depending on your hosting company, AWStats is often included as part of your self-hosting package, requiring no setup. The tracker provides detailed reports, such as the sample report in Figure 13-13, with information on every statistic from unique visitors and referring search engines to duration of site visits and internal keyword searches.

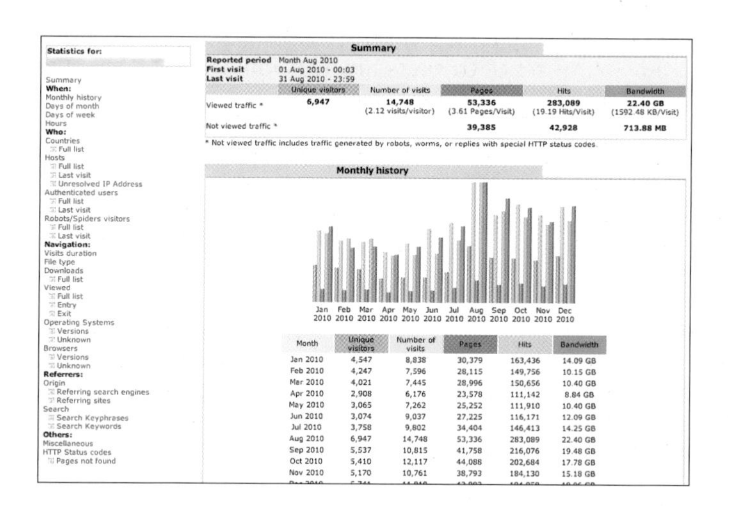

Month	Unique visitors	Number of visits	Pages	Hits	Bandwidth
Jan 2010	4,547	8,838	30,379	163,436	14.09 GB
Feb 2010	4,247	7,596	28,115	149,756	10.15 GB
Mar 2010	4,021	7,445	28,996	150,656	10.40 GB
Apr 2010	2,908	6,176	23,578	111,142	8.84 GB
May 2010	3,065	7,262	25,252	111,910	10.40 GB
Jun 2010	3,074	9,037	27,225	116,171	12.09 GB
Jul 2010	3,758	9,802	34,404	146,413	14.25 GB
Aug 2010	6,947	14,748	53,336	283,089	22.40 GB
Sep 2010	5,537	10,815	41,758	216,076	19.48 GB
Oct 2010	5,410	12,117	44,088	202,684	17.78 GB
Nov 2010	5,170	10,761	38,793	184,130	15.18 GB

Figure 13-13: Statistics results from an AWStats report.

Decoding basic blog statistics

After you implement your statistics tracker, allow it to catalog your traffic for a minimum of one month before reviewing and digesting the results.

Here are two main elements to focus on regarding traffic:

- **Unique visitors:** Also known as *unique users,* or just simply as *uniques,* unique visitors are a measure of the number of people who frequent your blog in a certain timeframe (generally 30 days). For example, one person who visits your blog four times in one day counts as one unique visitor because she's associated with one distinctive IP address.
- **Pageviews:** Pageviews are a measure of the number of pages on your blog that are accessed by Internet users. Unlike unique visitors, one person who visits four pages equals four pageviews. Pageviews are not the same as *page hits,* which are an inaccurate gauge of traffic because they count each individual graphic on a page that's accessed as an individual hit, and in doing so, they skew traffic results.

Depending on your specific meters for success, other informative analytics to assess include the following:

- **Traffic sources:** Traffic sources include where your inbound links are coming from and the quantity of traffic from search engines, referring sites, and direct traffic.
- **Content:** Gauge which posts are most popular, as well as which pages are the biggest points of entry to and exit from your blog.
- **Traffic over time:** Figure out which days are associated with the most traffic, as well as the times of day users most frequently visit your blog.
- **Time spent:** Discover the average amount of time readers spend on your blog.
- **Location:** Find out the location of your readers with the ability to then angle your content toward a variety of global palates.

14

Bringing Home the Bacon

In This Chapter

- Setting realistic financial goals for your blog
- Tweaking your content
- Exploring available ad network options
- Attracting and interacting with potential sponsors
- Diversifying your sources of online income
- Accepting and disclosing swag

Food bloggers of every skill level can monetize their blogs. For some, that means enough revenue to fund your next gourmet coffee run, and for others, it means a check fat enough to fly you to Colombia to harvest the beans yourself.

Where your hopes and ambitions rest on that spectrum is entirely up to you. But if you're interested in earning any sort of income from your blog, you have to view your blog as a full-blown business. That means you're the all-powerful CEO. You call the shots, you bask in the glory of success, you take your cut, and you own the consequences of defeat.

Approaching your blog from a business frame of mind should motivate you to explore every angle possible for how to make it worth more than the price you paid to register your domain. And this is when the numbers really start to matter, from your pageviews to your ad impressions to the cost of sponsorships, and more. But before assessing the numbers and evaluating your worth, you need to approach your newfound blogging business with a strategy that aligns realistic goals with financial victory.

To that end, in this chapter, I introduce you to the wide array of options for making pennies to banking big dollars from your blog. From setting realistic financial expectations to tapping into the world of ad networks, you find out how to mix up a calculated combination of strategies and techniques to discover the most effective approach to a profit.

(Reality) Check, Please!

Before reading another word in this chapter, here's a bite of reality pie — you might not like the way this tastes, but just try to get it down: There is no easy, effortless way to generate a million dollars a year from your food blog.

Shocked? Stumped? Unfazed? Annoyed? Let it all out now because after you accept that fact, you're infinitely closer to setting yourself up for money-making success. Sporting rose-colored glasses when it comes to food blogging and earning an income will lead you on the road to disappointment — and that's a road that far too many naive bloggers travel. The key is not only staying focused on the financial dreams for your blog, but also staying in touch with the reality of those dreams. And remember that it was a passion for food, and hopefully not finances, that led you into the food blogosphere in the first place.

The money every food blogger needs to earn to live solely off their blog obviously differs. But before you run to quit your day job, keep in mind that earning even the minimum amount needed for survival (living outside of New York City, eating ramen noodles, walking everywhere) requires the following:

- Hard work
- Extreme dedication
- A bit of luck
- Unwavering perseverance
- Even more hard work
- Even more luck

You have to proactively position yourself and your blog in a way that not only makes you money, but also makes you attractive to people who are willing to help you make money. I think of earning an "acceptable" (a relative term) income from a blog like trying to lose weight. No secret solution will make it happen overnight. You need to know and accept this reality. So with the ugly truth out on the table, it's time to evaluate all the possible money-making avenues from your blog and beyond.

Making the Most of Your Content

Because of the surge in the popularity of food blogging over the past five years, readers have their choice of countless food blogs covering every topic from raw food diets to culinary adventures in Asia. So what's going to get them to swing by your corner of the digital world, and more importantly, swing by more than once? The answer lies in the impact of your content.

Figure 14-1 illustrates the flow of readers to and from a food blog. Readers have two choices for types of content to interact with. Bland and unappealing content turns off readers, and they never become repeat visitors; the cycle ceases to exist as a continuously flowing chain of involvement, exposure, and blog growth. Useful, engaging, and entertaining content entices readers to keep coming back. And so the key transition in the diagram is when a new reader becomes a repeat visitor, which triggers him to become a loyal fan and share your content.

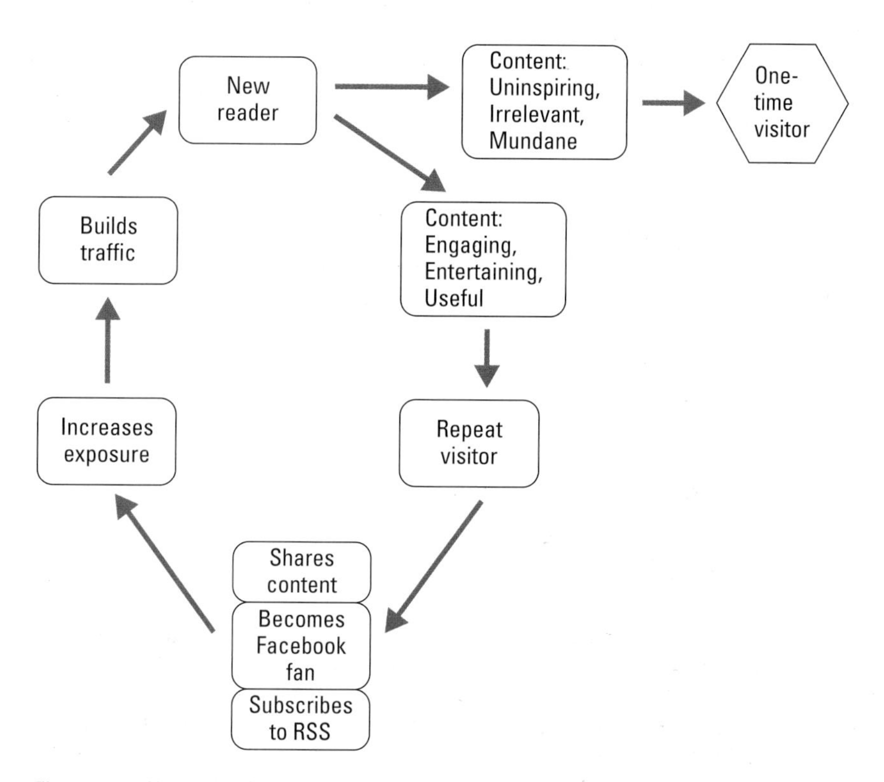

Figure 14-1: Useful, engaging, and entertaining content keeps the cycle of readership and traffic flowing.

Why obsess over repeat visitors? Because repeat visitors are the launching pad to profits. Online advertisers and sponsors have one-track minds leading them to their main goal: to get their product in front of as many eyeballs as possible. So the more visitors you have to your blog, the more enticing you appear to companies looking to promote their goods and services.

But there's no sense in promoting their products for free. Enter money. In the following section, I outline the two main ways to run ads on your blog, through direct advertising or an advertising network. Both options value your blog (as in, put a price tag on it) based on a variety of metrics tied to traffic. See how quality content, traffic, and profits are all coming together? Higher-quality content leads to more traffic, which creates a larger payout from advertisers and sponsors, which leads you straight to the bank.

And that's why the goal in creating useful, engaging, and entertaining content is to get the most traffic possible for every post you publish. It takes time to build up your fan base, and you have to put in the work from an editorial standpoint to ensure that what you're creating isn't attracting only one demographic, but as many demographics as possible. (See Chapter 5 for more on planning your content menu.)

Tapping into the Ad World

Online advertisements, which are text and graphic units promoting a good or service, are one way bloggers generate income from their blogs. The process is straightforward: You feature an ad somewhere on your blog promoting a company and then you get paid based on a specified metric, such as

- **Impressions:** Impressions are the number of times an ad loads onto a page. For example, if I visit a page on your blog and an ad displays on that page, that counts as one impression. Impressions provide an estimate for how many people view an ad.
- **Click-through rate:** The click-through rate of an advertisement is a percentage measurement of how many users click an ad, divided by how many times that ad appears (the number of *impressions*). So if 100 people click an ad that appears on my blog 1,000 times, my click-through rate would be 100 divided by 1,000, which expressed as a percentage would be 10 percent.
- **Pageviews:** Pageviews are a measurement of the number of web pages that display. The difference between pageviews and impressions can be confusing, but remember that pageviews measure strictly the number of pages that load, whereas impressions measure the number of times the ads on those pages load. The number of pageviews will not always equal the number of impressions because an ad may be only on your blog's home page and not on any other pages.

Here are two main ways to run advertisements on your blog:

- **Direct advertising:** In the direct advertising approach, you control all facets of advertisements, such as size, placement, and cost, that appear on your blog by selling ad space to advertisers.
- **Advertising networks:** Advertising networks serve the role of middleman to take over all the responsibilities involved in direct advertising. You join an ad network and then the ad network supplies the ads. For their services, the ad network receives a portion of the revenue you earn from your ads.

I discuss the pros and cons of both options later in this chapter, but for now, just remember that you're essentially faced with two main options when it comes to running ads on your blog.

In The State of the Food Blogosphere survey, about 45 percent of participating bloggers reported that they were running ads on their blog. But before you contemplate taking the ad plunge, consider an ad's impact — both positive and negative — on your blog-turned-business.

Evaluating the impact of ads

Ad revenue depends entirely on the amount of traffic your blog receives. If you launch your blog and instantly put up ads, consider whether the revenue they generate is worth the tradeoff of their presence. Ads often require placement above the fold (see Chapter 8) of your blog, as shown in Figure 14-2, which means prime real estate that could be home to your engaging content is occupied by content promoting another brand.

So how do you know when ad revenue is worth the potential eyesore? Start with the actual revenue ads generate, which is generally based on the *cost per thousand impressions*, known as *CPM* (the *M* stands for *mille,* which means *one thousand* in Latin). If you're running ads through direct advertising, you can structure your payment model and set the CPM at whatever price you see fit. If you're part of an ad network, it dictates the CPM based on the size and scope of your blog as well as on the specific network.

For example, say your CPM is $2, which means every 1,000 ad impressions is worth $2. If you're running ads through direct advertising, you would pocket $200. But if you're using an ad network, you aren't getting the full $2 because that amount is your *gross CPM.* The amount you actually pocket, your *net CPM,* is less than $2 because the ad network takes a cut. So if you get 100,000 impressions in one month and your net CPM is $1, your take away is $100.

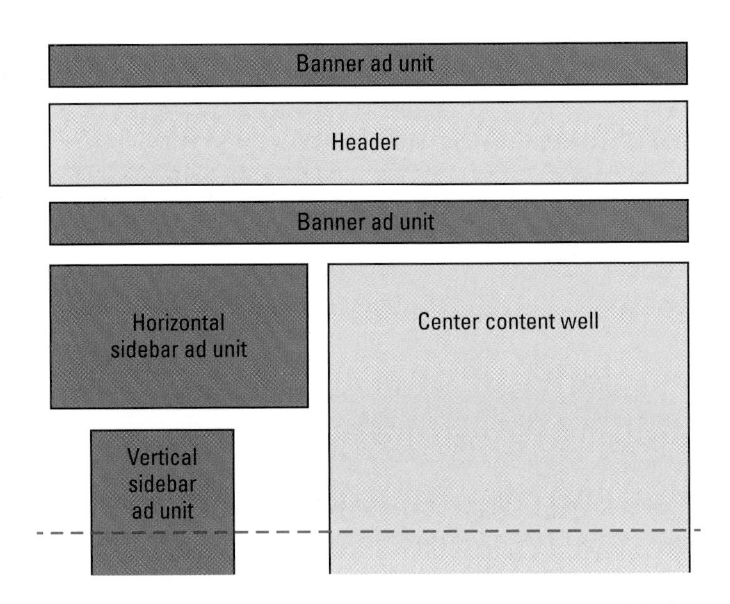

Figure 14-2: A wireframe of a basic blog layout highlights potential ad placements in prime real estate locations above the fold.

Whether $100 or $200 per month is worth giving up the prime real estate on your blog, which would otherwise be home to additional content, is your decision. The bottom line is that ad revenue depends entirely on traffic. More traffic, more impressions, more profit.

So is running a large ad unit on day one of your food blogging career worth it? If you do the math, the answer is "no." When you begin your blog, you're better off filling that space with content and building your traffic to a point where putting ads on your blog (should you decide to do that) is worth the sacrificed real estate. Ads also change the entire look and feel of your blog, which often makes them more of a distraction than what they're worth. When you initially design your blog, I recommend that you consider potential space for ad units so you can seamlessly add them later, if or when need be, without disrupting the overall aesthetic of your blog.

Putting profits in perspective

Asking another blogger how much money she makes from ads on her blog is like asking someone how much she weighs. Most bloggers aren't willing to share that number, nor is it a subject that's often discussed in the public realm.

However, I included the question on The State of the Food Blogosphere survey. I, like everyone else, was genuinely curious about the current industry average. I also wanted to share these numbers with you in the hope they'd provide perspective for realistic ad revenue earnings. Because I also felt it was important to allow bloggers to decline answering the question, I included an I'd Rather Not Share option. As the results in Figure 14-3 indicate, 25 percent opted out of the question, but the other responses can still provide insightful results.

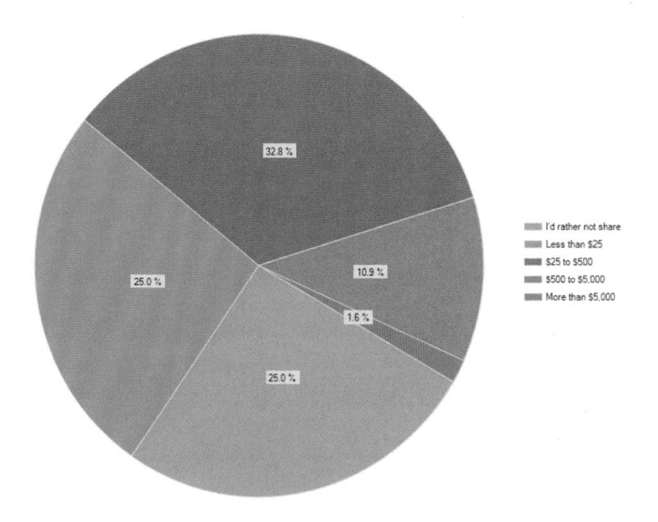

Figure 14-3: One-third of food bloggers reported earning between $25 and $500 in monthly ad revenue.

Roughly one-third of the food bloggers participating in the survey reported earning ad revenue between $25 and $500 per month, and less than 2 percent reported a monthly ad income of more than $5,000.

If you decide to run ads on your blog, consider your financial goals. Aiming to make enough money in your first year to pay for the groceries is a much different goal than aiming to open your own restaurant. Why does that matter? If you run ads on your blog, you must set clear monthly financial goals. Those goals are tied inevitably to traffic because a greater number of visitors translates to a greater number of impressions and pageviews, which increase your ad revenue. When you meet the month's goal, set the amount higher; then continue to produce the engaging, useful, and entertaining content that helps you meet the higher goal and keeps the cycle running.

Filed under the Things I Wish Someone Told Me Five Years Ago category is to always save your grocery store receipts for ingredients you buy and use for your blog. Depending on your personal taxes and blog revenue, you may be able to write off the cost of the ingredients if your blog operates at a *loss* (or you spend more on ingredients than what you make in blog-related revenue).

Keeping the Control with Direct Advertising

If you're interested in overseeing all the elements of your online ad campaign, direct advertising may be the best route for you. But with control also comes a tremendous amount of responsibility because you add the role of Ad Sales Director to your food blogging résumé. Table 14-1 outlines the pros and cons associated with direct advertising.

Table 14-1 Direct Advertising Pros and Cons

Pros	*Cons*
You build relationships with advertisers because you're in direct contact with them.	You have to find and contact potential advertisers.
You set the duration of the ad campaign.	You handle all interactions with advertisers, which can be a timely endeavor.
You have total control over the types of ads running on your blog because you've specifically approached or responded to only the advertisers you're interested in working with.	Implementing ads may require additional technical knowledge to properly display ad codes.
You earn all the revenue from the ads and dictate the payment date.	You keep track of payment deadlines and deal directly with advertisers if there are any issues.

The most challenging aspect of direct advertising is undoubtedly the time it takes not only to oversee your ad campaigns, but to even find and approach advertisers. You also need a certain degree of confidence to blindly contact a company and really put your brand and yourself out there. If you're up for the challenge, read on for an essential checklist that will ensure you're viewed as a passionate professional rather than a bewildered blogger.

At some point in your life, you've likely experienced that dreaded feeling of being called on by a teacher, only to allow your blank stare to give away the fact you didn't do your homework. Not preparing before approaching advertisers will evoke that same feeling, except the missed opportunities are much larger than a less-than-stellar grade in Chemistry class.

As you contemplate potential advertisers, either by making a list of a few of your favorite brands or by scoping out your fellow food bloggers' ads, keep this checklist close by and begin quizzing yourself until you're cool as a cucumber when it comes to your responses:

- **Traffic:** Know your blog traffic numbers, particularly your monthly unique visitors and your pageviews. Advertisers are enticed by an active, engaged, and most importantly, large blog community because it means more people view their good or service. (See Chapter 13 for a refresher on tracking your traffic.)
- **Price:** Know your CPM so you don't hesitate when an advertiser starts talking pricing. Similar to effective salary negotiation tactics, you want to pick a number and then stick to it.
- **Ad size:** Decide on the variety of ad sizes and placements that best suit the aesthetics and layout of your blog. The last thing you want to do is promise a 600-pixel-wide sidebar ad, only to discover your sidebar is actually 400 pixels wide.
- **Timeline:** Know the next step in the process, whether that means you follow up with an advertiser by e-mail or you arrange for a call to discuss the logistics of the ad placement. Remember that you're courting them and need to put in the effort to ensure a potential advertiser turns into a long-term client.

Does all this seem like too big of a burden to bear? The truth is, direct advertising is incredibly time-consuming and you'll likely have to take some time away from the cooking, photographing, and other fun stuff to ensure your advertisers are happy and you're getting your checks on time. It's for this reason, and many others, that most beginner food bloggers opt for the ad network route, if or when they decide to run ads on their blog.

Joining an Ad Network

Online advertising networks are companies that facilitate the process of connecting advertisers with businesses interested in featuring their ads. Running ads on your blog in exchange for payment is one of the fastest and easiest ways to bring home the bacon. But before your eyes turn into dollar signs, consider these possible barriers to entry:

- **Applications:** You have to apply to become a member of an ad network, and some are easier than others to join.
- **Contracts:** You have to sign a contract, and may have to agree to run their ads for a specific minimum amount of time.
- **Minimum requirements:** Each ad network varies with their requirements related to the age of your blog, the frequency with which you post, the ability for readers to leave comments, and even your number of unique visitors.

Table 14-2 further outlines the pros and cons associated with joining an ad network.

Table 14-2 Ad Network Pros and Cons

Pros	*Cons*
It handles all interactions with advertisers.	You have limited control over the types of ads running on your blog, and it may not allow you to run ads from other companies.
Implementing ads is fast and simple.	Its contracts may require minimum time commitments.
It may link to your blog or feature your content, which can increase traffic.	It takes a cut of your profits and dictates the payment date.
It may provide other benefits, such as large communities, resources, or special marketing opportunities.	It likely requires placement above the fold on your blog.

A quick search online returns countless ad network options, some of which focus specifically on food sites, and others that accept applications from sites in every niche imaginable. Each ad network has its own guidelines for eligibility, minimum contract length, and revenue model, so make sure you visit the individual network sites for full details.

In this section, I provide a summary of the identifying elements of five popular ad networks that offer a wide range of benefits and services. But don't let this short list deter you from applying to networks not mentioned, such as Blogads, Glam Media, Martha's Circle, and more. In addition to the networks I discuss, check out your favorite food blogs to see what networks they've joined and then decide which network best fits your unique needs.

Google AdSense

Google AdSense (www.google.com/adsense) is an advertising network in which participants are approved to feature Google ads on their blog, in addition to ads from other networks. AdSense users can view instant and accurate statistics in the form of performance reports, which indicate pageviews, clicks, estimated earnings, and more.

The amount of revenue generated by AdSense depends on a variety of factors, including the type of ads you run and the pricing of those ads (not all ads are priced equally). You also have endless options for customizing the color scheme and style of the ads appearing on your blog, as shown in Figure 14-4.

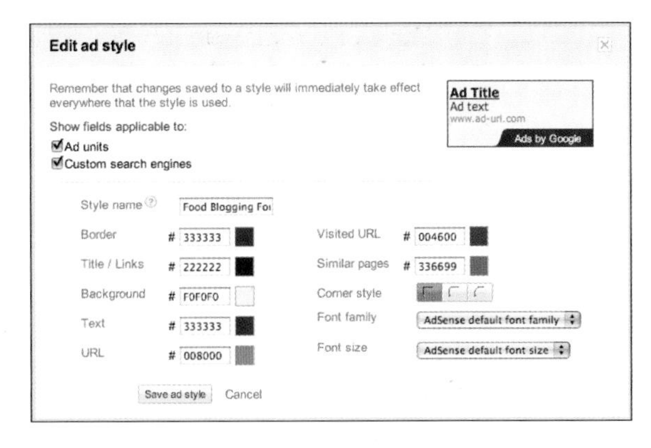

Figure 14-4: Customize the color and style of your Google AdSense ads with a few simple clicks.

PlateFull

PlateFull (www.platefull.com) is an entirely food-focused ad network with a portfolio of more than 1,000 blogs and sites selected and approved by General Mills. PlateFull counts national brands and independent bloggers among its clients, including 22 percent of The Babble 50: Mom Food Bloggers (www.babble.com/babble-best/top-50-mommy-food-blogs).

Because PlateFull works with larger brands, independent bloggers can have their content affiliated with and even featured on the sites of brands like Betty Crocker and Pillsbury.

BlogHer advertising network

BlogHer (www.blogher.com) is the largest online community of women bloggers, and as of December 2011, attracts 37 million unique visitors per month (Nielsen Site Census). The BlogHer advertising network is composed of 3,000 bloggers.

In addition to earning revenue by featuring BlogHer network ads on your blog, you also can meet and interact with bloggers on the BlogHer site, as shown in Figure 14-5, and at BlogHer events. The BlogHer Food Conference is one of the biggest food blogging events of the year, featuring panels and networking events with some of the best food bloggers in the business.

BlogHer's Food Topic Page (http://www.blogher.com/blogher-topics/food)

Figure 14-5: BlogHer is a robust blogging community attracting more than 37 million unique visitors per month.

An added perk of joining the BlogHer advertising network is you can have your content curated and displayed in the additional links featured below the BlogHer ad units. This increases your reach while bringing in additional traffic. (For full disclosure, I am currently under contract with the BlogHer Ad Network.)

Federated Media Publishing

Federated Media Publishing (`www.federatedmedia.net`) was launched in 2005 and has since established itself as a premiere ad network for independent publishers across four major categories: living (which includes food), business, technology, and real-time.

In 2010, Federated Media Publishing acquired Foodbuzz, which still maintains its own ad network through the Foodbuzz Featured Publisher program.

Interested bloggers can apply to either the Federated Media Publishing network or to Foodbuzz, which has less strict requirements for eligibility in terms of your blog's current traffic.

Foodbuzz Featured Publisher program

Foodbuzz (www.foodbuzz.com) is a blogging community that collects and curates content from more than 20,000 food blogs across the web. The Featured Publisher program includes more than 4,000 of those bloggers who are pre-approved publishers running Foodbuzz network ads on their blogs.

Your blog must be at least 30 days old to be considered for the Featured Publisher program, and it must be updated at least once or twice per week with at least 90 percent food-centric content. Extended editorial guidelines are detailed on the Foodbuzz site.

In addition to earning revenue from posting Foodbuzz network ads on your blog, you also become a part of the expansive online network of food bloggers. The community provides opportunities for meeting fellow bloggers, exchanging recipes, and participating in the annual Project Food Blog competition.

Interacting with Sponsors

If advertising is all about traffic, sponsorships are all about relationships. *Sponsors* are companies that support your blog either financially or through providing goods or services, and in return, they're granted a degree of access to your readership or association with your brand.

For example, if KitchenAid sponsored my blog post about making homemade pasta with a KitchenAid stand mixer, I could receive either money or goods in exchange for featuring some combination of its logo, a link to its products page, or a plug for its social media sites. The details of a sponsorship, whether monetary or in-kind, depend on the specific terms agreed upon between the sponsor and the blogger.

Establishing effective relationships with sponsors

Having a large audience is enticing for a sponsor. The underlying element that drives a successful relationship between you and a sponsor, however, is your genuine interest in the good or service the sponsor promotes. Therefore, establishing relationships with sponsors whose products are aligned with your editorial mission is critical. For example, if you're a vegan blogger who loves a certain brand of vegan salad dressing, having that brand sponsor your blog makes sense because you're a genuine supporter of the product.

If and when you do get approached by sponsors, remember that this is a professional working relationship. Your blog is a business, and the sponsor is a client. Define your specific terms for sponsorship by creating a written contract that addresses the following areas:

- **Duration:** What are the exact start and end dates of the sponsorship?
- **Promotion:** How will you promote the good or service? How many links and logos will you feature, and where will they be located on your blog? What role will social media play?
- **Goods:** Will the sponsor provide you with any goods or services in exchange for the sponsorship? Does the sponsor want to participate in a giveaway? (See the following section for more on giveaways.)
- **Payment:** Will the sponsor provide you with any monetary compensation in exchange for the sponsorship? When, through what form of payment, and in how many increments will any monetary compensation be provided?
- **Logistics:** If the sponsor's logo will be featured, what size should the logo be? What type of file should the logo be? What specific language should be included in any posts related to the sponsorship?

Using this checklist of questions ensures you cover all elements tied to creating a successful sponsorship, which is indicated not only by the money, goods, or services you receive, but also by the lasting relationship you establish with the brand. Depending on the size of the sponsorship, it's a good idea to have a lawyer review the contract you create to ensure it's accurate and legally binding.

Sponsors may not always be the first to make a move when it comes to kick-starting a relationship with you. If you're interested in having a company sponsor your blog, or even just a single post, take the first step and reach out to them.

Food blogger Jaden Hair of Steamy Kitchen champions the "you make the first move" approach, and even suggests bloggers start the conversation with something as simple as a direct message on Twitter, which is casual and straightforward. For example, if you're interested in KitchenAid sponsorship opportunities, send KitchenAid a direct message such as, "I'm a longtime user of your products and would love to discuss sponsorship opportunities on my blog. May I e-mail you with additional info?" The key is to think about which goods or services you'd be the best brand ambassador for, which is why contacting companies whose goods and services are already a part of your everyday life is critical.

Giving and taking with giveaways

Although giveaways don't necessarily have to involve sponsors, they're one type of sponsorship in which a company provides either a good or a service that you (you guessed it) give away on your blog. The post dedicated to the giveaway mentions the company sponsoring the giveaway and links to its site or social media platforms.

Collect entries for your giveaway by inviting readers to enter by

- Filling out an online form
- Leaving a comment on the giveaway post

Seems fair enough, right? At first glance, yes. But the second option for amassing entries can get cloudy when bloggers start inviting readers to earn additional entries by completing a variety of tasks, such as the post featured in Figure 14-6. (***Note:*** This was not a real giveaway.)

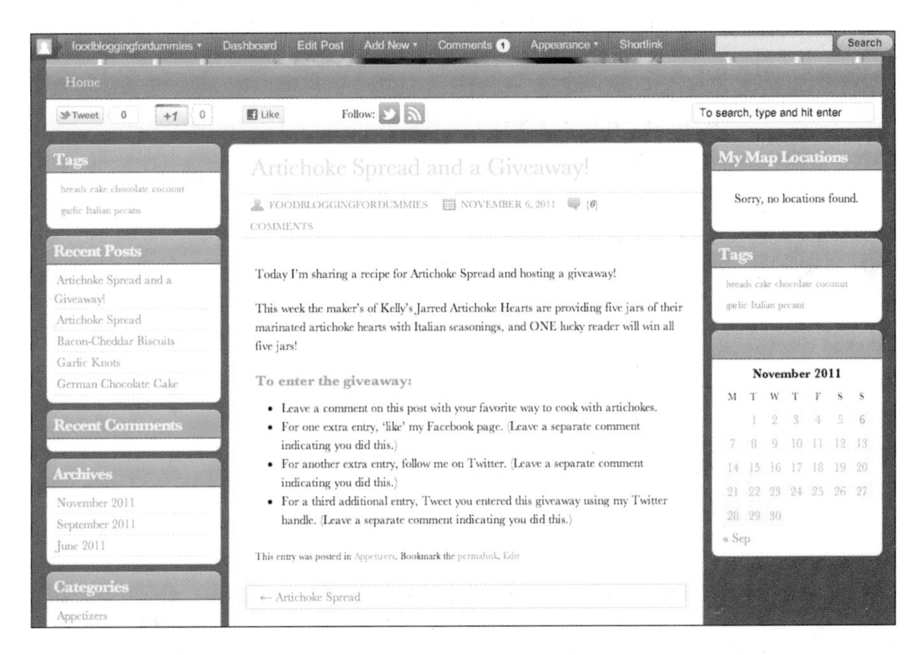

Figure 14-6: Bloggers encourage readers to complete tasks for additional giveaway entries.

Readers either have no problem completing these tasks because it increases their odds of winning the giveaway, or they find fault with the solicitation for loyalty. Beyond the gray zone of solicitation, giveaways also come with a side of legal considerations based on whether they qualify as a lottery, a contest, or a sweepstakes.

As I mention in Chapter 4, this book doesn't provide legal advice. I simply give you a friendly warning that you're better off getting all your legal ducks in a row before you start participating in giveaways. Keep in mind several potential pitfalls regarding the monetary value of the prize, how you collect entries, and even compliance with state and federal laws.

After considering the legal elements, you'll discover the positive side of giveaways as a tried and tested way to increase your blog traffic and generate hundreds, if not thousands, of comments. But keep in mind the traffic may be only temporary because giveaway lovers will come and go with the prizes, whereas devout fans will stick around for the intellectual freebies, too.

Diversifying Your Online Portfolio

Although advertisements and sponsorships are two mainstream ways to generate income from your blog, the key to really bringing home the bacon (or *facon,* for the fake bacon-loving vegetarians) is to generate income from four or five different avenues either directly or indirectly tied to your digital home base.

As you begin exploring the various options for diversifying your income portfolio, which I discuss throughout this section, always keep your own value in mind. I'm not talking about morals; I'm talking about cold hard cash. As in how much you'd expect to be paid for writing an article, creating a recipe, writing a cookbook, or speaking at a conference.

It's absolutely acceptable for that amount to be zero. After all, everyone has to start somewhere. But be aware that when you don't charge a company for your work, it's very hard to go back six months and five articles later and state your fee. Be mindful of who you are — and are not — willing to work for when payment comes in the form of a published byline or a local TV appearance.

Squeezing income from your skill set

Launching and creating a food blog equips you with valuable skills, but best of all, it provides an online home for displaying your creative talents. Your blog is a portfolio of your work, displaying your cooking abilities, your writing chops, and your artistic abilities in photography and videography. From freelance food writing to speaking engagements, the food blogging business creates countless opportunities to increase your income. Take the time to develop your talents and then tap into the potential of your single most lucrative asset — yourself!

Freelance food writing

Freelance food writing is about marketing and getting your name out to as many publications as possible, which makes your blog a prime place to point editors and publishers for a sample of your work (which is even more reason to quadruple check your spelling and grammar). Everyone has to start somewhere, even if your only published byline is the one on your blog. Pitching a local publication for available freelance writing assignments is a proactive and smart step for building your credibility and reputation in the world of food writing.

Your rate as a freelance food writer depends on the following factors:

- **Publication type:** Are you writing for a magazine, newspaper, or online publication?
- **Project type:** Will you be paid by the hour, by the number of words, or on a per project basis?
- **Skill level:** Have you written freelance articles in the past? How much experience do you have?

Each writer will have different answers to the preceding questions, which means it's impossible to state an average rate per hour or per word. But to estimate your own reasonable rate per hour, first consider your goal amount for an annual salary and then work backward by dividing by the number of weeks you'd work each year, the number of hours you'd work each week, and so on. Industry rates for projects paid by word-count range anywhere from 50 cents to $2 per word, but again, this number is subject to change based on the preceding factors.

So how do you catch the eye of an editor? You can grab their attention amid the sea of hungry writers by first and foremost avoiding these common pitfalls that prevent your pitch from having a fighting chance against the competition:

- **Initial e-mail:** Your initial e-mail to an editor is your first writing sample he reads. Pay careful attention to punctuation and grammar, and always address the e-mail to a name rather than "Dear Editor" or "To Whom It May Concern." It may take time to track down the correct name, but it makes all the difference, and he instantly knows you're detail-oriented.
- **Flawless résumé:** This one's a given, but ensure your résumé is free of any and all typos. A résumé typo in the writing world is akin to a scarlet letter. Don't let a silly mistake be the reason your genius pitch lands in the trash.
- **Succinct pitch:** I'm often asked what makes a great pitch, and my response is always, "One that's short and sweet!" Everyone is short on time, so the faster you get to your point, the better.

- **Working links:** If you include links in the body of your e-mail, make sure the links work. It might seem like common knowledge, but e-mail platforms do funky things to hyperlinks. When in doubt, send yourself a test e-mail first.
- **Inside access:** Don't leave an editor asking questions at the end of your pitch. Provide a list of the sources you intend to speak to or the industry experts you'd contact for comments. The more access you have, the better. I'm not saying you need to have Anthony Bourdain on speed-dial, but be ready to list your sources — big and small.
- **Total package:** Sum up your pitch with a few sentences about possible art, such as photos, videos, or graphics, you can provide. Help the editor visualize the piece beyond the written words.

Don't be afraid to start by writing for free. I know what you're thinking: "Isn't this the chapter about how to make money?" Yes. But it's important to be realistic. I know countless food bloggers (including myself), who got their start by writing for free — whether in national publications or local newspapers. Although writing for free isn't the most attractive option, it's sensible when you have a day job, and it's a great way to bulk up your writing résumé.

Recipe development

Recipe development is a learned skill, and one that requires familiarity not only with flavor profiles and culinary techniques, but also with the art of recipe writing. (See Chapter 5 for more on recipe writing.)

Rachel Rappaport, creator of the blog Coconut & Lime (as shown in Figure 14-7), is a prime example of turning your culinary skills from a food blog into a full-blown career in food writing and recipe development. What began in 2004 as a way to share recipes with friends has morphed into a business that includes multiple cookbooks as well as frequent feature and recipe contributions to top sites, magazines, and newspapers across the country, including Real Simple, FoxNews.com, *The Baltimore Sun*, and National Public Radio online.

Much like the approach to food writing, begin by building up your blog as a hearty online portfolio of your work. Then start pitching small, local publications and sites that have a need for original recipes. Offer to provide photographs with the recipe, and you're twice as enticing.

Expanding your skill set to include photography along with recipe development and writing is one of the fastest ways to find success in the world of food media. The more talents you master, the more attractive you become to food brands and publications.

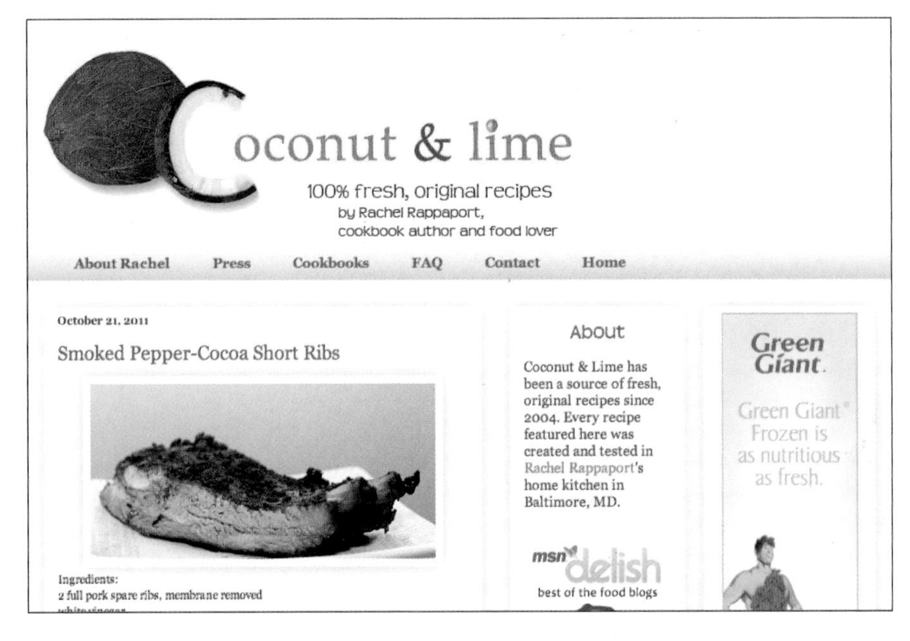

Figure 14-7: Rachel Rappaport grew her blog into a prime online destination for original recipes.

Food styling

The food-styling industry has exploded in recent times, shifting from a little known corner of the food media world to national headlines with behind-the-scenes features appearing in *The New York Times, The Wall Street Journal,* and beyond. If you can mold mashed potatoes like Michelangelo and (olive) oil paint like Picasso, food styling just might be your cup of (perfectly brewed and seductively steamy) tea.

Perfect your craft by studying the photos styled by some of the industry's best, such as Delores Custer, Denise Vivaldo, and Adam Pearson. Or to master the culinary cousins and turn them into a business, check out *Food Styling and Photography For Dummies* by Alison Parks-Whitfield.

Much like freelance food writing, food-styling rates vary greatly depending on your previous experience, as well as on the size and duration of the project. Guestimate your hourly rate based on your projected annual salary, and don't forget to ask your potential client whether food costs should be included in the hourly rate you provide.

Cookbooks

The list of food bloggers-turned-cookbook authors has grown dramatically in the past year, due in part to the growing popularity of food blogging as a business. Everyone from Ree Drummond and Angie Dudley to Lisa Fain and Matt Armendariz have done the reverse trek from digital to print.

But going from blog to book takes time and a demonstrated skill to create or photograph recipes, and preferably both. Every opportunity becomes more realistic with the wider array of talents you possess. If you can create and write recipes, style and photograph food, and maintain a food blog, you are essentially doing the jobs of five people.

Bee Yinn Low, creator of the blog Rasa Malaysia, as shown in Figure 14-8, is a great example of a food blogger who's also a professional recipe developer, photographer, and cookbook author. Low's first cookbook, *Easy Chinese Recipes: Family Favorites From Dim Sum to Kung Pao* (Tuttle Publishing), is currently one of the best-selling Chinese cookbooks on Amazon.

Figure 14-8: Bee Yinn Low launched her blog Rasa Malaysia and is the author of one of the best-selling Chinese cookbooks on Amazon.

Cookbook rates are generally structured in two parts: an *advance* (a sum of money paid to an author prior to her writing the cookbook) and *royalties* (a percentage of the cookbook's sales paid to the author after the book is published). Cookbook advances and royalties are based on the author's experience and notability, the length and subject matter of the cookbook, and the size of the publisher. The dollar range for cookbook advances truly spans the spectrum, especially when you consider that self-publishing comes with a hefty $0 advance, whereas James Beard award-winning authors can rake in six figures (and then some) before a single copy of their cookbook is sold.

Speaking engagements

From local food festivals to national culinary conferences, speaking engagements are a great way to not only earn some added cash, but also to enjoy face-to-face interactions with fellow food bloggers from across the web.

Large-scale events often draw bigger name speakers, so it's best to start small and work your way up to the main stage. Why not pitch yourself to your local TV or radio station for a segment on *insert your blogging niche here?* Or how about applying to speak at your town's summer food fest? Much like freelance food writing, you can't be afraid to start off as free talent with payment in the form of exposure, plus the added practice in public speaking.

Food bloggers speak at food and media industry panels and conferences across the country, such as at the BlogHer Food Conference and the International Association of Culinary Professional's conference, and although payment for such appearances isn't guaranteed, it's always a possibility. An even more likely possibility is that you won't actually be paid to speak, however, your event ticket, travel, and lodging may be compensated in exchange for your words of wisdom. But don't put all your money-making eggs in the speaker's basket because it takes some time to really establish yourself as a driving force in food media.

Opening up shop

An additional way to diversify your sources of online income is to join the *Amazon Associates program,* which is a free affiliate marketing program that anyone can register for and join. After you register, select Amazon products to feature on your blog and ultimately earn a cut of the profits for any item purchased via your link.

Amazon gives you total control over which products you feature, and it also provides three options — links/banners, widgets, and aStore — for how the content appears on your blog.

The sizes and styles of the links, banners, and widgets are easily customized to align with the aesthetics of your blog's design. For example, if I want to feature an Amazon banner on my blog, I simply log in to my Amazon Associates account, click Links & Banners at the top of the page, and then choose my ad category of choice. Similarly, you can create custom widgets via the Widgets tab, which allows you to personally select the products that appear in your widget.

Figure 14-9 depicts the Gourmet Food category banner, which is available in seven sizes. All you have to do is copy the provided HTML code, which contains your unique Amazon Associates ID, and paste it on your blog. The banner appears. Adding HTML code for banners and links is the same process as adding custom text widgets to your blog. (See Chapter 9 for more on implementing custom widgets.)

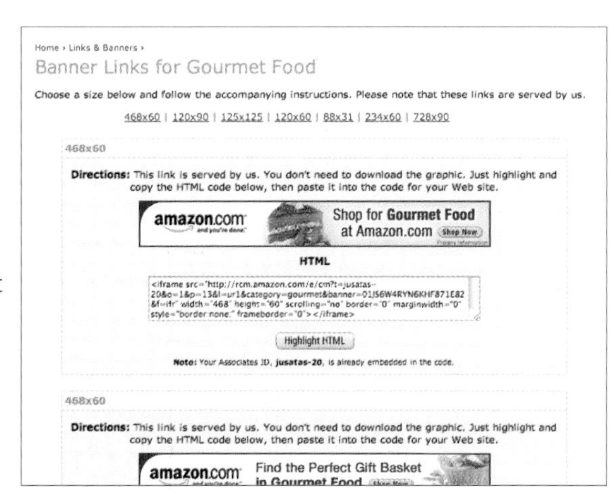

Figure 14-9: Copy and paste the provided HTML code to insert Amazon banners on your blog.

The third option for implementing Amazon products on your blog is via the *aStore,* which is a custom collection of products you curate and display in your personal online store. To create your store, click the aStore tab at the top of the Amazon Associates home page and then follow the step-by-step instructions detailed on the page that appears.

Amazon aStores can include any product listed on Amazon, such as cookbooks, cooking utensils, food items, and more. After you create a new aStore, create your custom categories, and then add items to each category. You can then personalize the look of your store page. Figure 14-10 depicts the editing page, which includes selecting colors for links and header text, as well as the option to upload a custom header. Adding a custom header is a great way to brand your page with your blog's name or logo.

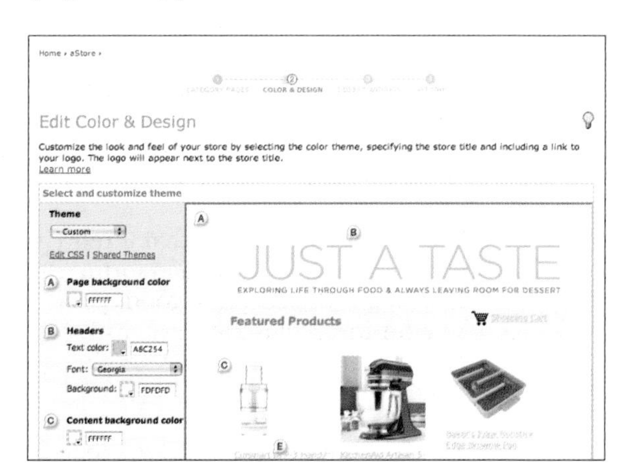

Figure 14-10: Take advantage of the ability to customize your aStore page by adding a custom header that features your blog's title.

After you finalize your design, click Continue, decide on the final placements for widgets, and then click Finish & Get Link. You can then link, embed, or integrate your aStore on your blog. Copy the provided HTML for your preferred option, paste it onto your blog, and let the aStore work its money-making magic.

You can keep careful watch on all the completed purchases via the Reports tab at the top of the Amazon Associates home page. This tab includes earnings reports, orders reports, and miscellaneous referrals.

Accepting Swag without Selling Out

Brands know the tremendous reach inherent in the food blogosphere. And there are few better people's hands to put products into than outspoken, engaging, and well-connected food bloggers.

Freebies in the form of goods and services are an inevitable perk of the business. Although the offers are enticing, it's important to realize that "free" gifts aren't often entirely free. Brands may gift products to food bloggers with the hope they'll write a positive review and endorse the product in return. So before you start your stockpile, consider your stance on swag.

Bloggers have strong opinions when it comes to swag, a topic that consistently stirs the food blogging pot. Some see no harm in accepting freebies, whereas others are adamantly against it. In The State of the Food Blogosphere survey, about 64 percent of bloggers responded they accept free products from companies in exchange for reviewing them on their blogs, but the important element of that 64 percent is that they do so only on the condition they can write whatever they want about the product (meaning, no forced-positive reviews).

The caveat is critical in that it represents food bloggers' belief in *transparency* (or upholding integrity and forthright values). First and foremost, nothing is wrong with accepting goods or services that have been gifted to you for free (or for as close to "free" as it gets). What matters is how you disclose those gifts to your readers and how you endorse (or don't endorse) them on your blog.

For example, if a bakery offers to send me a dozen cupcakes and encourages me to write about them on my blog, I'd maintain transparency with my readers by indicating in the post that I received the cupcakes for free and then provided my honest opinion, good or bad. That's not to say every food blogger follows this approach, but it's important to know where you stand on the topic of swag so the second you get your first offer, you can refer to your established policy on products and endorsements.

It wouldn't be a discussion on swag without a mention of the legal strings attached to freebies. Keep in mind that depending on the monetary value of your gifted items, there may be tax implications. Always consult the company providing the swag to determine the item's total cost. Remaining transparent and avoiding a tax audit should point your moral compass in the right direction when those decisions surface.

Julie Deily of The Little Kitchen is a perfect example of a food blogger who's given some serious thought to her blog's disclosure policy, as shown in Figure 14-11.

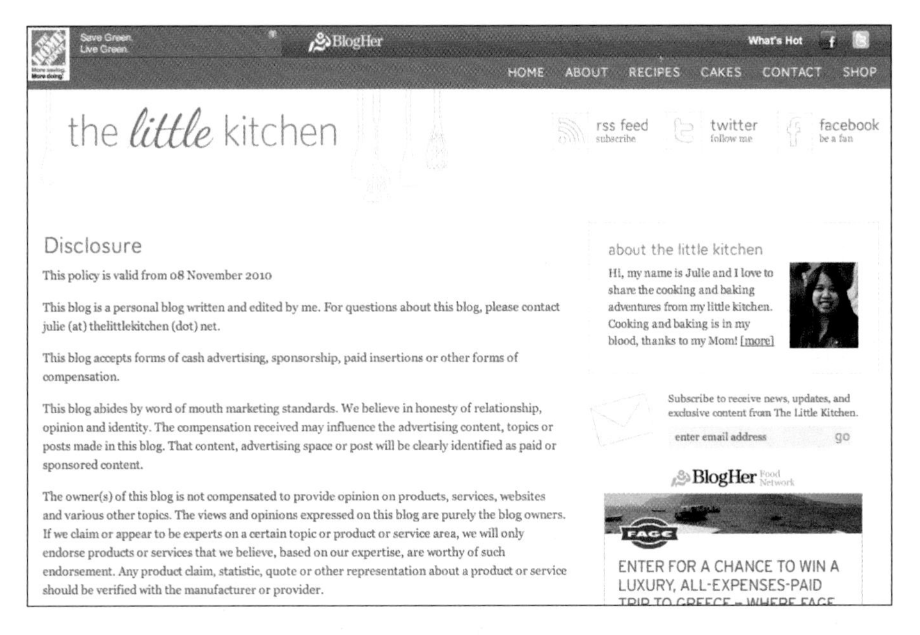

Figure 14-11: The Little Kitchen maintains transparency with her readers by featuring her personal disclosure policy about products and giveaways.

In addition to a separate page dedicated to her disclosure policy, Julie always maintains transparency with her readers by noting at the bottom of posts whether she received an item for free and whether she's being paid by a sponsor to write the post. You can include disclosure information at the top or the bottom of a post, based on your stylistic preferences.

Ultimately, the decision as to whether you accept free products from brands big and small is yours. If or when you do, take some time to establish your own disclosure policy by using resources like `www.disclosurepolicy.org`, which allows you to generate the specific language of your blog's product and giveaway guidelines.

Part VI
The Part of Tens

In this part . . .

This wouldn't be an iconic *For Dummies* book without the Part of Tens. In this part, I dish out a double serving of ten-tip guides, the first of which highlights the many things I wish I'd known before starting my food blog.

Avoid the common beginner mistakes and then dive in to Chapter 16, which puts you face to face with the hardest foods to photograph. Meet the prima donnas of the food world and find out how to prevent them from having meltdowns while maximizing their appeal on set.

15

Ten Things to Know before Starting Your Food Blog

In This Chapter

- Paying attention to the technical considerations pre-launch
- Taking advantage of free online resources
- Avoiding a total blog breakdown with one click

From the technical considerations and logistical strategies, to the ethical deliberations and practical plans, starting a food blog encompasses so much more than simply reviewing restaurants or photographing fajitas.

Although it's important to pay attention to the details, it's just as important to take a step back and look at your soon-to-be blog from a bigger perspective. The ten key tips I summarize in this chapter guide you through the pre-launch process and have you thinking like a food blogger long before you ever click Publish for the first time.

Many of the pointers are from my own Things I Wish I'd Known list — some of which are the result of studying countless blogs throughout the years, whereas others (fortunately or unfortunately) are the result of making mistakes and learning to live with the consequences. As great as learning from those mistakes has been, some errors are not worth your time or tears. (Hint: Back up your blog.)

Match Your Blog Name to Your URL

Save yourself the confusing stares and the missed traffic opportunities by matching the exact name of your blog to the domain (custom or hosted) you register. Aligning the two elements not only makes it easier for readers to find your blog, but it also creates a stronger brand for you and your blog to identify with.

If your blog's domain isn't available, I hate to be the bearer of bad news, but you should think of another title. Having one without the other creates confusion: It's like having a cheeseburger without the burger; it just doesn't work.

Look into Self-Hosting Your Blog

The endless debate between hosting and self-hosting: Do you give away the control and leave the maintenance up to the pros, or do you keep the control and inherit the technical headaches that come with it?

Unfortunately, this is not the type of decision that can be overturned easily if you choose Door A and realize two years later that you really meant to choose Door B. Hosting your blog with a platform, such as WordPress.com or Blogger, is without a doubt the easier route, but it's also much more limiting.

Although self-hosting requires a small budget and some technical know-how, I strongly encourage you to consider the self-hosting option available through WordPress.org. You'll be rewarded with the freedom to fully customize your blog, and most importantly, the ability to grow your blog's functionalities along with your budding readership.

Embrace Editing

Never fear the red pen. As a blogger, you're your own editor, and the biggest advantage you can give yourself is to embrace the editing process. At times, you will have crafted a sentence of perfect prose, and yet deep down you know it's just not right for the post. Take a deep breath, copy and paste it into another draft post, and remain confident that those words will grace your home page when the time is right.

I've cut words, sentences, and even entire paragraphs that I've been so in love with it was actually painful to part with them. But in the end, editing is always the right decision. Remember my editing mantra, "Follow your gut and don't be afraid to cut."

Log Your Ideas and Inspirations

You might be thinking, "What if you run out of ideas to post about?" The thought has likely crossed every food blogger's mind at some point or another. But any time I wonder where my next post is coming from, I dive headfirst into my backlog of draft posts.

Any time you have even the faintest hint of an idea or inspiring thought, create a new post in your Post editor and save it as a draft. Doing so logs the idea into your platform's records, and more importantly, into your very own digital memory. Even if the drafts never see your home page, they're always prime fodder for inspiring other thoughts or even just providing a virtual scrapbook of your ideas throughout the weeks, months, or even years.

Establish a list of ten drafts before you ever publish your first post. Not only will this give you a roadmap of where your content lineup is heading, but it will also serve to calm any nerves tied to the thought of an editorial drought. Save the list both on your blog platform as well as on your desktop so you can access the ideas even if your blog has a technical meltdown.

Get Social Early in the Game

It's never too soon to join the online social circles that exist on Facebook, Twitter, foursquare, and beyond. Taking part in the countless community exchanges happening in social media keeps you in the loop about industry-wide developments and trends, and puts you in touch with a whole host of your fellow food bloggers.

Know Your Free Resources

There may be no such thing as a free lunch, but there definitely are free blogging resources online. Taking advantage of the countless available sites helps troubleshoot any stumbling points by providing valuable advice on every topic from photo-editing software to SEO strategy:

- **Photo editing:** GNU Image Manipulation Program (GIMP; `www.gimp.org`) is a free program for photo retouching and image composition.
- **SEO:** Google Insights for Search (`www.google.com/insights/search/#`) allows you to compare what phrases are most searched for across regions, categories, or times. For example, Insights tells you whether the phrase *vanilla frosting* has been searched for more than *vanilla icing,* and the results can then shape how you title your posts for maximum search engine optimization (SEO) value.
- **Food safety:** FoodSafety.gov (`http://foodsafety.gov`) is your one-stop shop for all questions tied to proper cooking temperatures, sanitation, and more. When in doubt, consult the government's source for all things food safety.

- **Ethics:** The Food Blog Code of Ethics (`http://foodethics.wordpress.com`) and the Food Blog Alliance (`http://foodblogalliance.com`) address accountability, civility, and transparency in the field of food blogging. The Food Blog Alliance, as shown in Figure 15-1, also provides commentary tied to etiquette, copyright, content strategy, and community guidelines.

Figure 15-1: The Food Blog Alliance is a comprehensive resource for ethics, etiquette, and more.

Blog with a Conscience

The ethical and legal considerations tied to blogging, which I discuss in Chapter 4, are vast and varied. From recipe copyright to image usage, the lines are often blurred among borrowed, stolen, and rightfully reused. I always consider the crediting process from the perspective of the creator. For instance, how would you want to see your work attributed if you came across it on another blog?

The same ethical considerations exist for your community guidelines. Lay down the rules early to avoid getting caught without a code of ethics. Even if your considerations change drastically over time, it's better to establish them in some form than to not establish them at all.

Let You Be You

No way I could divulge ten critical tips for food blogging without serving up a scoop of the emotional elements. As cliché as the "let you be you" advice is, putting forth a false front happens to be one of the biggest slip-ups for first-time food bloggers.

Before you launch your blog, you're likely reading other food blogs that you find interesting or inspiring — so inspiring, in fact, that you want to get in on the fun. But getting inspired and emulating are two very different things, and it's easy to fall into the copycat trap.

There is only one Elise Bauer, and only one Simply Recipes. To try to copy the approach, tone, and even the aesthetics of another blog will lead to trouble, and more grimly, failure. First and foremost, you are not Elise. You don't have Elise's family history. You don't have Elise's background. You don't have Elise's life experiences that combine to form the basis of Simply Recipes.

And now that Debbie Downer has left the building, focus on what you *do* have — your family history, your background, and your own life experiences. Those elements, which are uniquely yours, stamp your blog with authenticity. Letting you be you is not only better from a branding perspective, but it's also much easier than keeping up a façade.

Avoid an Obsession with the Numbers

Plain and simple: Don't let your blog's unique visitors or pageviews get the best of you. Granted, this is easier said than done because traffic is the clearest indicator of success or failure, regardless of your scale.

However, the more you stress about getting traffic, the less authentic your blog will be because you'll spend more time trying to read your audience's mind than producing high-quality content. No food blog starts as a success; rather it becomes a success over time.

Back Up Your Blog

There may be no use crying over spilled milk, but I guarantee you tears will fall over failing to back up your blog. It's every blogger's worst nightmare — a routine technical update goes awry, a random plug-in malfunctions, a database is deleted accidentally. No matter the scenario, losing all or even a portion of your blog is devastating.

You're in the perfect position to never have to learn this lesson firsthand. How and when you back up your blog is a personal decision, but I do a manual backup via my hosting site every time I publish a new post. Doing so takes all of five minutes, and it saves you potential heartache.

If you host your blog (such as on WordPress.com or Blogger), your hosting platform takes care of any and all backups. But if you self-host your blog, here are several options for how to either manually or automatically create a backup:

- **Your host:** Utilize the available backup options provided by your specific hosting company. Although a host almost always keeps backup files of your blog, I prefer knowing the who, what, why, when, and how of my backup plan, so I manually download my database once a week. Consult your host for the available backup options.
- **WordPress.org:** WordPress.org provides detailed (read: very technical) directions for how to manually back up your blog. If you aren't comfortable performing the backup, opt for one of its available plug-ins that automatically does the work for you. For more information on manual and automatic backups on WordPress.org blogs, visit `http://codex.wordpress.org/WordPress_Backups`.
- **Dropbox:** Dropbox is a premiere online file-sharing and storing service that also offers an easy automated way for backing up your self-hosted blog. Sign up for an account on `www.dropbox.com`, and then download and install the Dropbox backup plug-in, as shown in Figure 15-2. The plug-in provides easy setup instructions, and enables you to set a date and time for routine, automatic backups of your blog's database.

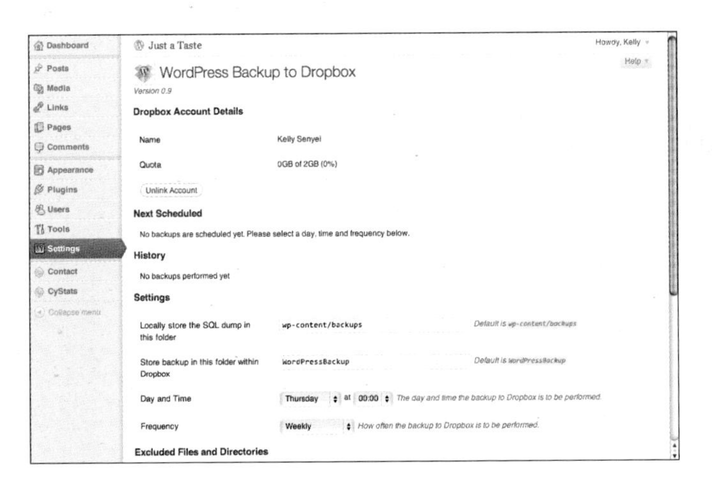

Figure 15-2: Utilize the Dropbox plug-in to routinely and automatically back up your blog's database.

16

The Ten Hardest Foods to Photograph

In This Chapter

- Adding shape to shapeless foods
- Enhancing the appeal of neutral-colored cuisine
- Working with time-sensitive ingredients
- Transforming textures from unappetizing to appealing

No matter how delicious a dish tastes, the reality is that people won't go near a meal if it doesn't pique their visual interest first. This tendency to eat with our eyes before our stomachs means food photography should be at the top of your list when it comes to enticing readers.

But a photo shoot just wouldn't be a photo shoot without a resident diva. And food photo shoots are no exception to the presence of prima donnas. Much like real-life divas, food divas have meltdowns, too.

In this chapter, I tackle ten of the hardest foods to photograph. From ice cream to enchiladas and every shapeless, colorless blob in between, you discover how to make the most of un-photogenic ingredients by transforming them from unappetizing to appealing with a few simple tricks.

Beef Stew

The problem: Shapeless stews of any variety are difficult to photograph, but toss in a few cubes of seared meat and you're destined for a dismal mess. It's a trying task to translate the appeal of thick gravy-soaked meat that's typical to stew-like dishes, including beef bourguignon, and even braised short ribs paired with a beef stock reduction. In addition to having no real shape, beef stew is often an unappetizing shade of brown that rests somewhere between shoe polish and mud. If only its looks could match its rich and hearty taste.

The fix: To usher this dish out of the throes of ugliness, draw attention to the other ingredients bobbing alongside the beef cubes, such as bright-orange carrots or glossy pearl onions. And don't forget to garnish! A chopped parsley or rosemary shower does wonders by adding a green accent to the murky hue.

Hummus

The problem: Hummus is the master of food-styling disasters. Hummus is everything you want your camera-friendly food *not* to be: shapeless and one solid color (and an ugly color at that).

The fix: If you're lucky enough to photograph a red pepper or basil variety, you can highlight non-neutral colors. But if you're stuck with the tan goop that is traditional hummus, you have your work cut out for you.

Use the back of a spoon or an offset spatula to create peaks and valleys in the puréed chickpeas. Doing so adds texture to an otherwise textureless food and provides pockets for olive oil puddles and landing spots for chopped fresh herbs, nuts, and any other applicable garnishes (see Figure 16-1). When in doubt, pair your dreary dip with crudités to add an array of bright colors and shapes to the spread. Apply this same approach to any variety of creamy white or neutral color foods, including sour cream- and yogurt-based dips, as well as cream cheese spreads.

Figure 16-1: Turn drab into fab by adding shape and color to traditional hummus.

Raw Meat

The problem: From ground beef and skirt steak to pork chops and whole chickens, raw meat is one of the most difficult foods to make look appetizing. Raw meat often appears slimy and bloody, fleshy and freshly plucked.

Despite its less than alluring appeal, capturing meat in a raw state can be valuable when demonstrating cooking techniques.

The fix: Each protein requires a different approach, but if possible, include some sort of action in the photograph to demonstrate that the meat is on its way to edibility. Consider the following photo prop pairings for a wide variety of raw proteins:

- **Beef and veal:** Beef and veal are available in a wide variety of cuts, which means it's critical to highlight the qualities that are specific to the cut in your recipe. For example, draw attention to the rich fat that characterizes a rib-eye steak by positioning it alongside a chef's knife for size context and angling your camera above the steak to capture the fat marbling. Similarly, provide perspective for just how thin your veal scaloppine is by featuring your hand or a pepper mill alongside the raw meat.
- **Game:** Depending on your recipe, aim to accentuate the rarer forms of wild game, such as poussins and ducks, by showcasing them as a whole animal, rather than as fabricated sections. Even if you feature only a solitary duck breast, draw attention to the contrast in colors between rich pink meat and cream-colored skin by photographing the breast on a dark background or capturing it sizzling skin-side down in a sauté pan.
- **Pork and lamb:** Make the most of lamb and pork cuts by highlighting, rather than discarding, the impressive bones that comprise thick-cut chops and roasts. If it applies to your recipe, french the bones to provide a clean, striking visual contrast to the tender pink meat and shiny fat.
- **Poultry:** Kitchen twine, scissors, and a good slick of olive oil or butter make drab raw poultry shine. Depending on your recipe, photograph the poultry in the marinating or seasoning stage to take advantage of the bright colors and contrasting textures afforded by spices and fresh herbs.

Melted Cheese

The problem: The melted stage of any food creates issues when translating the real-life texture through your lens. And cheese is no exception to this rule because it congeals not long after it goes from the solid to semi-solid stage. The result is a rubbery-looking substance that takes on a sheen while it sits and sweats. Sweaty cheese pizza. Need I say more?

The fix: You can photograph melted cheese in its prime using two methods. The first is simple: Work faster. As blunt as the advice may be, it gets you the best results. Melt the cheese last in your setup so that a quick run under the broiler or a ten-second spin in the microwave results in oozing rather than congealing.

If all else fails, rely on a relevant garnish to take away some emphasis from the melting matter. Figure 16-2 depicts cheesy garlic bread (quite possibly the most melt-worthy food on the planet), which I captured at its peak by using both of my suggested techniques. In this case, the bread was piping hot and scallions were mixed into the cheese base, so I simply saved the green tips and used them as a colorful garnish (with the added bonus of a final punch of oniony flavor).

Figure 16-2: Capturing melted cheese in its prime requires swift photography skills.

Oatmeal

The problem: Oatmeal is colorless and creamy. (Are you sensing a pattern here?) But at least oatmeal has the added benefit of being composed of individual oats . . . that are then cooked until they're mushy and shapeless.

The fix: The only real way to make oatmeal camera-ready is to rely on the toppings as strong supporting characters. Opt for brown sugar, fresh and dried fruits, honey, nuts, or essentially any garnish that contrasts with the gray palette and provides a welcome pop of color and texture.

Ice Cream

The problem: You probably aren't surprised as to why ice cream makes the list — any food with time-sensitive qualities is a diva by its own right. You need a certain touch to mold the ultimate scoop, and varieties like vanilla or other pale-colored flavors don't help the situation.

The fix: Opt for one of two methods, the fake food way or the pre-scooped way. Chapter 12 covers the powdered sugar and frosting option for creating real-life, melt-averse renditions of the real deal. But if you want to stay *au naturale,* which you most likely will if you're eating what you're blogging about, simply pre-scoop portions of the ice cream onto a metal sheet tray lined with parchment paper and stash the tray in the fridge until the scoops are firm.

When you're ready to assemble your cone or cup, grab the pre-frozen portions and start styling. I've used this technique when stacking multiple scoops skewered together, and the tower-o-dairy, as shown in Figure 16-3, actually lasted a full three minutes before collapsing. Pre-freezing ice cream is also a great time-saving tip when dishing out slices of cake or pie for any size crowd. The technique allows you to get your scooping work-out in ahead of time, which frees you up to quickly slide each serving onto waiting plates.

Figure 16-3: Freezing pre-scooped portions of ice cream extends the food's photographic lifespan and helps it hold its shape.

Chocolate Pudding

The problem: Dry chocolate is a notoriously finicky food to photograph because of its dark color and its propensity to *bloom* (or turn white) if not stored properly. The pudding form doesn't fare much better under the lights, and it has the added shapeless strike against it.

The fix: Similar to hummus and oatmeal, chocolate pudding is best captured with a variety of toppings, such as a wave of whipped cream or a sprinkle of chopped nuts. But if a garnish isn't appropriate for your recipe, consider the serving dish and the camera angle at which you photograph the pudding. Lighter-colored dishes provide better contrast against the monotone food, and eye-level or overhead angles make the most of its wiggly form.

Meatloaf

The problem: The camera does not love meatloaf in all its ground meat and gray-hued glory. Meatloaf is unfortunately dreary and non-descript, save its rectangular slices. Even a ketchup crust can't create the illusion of an appetizing meal straight from iconic American cuisine.

The fix: Don't steer clear of photographing meatloaf simply because it's unattractive. A brush of vegetable oil as a post-slice touchup is a nod to a moist, appealing meal. Serving the slices alongside brightly steamed veggies or a tower of butter-soaked mashed potatoes also helps place the meatloaf in a composed scene and draws less attention to the gloomy centerfold.

Poached or Fried Eggs

The problem: Scrambled, and even hard-boiled, eggs are stunning models for the sheer fact they hold their shape. But poach or fry the egg, and you're staring down a shiny white, translucent specimen that jiggles as it slides across a plate.

The fix: The poached or fried varieties are begging to be photographed only after they've been cut open to expose their inner beauty — a bright yellow river of yolk. Take advantage of the color intensity by serving the eggs on a white surface, whether on a plate, bowl, or slice of golden brown toast, as shown in Figure 16-4. Work quickly and don't cut into the egg until all the other elements are set. And don't forget the star power of a few turns of coarsely ground black pepper for a contrast in color and texture.

Figure 16-4: Capitalize on the striking yellow of egg yolks by pairing them with a white background.

Enchiladas

The problem: Enchiladas have what I refer to as *Burrito Syndrome*. Much like their rolled up culinary cousins, photographing a halved enchilada, or any other food rolled up in a tortilla or wrap, results in an unidentifiable mess of shredded meat, beans, vegetables, and cheese. The mash-up doesn't even include the brick red or neon green sauce slathered over the off-white tortillas topped with more cheese that's been, you guessed it, melted. The enchilada is the Holy Trinity of food-styling horrors: uncomplimentary colors, shapeless ingredients, and congealed dairy.

The fix: In addition to picking up the pace, your best bet is to not attempt to feature a cross-section of an enchilada. Instead, photograph the entire pan garnished with cilantro sprigs, chopped olives, and any other relevant toppings. A second approach is to plate two of the enchiladas and position your camera at a 75-degree angle to capture the round curve of the tortilla with just a hint of the filling spilling out. Top the duo with a slick of sauce and sprinkle of cheese, and then zap them with heat for a freshly melted appeal.

Index

• A •

A (Aperture-Priority) mode, 184
ability restrictions and requirements, 90
About page, 141–144
above the fold, 145–148
accessibility
  due to RSS feeds, 243
  for editors, 276
  restrictions and requirements, 90
acronyms, for naming blogs, 37
acrylic ice cubes, 213
"adapted from," 79, 104
AddThis, 167
adjectives in food writing, 67–79
ads
  Google Blogger, 42, 52–54
  TypePad, 42, 54–55
  WordPress. *See* WordPress.com; WordPress.org
advance (for books), 278
advertising
  about, 145, 160
  direct, 266–267
  Expression Engine, 43, 56
  networks, 267–271
  online, 262–266
advertising networks, 263, 267–271
Affiliate Programs, 146
Ahern, Shauna James (blogger), 64
alerts, creating, 242
Amateur Gourmet (blog), 11, 20–21
Amazon, 146
Amazon Associates program, 279–281
anchor text, 253
Annie's Eats (blog), 17–18
aperture, 179–180
Aperture-Priority (A) mode, 184
appearance, enhancing with widgets, 160
Apple's MacSpeech Scribe, 66
Armendariz, Matt (blogger), 278
artificial food styling, 210, 212–214
artificial light, 191–193
Associated Press Stylebook, 103
aStore, 280–281
attention to detail, 90
attribution, style guide for, 104
audience
  engaging, 87–89
  knowing your, 32–34, 90
  loyalty of, 100
Auto mode, 184
auto-timer, 205
AWStats, 34, 115–116, 257

• B •

The Babble 50: Mom Food Bloggers (website), 269
backgrounds, 191
backup, 289–290
badges, 167–168. *See also* widgets
Bakerella (blog), 11, 83, 129
bandwidth, 49
Bartoli, Jennifer (blogger), 246
Bauer, Elise (blogger), 156–157
<b></b> tag, 172
beef, 291–292, 293
behind-the-scenes, as blog posts, 87–88
"being yourself," 288–289
below the fold, 148–150
Bev Cooks (blog), 178–179
Bhide, Monica (blogger), 22
Birley, Shane (author)
  Blogging For Dummies, 147
Bitten Word (blog), 166
.biz extension, 47
black fill cards, 200
Blog Polls (website), 88
Blogger (Google)
  about, 42, 53–54
  adding gadgets, 163–164
  adjusting comment settings, 155–156
  blogroll widget, 149, 173
  categories, 93–94
  creating pages, 95–96
  editing views, 72
  implementing custom widgets, 165–166

Blogger (Google) *(continued)*
inserting links, 106–107
inserting videos in posts, 111–112
inserting visuals, 110–111
installing templates from external sites, 126–127
popularity of, 52
publishing your first post, 74–75
style and design, 120
templates, 124
Bloggeries (website), 88
The Blogger's Legal Guide (Electronic Frontier Foundation), 80
Blogging For Dummies (Gardner and Birley), 147
blogging platforms, 50–57
blogging software, 56–57
BlogHer, 11, 269–270, 279
Bloglines (website), 244
blogroll, 149, 173
blogs. *See also specific blogs*
hosting, 41–50
naming, 36–40
registering, 41–50
self-hosted, 42–44, 286
blowtorch, 207
Bluehost, 49
Born Round: The Secret History of a Full-Time Eater (Bruni), 66
bottles, 223–224
Bottoms, Kevin and Amanda (bloggers), 18–19
bounce cards, 200
bowls, 207, 221–222

 tag, 172
brand identity, 101
branding
about, 99, 101–102
attribution, 104
consistency, 100–101
envisioning your brand, 65, 100–102, 240
frequency, 112–116
grammar, 69–70, 108–109
images, 104–105
links, 105–107
post length, 103–104
recipes, 107–108
spelling, 69–70, 108–109
style guide, 102–109
visuals, 109–112
brightness, 233
Bruni, Frank (author)
Born Round: The Secret History of a Full-Time Eater, 66
BTemplates, 125
budget, 90, 214
Burton, Brooke (blogger), 80, 288
buttons, displaying, 167–168

Cake Wrecks (blog), 86–87
camera phones, 196, 197
candle wax, 208
Cannelle Et Vanille (blog), 133
capacity, of web hosts, 49
capitalization, 108
categories, 92–94, 148–149
Celiac Team (blog), 28
center content well, 149
<center></center> tag, 172
Champagne, 208
cheese (melted), photographing, 293–294
Chez Pim (blog), 130
Chief Financial Officer, as role of food blogger, 15
Chocolate & Zucchini (blog), 11, 133
chocolate pudding, photographing, 295
classic recipe, 79
Clay, Bruce (author)
Search Engine Optimization All-in-One For Dummies, 248
cleaning, 98
click-through rate, 262
Coconut & Lime (blog), 276, 277
Color Hunter, 131
color palettes, selecting, 129–131
Color Scheme Designer, 131
.com extension, 47
commas, 108
comments, 154–157
commitment, 24
communication, 244
community, 31–32, 58, 254–255
composition, 186, 188–189, 231
conferences, 255

confidence, projecting, 64
conscience, blogging with a, 288
consistency, creating, 100–101
Contact pages, 144
content
  about, 81
  accessing, 160
  defining, 81–89
  gauging, 96–98
  optimizing, 261–262
  organizing, 91–98
  promoting visual, 246–248
  protecting, 76–78
  sharing, 243–248
  tracking, 258
  writing and creating recipes, 89–91
  for your niche, 71
contracts, for advertising networks, 268
contrast, 131–133, 233
conventions, explained, 2
cook, as role of food blogger, 14
cookbooks, 278–279
cooking, 98
cooking equipment, 224–225
Cooking with Amy (blog), 11
copyright, 76–78
cost
  ExpressionEngine, 56
  Google Blogger, 54
  TypePad, 55
  WordPress.com, 53
  WordPress.org, 56
cost per thousand impressions (CPM), 263
cotton balls, 212–213
Creative Commons licensing, 77
creativity, for naming blogs, 37
credibility, 78–80, 101, 242
cropping, 233
cross-testing, 98
custom widgets, 164–167
customer service, of web hosts, 49
cutlery, 222–223

Dailymotion, 60
dashboard, 50
David Lebovitz (blog), 133, 240
daylight bulbs, 192
Deily, Julie (blogger), 282
delicious:days (blog), 133
Denny, Kalyn (blogger), 17
depth of field, 184–185
descriptions, 67–79
design
  considerations, 24
  ExpressionEngine, 56
  extensions for naming blogs, 37
  Google Blogger, 54
  headers, 133–134
  TypePad, 55
  WordPress.com, 53
  WordPress.org, 55
Desserts for Breakfast (blog), 178–179
dietary restrictions and requirements, 90
Digg, 245
digital duplicate, for naming blogs, 38
Digital Photography For Dummies (King), 181
dining mates, for restaurants, 231
direct advertising, 263, 266–267
directional light, 179
disclosure policy, 282
discretion, for restaurants, 230
domain name
  ExpressionEngine, 56
  Google Blogger, 54
  registering, 45–48
  TypePad, 55
  WordPress.com, 53
  WordPress.org, 55
domain registrar, 45–48
double right rail, 150
Dragon NaturallySpeaking 11.5 Home, 66
DreamHost, 49
drive space, 49
Dropbox, 290
Drummond, Ree (blogger), 11, 101–102, 278
dSLR cameras, 196, 198
Dudley, Angie (blogger), 11, 83, 278
duration, of sponsorship, 272
Dusoulier, Clotilde (blogger), 11

• E •

earplugs, 208
Easy Chinese Recipes: Family Favorites From Dim Sum to Kung Pao (Low), 278
EatingAsia (blog), 28

eat-ups, 255
editing, 65, 91, 233–235, 286
editor, as role of food blogger, 15
eggs, photographing, 296
Electronic Frontier Foundation, 80
e-mail, 245, 275
embedding widget code, 164–165
enchiladas, photographing, 296
entertainment value, providing, 160
equipment and tools
  about, 195
  camera options, 195–198
  camera phones, 196, 197
  cooking, 224–225
  dSLR cameras, 196, 198
  enhancing light, 200–201
  freeing up your hands, 204–205
  point-and-shoot cameras, 196, 198
  repurposing household items, 201–204
  studio, 199–205
  toolkit, 205–208
errors in design, 135
Esparaza, Susan (blogger)
  Search Engine Optimization All-in-One For Dummies, 248
ethics, 288
events, 255
exposure, 233
ExpressionEngine, 43, 56
extensions, 47
external links, 105
eyedroppers, 206
eye-level perspective, 189–190

• F •

Facebook, 60, 151–154, 166
Fain, Lisa (blogger), 148, 278
false bottom, 207–208
Family Fresh Cooking (blog), 15–16
FAQ (Frequently Asked Questions), 146
Federated Media Publishing, 270–271
FeedBurner, 147, 245–246
File Transfer Protocol (FTP), 57, 125, 127
fill cards, 200
financial reward
  about, 259–260
  accepting freebies, 281–282
  direct advertising, 263, 266–267
  diversifying online portfolios, 274–281
  online advertisements, 262–266
  online advertising networks, 263, 267–271
  optimizing content, 261–262
  reality of, 260
  sponsors, 271–274
finding your niche
  about, 25
  getting started, 25–31
  joining food blogging community, 31–32
  knowing your audience, 32–34
  measuring success, 35–36
  naming your blog, 36–40
first impression, 64–65, 121–123
$5 Dinners (blog), 28
Flake, Jenny (blogger), 150
flash, using in restaurants, 230
flea markets, 203
Flickr, 60, 85, 166
f-number, 180
focus, 234
font, selecting size, style, and contract of, 131–133
Food Blog Alliance (website), 288
food blogging. *See also specific topics*
  accessing blogosphere, 9–14
  finding your niche, 19–21
  owning your voice, 21–23
  rise of, 10–12
  roles, 14–16
  tips, 23–24
  well-known food bloggers, 16–19
Food Blogging For Dummies (blog), 121, 122
Food Channel, 11
food news, as blog posts, 84
Food Porn Daily (blog), 248
food safety resources, 287
food styling and photography
  about, 209, 277, 291–296
  artificial, 210, 212–214
  constructing setup, 227–230
  editing programs, 233–235
  finding your style, 210–214
  propping, 220–226
  in restaurants, 230–232
  tips, 214–219

Food Styling and Photography For Dummies (Parks-Whitfield), 277
food stylist, as role of food blogger, 14
Food Wishers (blog), 84
Foodbuzz Featured Publisher program, 270–271
foodgawker (blog), 178, 247–248
FoodSafety.gov (website), 287
The Food Blog Code of Ethics (Burton and Greenstein), 80, 288
footer, 150
framing, focus on, 234
freebies, accepting, 281–282
freelance food writing, 275–276
frequency of posts, 112–116
Frequently Asked Questions (FAQ), 146
fried eggs, photographing, 296
f-stop, 180
FTP (File Transfer Protocol), 57, 125, 127

• G •

gadgets. *See* widgets
game (meat), 293
Gandi.net, 46
Gardner, Susannah (author)
Blogging For Dummies, 147
garnishes, 168–174, 215
getting started, 25–31
Gim, Sarah (blogger), 246
GIMP (GNU Image Manipulation Program), 234, 287
giveaways, 88–89, 273–274
glasses, 223–224
Gluten-Free Girl and The Chef (blog), 64
glycerin, 213
GNU Image Manipulation Program (GIMP), 234, 287
Go Daddy, 46
goal setting, 24
gold fill cards, 200
goods, from sponsorship, 272
Google AdSense, 269
Google Analytics, 33, 256–257
Google Blogger. *See* Blogger (Google)
Google Insights, 250–252, 287
Google Reader, 244
Google Recipe View, 251
Google Rich Snippets, 251
Google Webmaster Tools Help page (website), 251
grammar, 69–70, 108–109
graphics, 133, 169–172
Greenstein, Leah (blogger), 80, 288
gross CPM, 263–264
guest posts, 88

• H •

Hair, Jaden (blogger), 66, 129, 272
headers, 133–134, 138
headnotes, 70, 103
holidays, paying attention to, 90
home page, 140–141
home repair stores, 203
Homesick Texan (blog), 147–148
hosted videos, 111
hosting company, 57, 290
household items, repurposing, 201–204
how to's, as blog posts, 83
HTML tags, 172–174
hummus, photographing, 292
hyperlinks, 105–107, 169–172, 252–254, 276

• I •

IACP (International Association of Culinary Professionals), 79, 279
ice cream, photographing, 294–295
ice cubes (acrylic), 213
icons, explained, 5
ideas, generating, 90
Identifont (website), 132
identity, 100
<i></i> tag, 172
images, 22–23, 80, 104–105, 134, 233–235, 247
impressions, 64–65, 262
inbound links, 252–254
income, from skill set, 274–279
informational links, 149
ingredient lists, 89
Insert Custom Character option (WordPress), 73, 74
Insert More Tag option (WordPress), 73, 74
inside jokes, for naming blogs, 37

inspiration, from social media, 58
"inspired by," 79, 104
interactiveness, 160
interests, streamlining your, 27–29
internal links, 105, 252–254
International Association of Culinary Professionals (IACP), 79, 279
International Organization for Standardization (ISO), 179–181
interviews, as blog posts, 86
introduction, 71
iPage, 50
ISO (International Organization for Standardization), 179–181
italics, 108

• J •

Joy the Baker (blog), 133
Just a Taste (blog), 123, 143

• K •

Kalyn's Kitchen (blog), 17, 79
Kevin & Amanda (blog), 18–19
keyword density, 249
keywords, 105, 249–252
King, Julie Adair (author)
  Digital Photography For Dummies, 181
kitchen, 204
kitchen bouquet, 212
kitchen failures, as blog posts, 86–87
knives, 206
Kuler, 131

• L •

La Tartine Gourmand (blog), 23
Lai, Chuck (blogger), 247
lamb, 293
Landis, Lindsay (blogger), 131–132
leading lines, 188
Lebovitz, David (blogger), 133, 240
left rails, 138
legal issues, 75–80
length of posts, 103–104
A Life of Spice (blog), 22
lighting
  artificial/natural, 191–193
  directional, 179
  enhancing, 200–201
  for restaurant shooting, 232
Limited Liability Company (LLC), 78
link exchange, 254
link roundups, as blog posts, 87
LinkedIn, 60
links, 169–172, 252–254, 276
LinkWithin, 167
liquids, 206
The Little Kitchen (blog), 282
LLC (Limited Liability Company), 78
location, tracking, 258
logistics, during sponsorship, 272
logo, 100
Love and Olive Oil (blog), 131–132
Low, Bee Yinn (author)
  Easy Chinese Recipes: Family Favorites From Dim Sum to Kung Pao, 278
loyalty of audiences, 100

• M •

M., Annie (blogger), 17–18
M (Manual) mode, 182–184
MacSpeech Scribe (Apple), 66
maintenance
  ExpressionEngine, 56
  Google Blogger, 54
  TypePad, 55
  WordPress.com, 53
  WordPress.org, 55
management provider, 245
managing editor, as role of food blogger, 15
Manual (M) mode, 182–184
marketability, for naming blogs, 37
marketing
  about, 160, 239
  branding, 69–70, 99–116, 240
  community-building, 254–255
  Google Recipe View, 251
  meeting bloggers offline, 255–256

publicists, 241–243
search engine optimization (SEO), 248–254
sharing content, 243–248
tracking, 256–258
Matt Bites (blog), 121
maximalist, 220
McCord, Garrett (blogger), 77, 151–152
measurements, knowing your, 89
meat (raw), photographing, 292–293
meatloaf, photographing, 295
medium shot, 190
melted cheese, photographing, 293–294
Meridith, Marla (blogger), 15–16
microblogging platform, 52
mimicking, avoiding, 65
minimalists, 220
minimum requirements, for advertising networks, 268
Mitzewich, John (blogger), 84
Moniker, 46
MOO (website), 256
My Baking Addiction (blog), 152

• N •

name, matching to URL, 285–286
Namecheap, 46
natural food styling, 210–211
natural light, 191–193
NaturallySpeaking 11.5 Home (Dragon), 66
navigation
about, 137
About page, 141–144
above the fold, 145–148
below the fold, 148–150
categories, 148–149
center content well, 149
comments, 154–157
Contact page, 144
essentials, 138–144
example, 150
footer, 150
home page, 140–141
informational links, 149
organizing elements, 147–148
RSS feed, 147
social media, 151–154
subcategories, 148–149
tag clouds, 149
Navigation bar, 145–147
negative fill card, 201
negative space, 134–135
net CPM, 263–264
.net extension, 47
Network Solutions, 46
NewsGator (website), 244
niche, finding your
about, 19–21, 25
content, 71
getting started, 25–31
joining food blogging community, 31–32
knowing your audience, 32–34
measuring success, 35–36
naming your blog, 36–40
noise, 182
nonhosted videos, 111
Not Without Salt (blog), 146
notes, for restaurant shooting, 232

• O •

oatmeal, photographing, 294
101 Cookbooks (blog), 20
one-click installation, 57
one-person band, 113
online advertising
about, 262–263
evaluating impact of, 263–264
profits, 264–266
online advertising networks, 263, 267–271
online portfolios, diversifying, 274–281
online shop, opening an, 279–281
Orangette (blog), 103–104, 129
.org extension, 47
organic SEO, 249
original recipe posts, 97–98
originality, 37, 76
outbound links, 252–254
overhead perspective, 189–190

P

P (Programmed Autoexposure) mode, 184
page hits, 258
pages, compared with posts, 94–96
pageviews, 258, 262
paid SEO, 249
PainShop Photo Pro, 234
paintbrush, 208
Panini Happy (blog), 28
paper towels, 207
Parks-Whitfield, Alison (author)
  Food Styling and Photography For Dummies, 277
patina, 202
payment for sponsorship, 272
pay-per-click campaigns, 249
Peltre, Béatrice (blogger), 23
people, as props, 225
permission, asking for in restaurants, 231
personal affinity, for naming blogs, 37
perspective, 189–191, 232
photo editing resources, 287
Photobucket (website), 85
photographer, as role of food blogger, 14
photography. *See also specific topics*
  about, 177
  aperture, 179–180
  Auto mode, 184
  backgrounds, 191
  basic rules, 185–191
  composition, 188–189
  depth of field, 184–185
  developing your style, 177–179
  food, 291–296
  fundamentals, 179–185
  ISO, 179–181
  lighting, 191–193
  Manual mode, 182–184
  perspective, 189–191
  Rule of Thirds, 186–188
  shutter speed, 179–180
photos, 22–23, 80, 104–105, 134, 233–235, 247
Photoscape (website), 234
photo-sharing site, 85
Photoshop Elements, 234
Picasa (website), 234
Picky Palate (blog), 150
Pinterest, 153
The Pioneer Woman (blog), 11, 101–102
pitch, to editors, 275
Pixlr (website), 234
PlateFull, 269
plates, 221–222
platforms (blogging), 50–57
plug-ins. *See* widgets
poached eggs, photographing, 296
podcasts, as blog posts, 84
point-and-shoot cameras, 196, 198
polls, as blog posts, 88
pork, 293
portlets. *See* widgets
post editor (Google Blogger), 53–54
Posterous, 42
posting schedule, 113–115
posts
  brainstorming ideas, 83–87
  compared with pages, 94–96
  dictating, 66
  frequency of, 112–116
  inserting visuals into, 109–112
  length of, 103–104
  original recipe, 97–98
  publishing your first, 71–75
  step-by-step recipe photo, 98
  video, 98
poultry, 293
powdered sugar, 213
`<p></p>` tag, 172
Press Announcements and Awards, 147
Press page, 241–242
price, in direct advertising, 267
process, 216–219
profits, 264–266
Programmed Autoexposure (P) mode, 184
promotion, during sponsorship, 272
proofreading, 89, 91
prop stylist, as role of food blogger, 14
proportion, 133
propping, 220–226, 232
public, going, 70–71
publicist, 15, 241–243
publishing, 71–75, 91
punctuation, 69–70

Q

Q-tips, 206

R

Rappaport, Rachel (blogger), 276
Rasa Malaysia (blog), 278
raw meat, photographing, 292–293
reach, due to RSS feeds, 244
reality of financial rewards, 260
Really Simple Syndication (RSS), 145, 147, 243–246
Recipe Copyright (U.S. Copyright Office), 80
recipe developer, as role of food blogger, 14
recipe development, 276–277
Recipe Index, 146–147
recipe tester, as role of food blogger, 14
recipes
  attributing, 80
  creating, 89–91
  measurement abbreviations, 107–108
  style guide for, 107–108
  testing, 90–91
  writing, 89–91
Reddit, 153
reflectors, 200
relevancy
  for naming blogs, 37
  of props, 221
reliability of web hosts, 49
Remember icon, 5
Remove Formatting option (WordPress), 73, 74
resources (free), 287–288
restaurants, photographing food in, 230–232
résumés, to editors, 275
revenue, 243
reviews
  as blog posts, 83
  trustworthy, 70
right rails, 138
Roberts, Adam (blogger), 11, 20–21
roles of food bloggers, 14–16
rotation, 233
royalties, 278–279
RSS (Really Simple Syndication), 145, 147, 243–246
RSS reader, 244
Rule of Thirds, 186–188

S

S (Shutter-Priority) mode, 184
salt, 208
saturation, 233
SAVEUR Sites, 242
Savory Sweet Life (blog), 241
scale of props, 220
Search bar, 145
search engine optimization (SEO), 101, 248–254, 287
Search Engine Optimization All-in-One For Dummies (Clay and Esparaza), 248
seasons, paying attention to, 90
security of web hosts, 49
self-hosted blogs, 42–44, 286
Senyei, Kelly (author), 5
SEO (search engine optimization), 101, 248–254, 287
series, as blog posts, 84
Serious Eats (blog), 86, 103–104, 174
setup
  about, 41
  choosing blogging platforms, 50–57
  constructing for photos, 227–230
  domain names, 47
  ExpressionEngine, 56
  Google Blogger, 53–54
  hosting your blog, 41–50
  installing blogging software, 56–57
  registering your blog, 41–50
  registering your domain, 45–48
  RSS feeds, 245–246
  selecting web hosts, 48–50
  social media, 58–60
  Tumblr, 52
  TypePad, 54–55
  WordPress.com, 53
  WordPress.org, 55–56

Sherman, Amy (blogger), 11
Shih, Stephanie (blogger), 178–179
shots, previewing, 234
Show/Hide option (WordPress), 73, 74
shutter speed, 179–180
Shutter-Priority (S) mode, 184
shutter-release cord, 204
shutter-release remote, 205
sidebars, 138
silicone earplugs, 208
silver fill cards, 200
Simply Recipes (blog), 10, 156–157
Simpson, Amanda (blogger), 248
Site Meter, 34, 257
size
  editing, 233
  font, 131–133
  in headers, 134
  of props, 220
skewers, 206
skills
  considering levels, 89
  developing, 30–31
slide shows, as blog posts, 85
Smitten Kitchen (blog), 10, 133
Snapfish (website), 85
social media
  about, 24, 58, 151–154, 287
  benefits of, 58–59
  extending content to, 160
  links, 145
  strategizing approaches to, 59–60
social media strategist, as role of food blogger, 15
software (blogging), 56–57
The Sophisticated Gourmet (blog), 121, 122
spatulas, 206
speaking engagements, 279
spelling, 69–70, 108–109
sponsors, 271–274
spray bottles, 206
Sprouted Kitchen (blog), 140–141
Starbucks, 100
The State of the Food Blogosphere survey, 12–13, 26
stationery stores, 203
statistics tracker, 10–11, 256–257, 289
Steamy Kitchen (blog), 66, 129, 272
stew (beef), photographing, 291–292
stockpiling, 114–115
StudioPress, 125
studios, building, 199–205
StumbleUpon, 153, 245
style and design
  about, 119–120
  custom templates, 124–128
  design errors, 135
  designing headers, 133–134
  finding your style, 210–214
  first impressions, 121–123
  font, 131–133
  negative space, 134–135
  selecting color palettes, 129–131
  selecting font size, style, and contrast, 131–133
  templates, 123–128
style guide
  about, 102–103
  attribution, 104
  grammar, 108–109
  images, 104–105
  links, 105–107
  post length, 103–104
  recipes, 107–108
  spelling, 108–109
subcategories, 92–94, 148–149
success
  measuring, 35–36
  setting yourself up for, 19–24
sugar (powdered), 213
Swanson, Heidi (blogger), 20

• T •

tag clouds, 149
tagging images, 247
taste tests, as blog posts, 86
TasteSpotting (blog), 178, 246–247
Techamuanvivit, Pim (blogger), 130
technical director, as role of food blogger, 15
technology, 24

Technorati search engine, 10, 153
templates, 123–128
themes, 123
three-quarters perspective, 189–190
tight shot, 190
time commitment, gauging, 96–98, 258
timeline, in direct advertising, 267
Tip icon, 5
tone setting, 65–67
top-ten lists, as blog posts, 85
traffic, 243, 258, 267
tripods, 204, 205
Tumblr, 42, 52
tweezers, 206
Twitter, 60, 151–154, 166
Two Peas and Their Pod (blog), 87–88
TypePad, 42, 54–55

• U •

uncommon extensions, for naming blogs, 37
unique visitors, 258
uniqueness, identifying your, 29–30
Unlink option (WordPress), 73, 74
URL, matching blog name to, 285–286
U.S. Copyright Office, 76, 80
user-friendliness, for naming blogs, 37

• V •

Vanilla Garlic (blog), 77, 151–152
veal, 293
Veggie Belly (blog), 28
video posts, 84, 98, 111
video sites, 60
videographer, as role of food blogger, 14
Vimeo, 60
virtual recipe events, as blog posts, 84
Vistaprint (website), 256
visuals, 65, 109–112
voice
  finding your, 63–67
  owning your, 21–23
  sharing your, 58

• W •

Warning! icon, 5
wax (candle), 208
web designer, 57
web hosts, 45–50
websites
  AddThis, 167
  AWStats, 34
  The Babble 50: Mom Food Bloggers, 269
  Blog Polls, 88
  Blogger (Google), 53
  Bloggeries, 88
  BlogHer, 269–270
  Bloglines, 244
  BlueHost, 49
  BTemplates, 125
  Color Hunter, 131
  Color Scheme Designer, 131
  Creative Commons licensing, 77
  Digg, 245
  disclosure policy, 282
  DreamHost, 49
  DropBox, 290
  Electronic Frontier Foundation, 80
  ExpressionEngine, 56
  Facebook, 60, 166
  Federated Media Publishing, 270–271
  FeedBurner, 147, 245–246
  Flickr, 85, 166
  Food Blog Alliance, 288
  Foodbuzz, 271
  FoodSafety.gov, 287
  The Food Blog Code of Ethics, 80, 288
  GIMP, 235, 287
  Google AdSense, 269
  Google Analytics, 33, 256
  Google Insights, 250, 287
  Google Webmaster Tools Help page, 251
  Identifont, 132
  iPage, 50
  Kuler, 131
  LinkWithin, 167
  MOO, 256
  NewsGator, 244

websites *(continued)*
  Photobucket, 85
  Photoscape, 234
  Picasa, 234
  Pinterest, 153
  Pixlr, 234
  PlateFull, 269
  Reddit, 153
  Site Meter, 34
  Snapfish, 85
  StudioPress, 125
  StumbleUpon, 153, 245
  TasteSpotting, 246-247
  Technorati, 153
  Tumblr, 52
  Twitter, 166
  TypePad, 54
  U.S. Copyright Office, 76, 80
  Vistaprint, 256
  WhatTheFont, 132
  WordPress.com, 53
  WordPress.org, 290
  WordPress.org Free Themes Directory, 125
  WP-Polls, 88
Weidner, Bev (blogger), 178–179
well-known blogs, 16–19
WhatTheFont (website), 132
white fill cards, 200
White On Rice Couple (blog), 129
wide shot, 190
widgets
  about, 159–160
  custom, 164–168
  implementing, 161–164
Windex, 206
Wizenberg, Molly (blogger), 168
word mark, 133
WordPress.com
  about, 42, 53
  adjusting comment settings, 153, 155
  blogroll widget, 173
  creating categories and subcategories, 92–93
  creating pages, 94–95
  editing views in, 72
  embedding widget's codes in, 164–165
  implementing pre-loaded widgets, 161–162
  inserting links in, 105–106
  inserting videos in posts, 111–112
  inserting visuals in, 109–110
  popularity of, 51–52
  publishing your first post in, 72–74
  style and design, 120
  templates, 123–124
WordPress.org
  about, 43, 53, 55–56
  adjusting comment settings, 153, 155
  backup, 290
  blogroll widget, 173
  creating categories and subcategories, 92–93
  creating pages, 94–95
  editing views in, 72
  embedding widget's codes in, 164–165
  five-minute install, 57
  implementing pre-loaded widgets, 161–162
  inserting links in, 105–106
  inserting videos in posts, 111–112
  inserting visuals in, 109–110
  Installation Guide, 56
  plug-ins, 162–163
  popularity of, 51–52
  publishing your first post in, 72–74
  style and design, 120
  templates, 123–124
WordPress.org Free Themes Directory, 125
words
  choosing wisely, 64
  developing your voice with, 21–22
WP-Polls (website), 88
writer, as role of food blogger, 15
WYSIWYG interface, 72

YouTube, 60